12.00
1

Merger Politics

Local Government Consolidation in

Tidewater Virginia

Also published for the Institute of Government, University of Virginia:

Chester W. Bain, *Annexation in Virginia: The Use of the Judicial Process for Readjusting City-County Boundaries.* 1966. xiv, 258 pp.

Chester W. Bain, *"A Body Incorporate": The Evolution of City-County Separation in Virginia.* 1967. xii, 142 pp.

MERGER POLITICS

Local Government Consolidation in Tidewater Virginia

David G. Temple

West Virginia University

Published for
the Institute of Government, University of Virginia

The University Press of Virginia
Charlottesville

THE UNIVERSITY PRESS OF VIRGINIA
© 1972 by the Rector and Visitors
of the University of Virginia

First published 1972

ISBN: 0–8139–0389–0
Library of Congress Catalog Card Number: 72–181718
Printed in the United States of America

For Julia Ann

FOREWORD

THE Institute of Government of the University of Virginia is pleased to present the third in a series of monographs on selected aspects of Virginia government and politics. The first two monographs, which dealt with annexation and the evolution of city-county separation, will now be joined by the following study of the politics of local government consolidation in Tidewater Virginia. The appearance of the third volume is most timely in that, as the author demonstrates most effectively, local government consolidation in Virginia is intimately related to and affected by annexation and city-county separation. This volume also continues the previous practice of expanding the Institute's staff resources by attracting persons on leave from other institutions to work on specific projects.

WELDON COOPER, *Director*
Institute of Government

Charlottesville, Virginia
April 15, 1971

PREFACE

THIS is a study of the processes and politics of four local government consolidations that occurred in two of Virginia's Standard Metropolitan Statistical Areas between 1952 and 1963. Both of these metropolitan areas, Newport News–Hampton and Norfolk–Portsmouth, are located in the easternmost part of the state in that general geographic region which most Virginians call Tidewater.

In broad outline, this study attempts to sketch the why, what, and how of local government consolidation in Tidewater Virginia. In addition, an effort has been made to describe certain of the consequences of consolidation, with special emphasis upon common problems arising in the immediate postmerger period. In the pursuit of this goal, the study has eschewed a case-by-case approach in favor of one that dwells on each of the several factors identified as being included in the merger process from its inception to its implementation. The primary reason for this approach relates directly to the conclusions that emerged from this study of the Tidewater mergers. The main thrust of these conclusions is that local government consolidation, regardless of whatever else it may be, is primarily a political act. The word *politics,* when used in this manner, does not necessarily carry the connotation of partisan politics. Rather, to use selected definitions of politics already extant, merger is very much the "art of the possible"; its prospects are deeply involved with "who gets what, when, where, and how"; and it may win acceptance or be rejected on the basis of decisions dealing with "the pursuit and exercise of power." Although the promergerites from time to time employed the traditional rhetoric of local government consolidation, such as the benefits of economy and efficiency or the need for a broadened tax base, the fact is that in each merger there was an unrelated and overriding political reason for consolidation.

Without the assistance of the Institute of Government of the University of Virginia, this study would never have been done. The inquiry was originally undertaken in 1962–63 by the author to satisfy the Ph.D. dissertation requirement in the Woodrow Wilson Department of Government and Foreign Affairs. At the urging of Weldon Cooper, Director of the Institute, the author undertook the revision of the manuscript for publication. The Institute provided funds, office space, secretarial assistance, and other support.

Thanks are also due to the late William M. Griffin, Assistant Director of the Institute, who offered advice and encouragement in the early stages of the study. Ralph Eisenberg, then Associate Director of the Institute, read the manuscript and offered many critical and helpful suggestions. S. J. Makielski, Jr., also of the Institute staff, provided advice and helped the author to develop a perspective on consolidation. Finally, special thanks are due to the Institute's secretarial staff, especially Mrs. Janie Steorts, Miss Patricia Banks, Miss Laurel McGilvery, and the late Mrs. Grace Bellomy, who assumed responsibility for the typing chores.

So many people in public and private life contributed to the content of this study that it would be impossible to give them the credit they deserve. Most are identified in the list of interviews given in the Bibliography. Some persons who are not listed expressed a desire to remain anonymous, and this wish has been respected. A special debt of gratitude is owed the many elected and appointed officials of the consolidated cities who gave freely of their time, knowledge, and recollections of the mergers. Were it not for their courtesy, cooperation, and help, the story of the mergers could not have been told. Needless to say, none of the aforementioned persons can be held responsible in any way for any errors of fact or interpretation. These are the sole responsibility of the author.

Finally, the author admits to having a deep-seated affection for Tidewater Virginia that began early one morning in 1945, when, as a newly enlisted seaman in the United States Navy, he first entered the harbor of Hampton Roads. Time and repeated visits to the Greater Hampton Roads area have done nothing to diminish this affection, and, if anything, those months spent there reconstructing the mergers worked to intensify it. With its amiable people, national historic shrines, and fine recreational facilities, there can be no more pleasant place in the nation to study local government consolidation.

David G. Temple

Morgantown, West Virginia
July 1971

CONTENTS

TABLES

MAPS

Merger Politics

Local Government Consolidation in

Tidewater Virginia

CHAPTER I

CONSOLIDATION COMES TO TIDEWATER

THE past decade has witnessed a revival of interest in city-county consolidation in the United States. Between 1960 and 1970 there were seven city-county consolidations, more than in any other decade of the twentieth century.[1] During the 1960's eleven other proposed city-county consolidations were brought to local referendum; none, however, was able to win voter acceptance.[2] Nevertheless, in no other decade in the history of the United States have so many city-county consolidation proposals been brought to the referendum stage.[3]

Almost from the time scholars and reformers first discovered the governmentally fragmented metropolitan area, the merger or consolidation of governments was advanced as one solution to urban problems that seemed attributable to the proliferation of local units of government. Governmental consolidation, it was argued, would simplify the local government structure, provide a more realistic framework for approaching common problems, eliminate the duplication of functions and services, facilitate the establishment of uniform levels of services, provide a sound tax base, permit the realization of economies of scale, and otherwise establish a governmental structure capable of coping with urban development. But

[1] These included (1) Nashville–Davidson County, Tennessee, (2) Virginia Beach–Princess Anne County, Virginia, (3) South Norfolk–Norfolk County, Virginia, (4) Jacksonville–Duval County, Florida, (5) Indianapolis–Marion County, Indiana, (6) Carson City–Ormsby County, Nevada, and (7) Juneau–Borough of Juneau, Alaska.

[2] A list of defeats is provided in S. J. Makielski, Jr., "City-County Consolidation in the United States," 46 *University of Virginia News Letter* 5–8 (Oct. 15, 1969). Since Makielski's article appeared, there have been at least four other defeats: Roanoke–Roanoke County, Virginia; Winchester–Frederick County, Virginia; Bristol–Washington County, Virginia; and Charlotte–Mecklenburg County, North Carolina.

[3] The verbs *to merge* and *to consolidate* are used interchangeably throughout this study to describe the complete joining of separate governments. In this context, both mean to unite indistinguishably.

as far as complete local government consolidation was concerned, at least until the 1960's, merger was rarely effected. If a consolidation proposal somehow managed to reach the stage of a popular vote, it was usually defeated. This was not the case, however, in Tidewater Virginia between 1952 and 1963.

Focus on Tidewater

In four mergers between 1952 and 1963, the voters of three Tidewater Virginia counties, five cities, and one town abolished their existing local governments and formed four consolidated city governments. The option presented to the voters in each locality was between retention of existing governments or ratification of a merger in which the existing governments would disappear.[4] In all cases decisive majorities of city, county, and town voters responded favorably to full-scale consolidation.

Each of the local governments abolished by consolidation was located in one of the two Tidewater Virginia metropolitan areas—the Norfolk–Portsmouth and the Newport News–Hampton Standard Metropolitan Statistical Areas (SMSAs). The consolidating governments were part of that section of Virginia first settled by the adventurous English colonists. One of the former cities, the pre-merger City of Hampton, laid claim to being the "oldest continual Anglo-Saxon settlement in the New World," while the "newest" of the county governments, Princess Anne County, was formed in 1691. Despite the apparent presence of significant historic ties to county government, voters in the three counties gave overwhelming support to merger even though each of the counties disappeared completely following consolidation. The ratios for merger provided by county voters ranged from 2–1 to 8–1.

Certain of the vital statistics of merger in Tidewater Virginia are set forth in Table 1. Between 1952 and 1963 consolidation reduced the number of governments from nine to four. Two of the consolidated cities, Hampton and Newport News, are the "core" cities of that SMSA, while the other two consolidated cities, Virginia Beach and Chesapeake, are part of the Norfolk–Portsmouth SMSA.

The four Tidewater mergers display certain features that, on the surface, either contradict prevailing opinion about the prerequisites

---

[4] Much of the data for this study was gained through interviews with merger leaders and through access to certain quasi-public and private working papers dealing with the mergers. See Bibliography below.

Table 1. Merger in Tidewater Virginia

Consolidated city	Date of merger	Former units of government	Former land area (sq. mi.)	Population 1950	Population 1970
Hampton	1952	City of Hampton	1	5,966	120,779
		Elizabeth City County	56	51,334 [a]	
		Town of Phoebus	— [b]	3,694	
Newport News	1957	City of Warwick	71	39,875	138,177
		City of Newport News	4	42,358	
Virginia Beach	1963	City of Virginia Beach	2	5,390	172,106
		Princess Anne County	253	42,277	
Chesapeake	1963	City of South Norfolk	7	10,434	89,580 [c]
		Norfolk County	337	99,937	

SOURCES: Population figures are from the 1950 and 1970 *Census of Population.*

[a] Includes the population of the Town of Phoebus.

[b] Included in area for Elizabeth City County.

[c] Due to annexation suits, the population of former Norfolk County declined from 99,937 to 51,612 between 1950 and 1960.

for a successful merger or run counter to the experience with consolidation proposals elsewhere in the nation. First, any consolidation of general units of local government in a metropolitan area is a rare occurrence; for that matter, the consolidation of general units of government whether rural or urban is rare. Voters have usually rejected consolidation proposals for such reasons as loyalty to existing governments, fear of change, regard for tradition, concern about the cost of services, or simply desire to maintain local control. Yet in the two Tidewater metropolitan areas between 1952 and 1963, the voters behaved as if these reasons did not exist. Perhaps even more surprising, the Tidewater voters opted for unknown and untried consolidated city governments without any in-depth studies about the effect of merger on public services or finance, and in the face of consolidation agreements and charters that suggested the essentially political character of the merger proposals.

Second, the behavior of county voters in Tidewater on the merger issue was unusual. Elsewhere in the United States city-county consolidation has almost always been defeated by county voters. Typically, the county suburbanite has been persuaded that consolidation was not in his best interests, and his more rural counterpart has usually shared this viewpoint. In Tidewater, however, suburban voters gave firm backing to merger, and those county precincts that were entirely rural also recorded significant favorable majorities.

Finally, the role played by local government officials in the Tidewater mergers differed significantly from that played by local officials elsewhere. More often than not, in a merger campaign, local public officials are found in the anticonsolidation camp and are usually active in the struggle against change. Although the underlying motives for their opposition vary, consolidation does affect the political base from which local officials operate. It also threatens their continuation in office, alters existing administrative arrangements, encourages a restructuring of political alignments, and affects patronage, salary scales, and retirement benefits. Nevertheless, three of the four Tidewater mergers were initiated, supported, and led by elected local officials, who carried the full burden of the consolidation campaigns in each of the participating local governments. In the fourth merger, that of the cities of Newport News and Warwick, most public officials either supported consolidation or assumed a neutral stance.

What the Mergers Were Not

Because the merger proposals met success at the polls, and because the reaction of voters and officials to merger differed from that commonly exhibited elsewhere in the nation, the Tidewater response to consolidation necessarily arouses curiosity. A brief overview at this point will help to establish a framework for analysis, to dispel certain illusions about the mergers that may exist, and to underscore further the uniqueness of the consolidations. This can best be accomplished by exploring what the mergers were not.

The four consolidations display several paradoxical features since none of the traditional or historical reasons urged by metropolitan area reformers on behalf of local government consolidation were major considerations in the Tidewater mergers. If the former governments were too small and inefficient, or if overlap and duplication of services and functions existed, there was little suggestion that the voters were alarmed about these conditions. The existing local governments seem to have enjoyed the full confidence and support of their citizens. No financial breakdown appeared imminent, nor had any significant disruption in the provision of public services occurred. In each case the existing governments, including the counties, had developed programs to cope with increasing urbanization within the SMSAs and had achieved at least modest success in these efforts. Corruption in government, or even the taint of corruption, was never an issue. In sum, the size, nature, and operation of the participating local governments prior to merger provide no clue as to why consolidation was so readily accepted.

At the same time promerger advocates in the Tidewater area were not especially concerned with the need for developing a metropolitan area-wide approach to common problems. A metropolitan area-wide authority was, in fact, one of the more remote considerations in promoting the individual mergers. Public officials and voters never came to the realization that either of the metropolitan areas was cluttered with governments because such cluttering had in fact never occurred. Mergers were supposed to eliminate interjurisdictional disputes and problems, but this issue never really surfaced except in the Newport News–Warwick merger. Unequal levels of taxation and services were an important factor in consolidation, but only because the price of merger included retention of unequal taxes and services. Finally, the "enlightened promerger leadership" provided by local public officials during the merger campaigns seems to have stemmed as much from self-interest and self-perpetuation as from any other motive.

For these reasons, as far as the traditional theories, reasons, and goals of metropolitan area reorganization are concerned, one might well argue that the Tidewater mergers were undertaken for the wrong reasons and involved the wrong governments. Instead of enhancing a metropolitan area-wide approach, three of the four consolidations were clearly aimed at preserving localism and the political status quo. Although it may seem paradoxical, the merger alternative was presented to the voters at the time as the most effective way to minimize future governmental change and to preserve the status quo by abolishing the existing local governments and creating consolidated city governments.

Because the consolidations were essentially political exercises rather than deliberate attempts to achieve metropolitan area reform or to upgrade local services, the practice of interlocal politics serves as a broad focal point for this study of the Tidewater mergers. Although local government services cannot be entirely excluded as an issue, and the impact of merger upon the metropolitan area must also be considered, the significance of the Tidewater mergers lies in the circumstances that spawned the consolidations, why they were undertaken, and how they were achieved.

In a larger sense, a further question to be explored is why merger won acceptance in Tidewater when it has usually been rejected elsewhere. Admittedly, as will be seen, certain peculiar features of Virginia's local government system, most notably the scheme of city-county separation and annexation law and practice, contributed to promoting the mergers. But city-county separation and annexation alone do not explain the Tidewater mergers. The same or similar circumstances existing in Tidewater between 1952 and 1963 were also prevalent in other areas of the state and continue to prevail. Yet in these other parts of Virginia, consolidation proposals either have been rejected by the voters or have never passed beyond an initial exploratory stage. What was accomplished with apparent ease in Tidewater has not been duplicated elsewhere in Virginia.[5]

The Setting for Merger

The four consolidated cities are located in what is sometimes described as the Greater Hampton Roads Community, which embraces two metropolitan areas, the Norfolk–Portsmouth SMSA and the Newport News–Hampton SMSA, facing each other across Virginia's harbor of Hampton Roads. To a significant extent the economic lifeblood of the two metropolitan areas flows from the harbor, its ocean-going commerce and related industries, and the extensive naval facilities that border Hampton Roads. Although the economy of the area has been diversified significantly since World War II, maritime activity stemming from easy access to the sea continues to serve as the basis for area growth and development.

The Newport News–Hampton SMSA in 1970 was composed of the two consolidated cities of Newport News and Hampton, York County, and the Town of Poquoson. Located on what Virginians term the Lower Peninsula, the Newport News–Hampton SMSA is surrounded on three sides by water barriers—Chesapeake Bay to the north, Hampton Roads to the east, and the James River to the south. The metropolitan area contains 255 square miles and in 1970 had a population of 292,159.[6] Before the two consolidations that

[5] Consolidation proposals have been defeated in referendums involving Richmond–Henrico County, Roanoke–Roanoke County, Winchester–Frederick County, Charlottesville–Albemarle County, and Bristol–Washington County.

[6] U.S., Bureau of the Census, *1970 Census of Population, PC (Va) -48, Virginia* (Washington, D.C., Feb. 1971).

occurred in this SMSA, the area included the counties of Elizabeth City and York, the towns of Phoebus and Poquoson, and the former cities of Hampton, Newport News, and Warwick.

The Norfolk–Portsmouth SMSA on the eastern and southern shores of Hampton Roads is a partial peninsula bordered on the north by the entrance to Chesapeake Bay and on the east by the Atlantic Ocean. Of the two metropolitan areas, this is by far the larger, with a land area of 667 square miles and a population in 1970 of 680,600. The City of Norfolk, in fact, with a population in 1970 of 307,951, is Virginia's largest city. Before the two mergers that occurred in 1963, the metropolitan area encompassed the counties of Norfolk and Princess Anne and the cities of Norfolk, Portsmouth, South Norfolk, and Virginia Beach.

Geography has been an important factor in the economic development of both areas as well as in the pattern of local government consolidation. Before World War II the cities of Hampton Roads were relatively small in both area and population, while the counties were predominantly rural. Although both SMSAs bordered on Hampton Roads, they were isolated from each other by the water barriers of the harbor and the James River; in addition, the Elizabeth River separated the cities of Norfolk and Portsmouth. During much of the area's history an elaborate ferry network served as the primary means of interlocal transportation. Not until 1950 were Norfolk and Portsmouth connected by a bridge-tunnel. In part because of the difficulties of interlocal travel and transport, the rate of growth in the two metropolitan areas prior to World War II was nominal, and each of the local governments was relatively free to work out its own destiny without treading heavily on the toes of its neighbors.

The impact of the Second World War upon the Greater Hampton Roads Community cannot be underestimated. Norfolk, Portsmouth, and Newport News had long been the site of miltiary installations, but with the coming of the war these installations were expanded and new major installations were built. Throughout the war Hampton Roads was crowded with vessels, war and other related industries experienced an upsurge, and the general atmosphere reflected boom-town proportions. A four-lane Military Highway was built around Norfolk's narrow streets and connected Portsmouth with the Norfolk Naval Operating Base and Naval Air Station. In 1942, partly as a response to military pressure, the Virginia General Assembly created the Elizabeth River Tunnel Commission to build a bridge-tunnel across the Elizabeth River connecting downtown Portsmouth and downtown Norfolk, which, on its completion in

1950, sounded the death knell for the ferry network. In 1957, the completion of the Hampton Roads Bridge-Tunnel across the harbor's entrance connected the two metropolitan areas for the first time.

Following the close of World War II the Greater Hampton Roads Community did not revert to its prewar condition. Although boom

Table 2. Population growth in the Hampton Roads Metropolitan Areas

Metropolitan Area	1940	1950	1960	% Increase or Decrease 1940–50	1950–60
Newport News–Hampton					
York County	8,857	11,750	21,583	32.7	83.7
Elizabeth City County	32,283	55,028	—	70.5	—
Hampton	5,898	5,966	89,258	1.2	46.3
Warwick County [a]	9,248	39,875	—	331.2	—
Newport News	37,067	42,358	113,662	14.3	38.2
Subtotal	93,353	154,977	224,503	66.0	44.9
Norfolk–Portsmouth					
Princess Anne County	19,984	42,277	77,127	111.6	82.4
Virginia Beach	2,600	5,390	8,091	— [b]	50.1
Norfolk County	35,828	99,937	51,612	178.9	−48.4
South Norfolk	8,038	10,434	22,035	29.8	111.2
Norfolk	144,332	213,513	304,869	47.9	42.8
Portsmouth	50,745	80,039	114,773	57.7	43.4
Subtotal	261,527	451,590	578,507	72.7	28.1
Total	354,880	606,567	803,010	70.9	32.4

SOURCES: 1950 and 1960 *Census of Population.*

[a] Warwick County was incorporated as a city of the first class in 1952. Unless otherwise noted, Warwick is tabulated as a city, its status at the time of merger.

[b] The population of the Town of Virginia Beach in 1940 was calculated as part of Princess Anne County.

conditions subsided, many of the wartime facilities became permanent, and there was a decided net gain in both industry and population.[7] The 1950 census showed that population growth had

[7] Carolyn Louise Haldeman, "National Defense Efforts and Their Effect on the Cities of Hampton and Newport News, Virginia" (Master's thesis, Department of Government and Foreign Affairs, University of Virginia, 1964).

been both real and significant. As Table 2 shows, the population continued to grow in the subsequent decade.

It is important to note that Norfolk County declined in population by 48.4 percent between 1950 and 1960 after an increase of 178.9 percent between 1940 and 1950. This striking decrease in population by 1960 was not the result of out-migration but was chiefly the result of annexation of parts of the county by the cities of Norfolk, Portsmouth, and South Norfolk. Up to the time of its merger with the City of South Norfolk, Norfolk County held the dubious distinction of being the state's most annexed county, which was one of the major factors contributing to the merger. In fact, the growth that did occur in the cities of Norfolk, Portsmouth, and South Norfolk between 1950 and 1960 was due in part to the extension of municipal boundaries by means of annexation. Between 1950 and 1960 the City of Norfolk, at the expense of Norfolk County and Princess Anne County, expanded its area from twenty-eight to fifty square miles, while the City of Portsmouth expanded from ten to eighteen square miles. The areas and population densities of the several local units of the Greater Hampton Roads Community in 1960 are shown in Table 3.

Table 3. 1960 population densities of the Greater Hampton Roads Community

County or City	1960 population	Land area (sq. miles)	% Urban	Population per sq. mile
Hampton	89,258	57	100.0	1565.9
Newport News	113,662	75	100.0	1515.5
Princess Anne County	77,127	253	56.1	300.9
Virginia Beach	8,091	2	100.0	4045.5
Norfolk County	51,612	337	54.4	153.2
South Norfolk	22,035	7	100.0	3147.9
Norfolk City	304,869	50	100.0	6097.2
Portsmouth	114,773	18	100.0	6376.3

SOURCE: 1960 *Census of Population.*

In the early stages of this study it was hypothesized that certain socioeconomic characteristics of the two SMSAs might shed some light on the acceptance of merger. Like most Southern communities, for example, the cities and counties of the Greater Hampton Roads Community contain significant nonwhite populations, as Table 4 shows. As nearly as could be determined, however, the size of the nonwhite population was a merger issue in only one instance. An increasing black population in former Newport News in the 1950's undoubtedly contributed to promerger pressures at work on whites in that city. Fear was expressed privately, and later openly, among white Newport News residents that the growing Negro population of Newport News might soon win control of the municipal government. Faced with the prospect of eventual black control of their city government, white Newport News residents became increasingly

Table 4. Nonwhite population in the Greater Hampton Roads Community, 1950–1960

| | 1950 | | 1960 | |
County or city	Nonwhite population	% of total population	Nonwhite population	% of total population
Elizabeth City County	11,266	20.5	—	—
Hampton	2,222	37.2	19,095	21.4
Warwick	12,435	31.0	—	—
Newport News	18,300	43.3	39,060	34.4
Princess Anne County	9,936	23.5	12,560	16.3
Virginia Beach	— a	—	534	6.5
Norfolk County	16,326	16.3	13,536	26.3
South Norfolk	2,398	23.0	5,806	26.4
Portsmouth	30,729	38.4	39,681	34.6
Norfolk	63,448	29.7	80,621	26.5

SOURCES: 1950 and 1960 *Census of Population.*
a Included with Princess Anne County in the 1950 Census.

interested in a merger with adjacent Warwick, which was predominantly white and suburban. Other reasons, of course, supported the promerger cause.

The effects of the presence of a sizable Negro community on merger elsewhere in Tidewater are difficult to gauge. In 1950, for instance, the population of the former City of Hampton was 37.2 percent nonwhite, yet several reliable sources have stated that racial control of government was not an issue in the Hampton–Elizabeth City County merger.[8] There can be no reason to doubt this claim

[8] Interviews with Robert B. Smith, Editor, *Daily Press*, Newport News, Aug. 22, 1963, and E. Sclater Montague, Hampton, Aug. 16, 1963. Mr. Smith was a former mayor of Newport News.

because in 1950 blacks posed no real threat to continued white control there. On the other hand, there is some basis for the belief that expanding black populations in the cities of Norfolk and Portsmouth contributed to vigorous annexation movements between 1950 and 1960, which in turn prompted two of the four mergers. But even here, racial considerations were by no means the chief reason for seeking annexation.

The nonnative population in the Hampton Roads area was significant also, although it was impossible to determine accurately the impact of this variable on merger. In 1960 the population of the former City of Virginia Beach was composed of only 43.7 percent of native Virginians.[9] Princess Anne County and the City of Norfolk also had more nonnatives than natives. Only the counties and cities in Northern Virginia immediately adjacent to Washington, D.C., registered consistently lower percentages of native population in the state. At the other end of the scale, even former Norfolk County had only 62.5 percent native population. Second to Norfolk County was the former City of South Norfolk with a native population of 60.6 percent.

The relatively large nonnative population can be explained by the presence of the sprawling military establishment in the Greater Hampton Roads area. The military installations include the Norfolk Naval Operating Base, Norfolk Naval Air Station, Armed Services Staff College, Portsmouth Navy Yard, Portsmouth Naval Hospital, Little Creek Amphibious Base, Langley Air Force Base, and Fort Monroe, the headquarters of the Continental Army Command. As a result of these and other military installations, the ratio of government workers and armed service personnel was and is high when set against the total number of civilian employees. Nevertheless, no direct connection between this ratio and the merger sentiment can be demonstrated.

These peculiar or unique socioeconomic characteristics of the two SMSAs do not seem to have had much part in the movement toward merger. On the other hand, factors that did contribute to the favorable acceptance of merger included (1) a simplistic governmental structure, (2) increasing urbanization, and (3) a restricted electorate.

The structures of government in the two metropolitan areas were and are simplistic in comparison to those of other metropolitan

[9] All figures taken from U.S., Bureau of the Census, *1960 Census of Population, Characteristics of the Population* (Washington, D.C., 1961), vol. 1, pt. 48, Table 35.

areas in the nation. Within the two SMSAs, encompassing more than
900 square miles, there were, prior to the first merger in 1952, five
counties, six cities, and one town. At present the two SMSAs contain one county, six cities, and one town.[10]

The number of special districts in the two SMSAs was likewise
insignificant, and their presence presented no barrier to merger.
The 1962 Census of Governments, for example, revealed a total of
seven special districts in both metropolitan areas, of which two were
soil conservation districts.[11] Since none of these special districts
levied taxes, they did not figure in any significant way in the success
of merger.

Second, significant urbanization was occurring in the counties at
the time the mergers were initiated. This urbanization had several
consequences for county government, especially those involving the
provision of services and the likelihood that the urbanized county
areas would be annexed by an adjacent city. These consequences
will be explained in greater detail in the following chapter.

Third, at the time of the mergers the electorate in Virginia was
restricted, chiefly through such devices as the poll tax, which, while
nominal, had to be paid cumulatively for three years. The voter
registration requirements tended to work against a short-term or
temporary resident's participating in the political process, and there
is no evidence that a transient vote was responsible for the mergers.
On the contrary, judging by the tenor of the promerger appeal made
during the campaign, the main thrust was directed at the long-time
county and city residents.

In large measure because the electoral restrictions worked to ex-
clude blacks and others of low income from broad-scale political
participation, the phenomenon of black bloc voting against merger
was not present in three of the four consolidations. In former New-

---

[10] The Town of Phoebus in former Elizabeth City County was abolished in the
1952 Elizabeth City County–Hampton consolidation. The Town of Poquoson in
York County of the Newport News–Hampton SMSA was incorporated in 1952.

[11] A count of both independent and dependent special districts in 1959 showed
37 districts in the Greater Hampton Roads area. See S. J. Makielski, Jr., and
David G. Temple, *Special District Government in Virginia* (Charlottesville: Institute of Government, University of Virginia, 1967), p. 112. The main purpose
of this study was to examine the nature and extent of functional disintegration
brought about by the use of special purpose boards, commissions, and authorities. For this reason, the study explored both dependent and independent districts. In his study of special districts, John C. Bollens devotes a chapter to the
dependent district. See his *Special District Governments in the United States*
(Berkeley and Los Angeles: University of California Press, 1957).

port News, where racial control of city government was an issue, this was reflected to some extent in the antimerger vote in certain identifiable black precincts. A contrary result occurred in the Princess Anne County–Virginia Beach referendum on merger when the predominantly black precinct of Seatack in the county led all other county precincts in the percentage of votes cast in favor of consolidation.

Yet a simple governmental structure, increasing urbanization, and a restricted electorate did not by themselves make the mergers. Additional factors were present, both locally and statewide, which contributed to each consolidation in its particular setting. Because these factors were unique or peculiarly Virginian, they will be explored in some depth in the next chapter.

CHAPTER II

THE ENVIRONMENT OF MERGER: THE STATE

E ACH of the Tidewater mergers was the product of a unique political environment, and as might be expected, no two mergers were alike in all respects. On the one hand, the process and politics of merger were clearly shaped by the local political environments. Yet, on the other hand, the politics of consolidation also transcended the boundaries of the involved local governments and, at times, even their respective metropolitan areas. In a strict sense, the consolidations were local undertakings, but several of the issues and circumstances that prompted and promoted merger were not merely local.

To understand the *raison d'être* of the Tidewater mergers, an examination of the legal, structural, and political characteristics of Virginia and Virginia local government is necessary. Merger politics was carried on against a backdrop of (1) city-county separation, (2) municipal annexation law and practice, (3) state statutes controlling local government consolidation, and (4) Byrd Organization politics. In some measure each was an important factor in affecting the outcome of consolidation.

City-County Separation

Perhaps the most distinctive feature of local government in Virginia is the statewide application of the principle of city-county separation.[1] Throughout the state, every city is politically independent of the county in which it is located. The county performs no functions within the corporate limits of the city and exercises no jurisdiction over city residents. City residents pay no taxes to and generally

[1] See, generally, Chester W. Bain, *"A Body Incorporate": The Evolution of City-County Separation in Virginia* (Charlottesville: Published for the Institute of Government, University of Virginia, by the University Press of Virginia, 1967).

receive no services from county government. For this reason, city dwellers play no part in the political life of the county; they do not vote for members of the county board of supervisors or any other county officer. Cities and counties in Virginia are independent of each other in the same manner as two counties elsewhere are independent and coequal local units.

City-county separation may be seen as a logical result of the dichotomous urban and rural concept of city and county government that has prevailed in Virginia. City government is held to be urban government, and cities are created primarily to perform services required by the conditions of urban life. County government, on the other hand, is intended, so it has been argued, to serve only rural and less densely populated areas. City-county separation is based on the premise that since the county is a rural unit of government, there can be no need for rural government in an urban place, and vice versa. This premise, and city-county separation itself, stems largely from practice and tradition, although both may be inferred from the Virginia Constitution,[2] and both have been confirmed in principle by the Virginia Supreme Court.[3] If Virginia's metropolitan areas are excluded, the urban-rural distinction between city and county government has been maintained with more than reasonable success throughout the Commonwealth.

Virginia in 1970 had ninety-six counties and thirty-eight cities. Because cities and counties are separate, the most obvious result of the system in operation is that no overlap of services and functions can occur. State functions, such as the administration of justice, which are undertaken by counties elsewhere in the United States, are performed by cities and counties alike in Virginia. When Virginia cities are viewed in this manner, as John A. Rush correctly observed, each city in Virginia is a consolidated city-county.[4]

At the time of the Tidewater mergers Virginia had three classes of municipal corporations: cities of the first class, cities of the second class, and towns. Population served as the basis for these classifica-

---

[2] The Virginia Constitution in effect at the time of the four consolidations was the Constitution of 1928, as amended. The pertinent section here is Sec. 116. The Virginia Constitution of 1971, which became effective at noon on July 1, 1971, made a small, though significant, change in the definition of a city. In this connection, see Weldon Cooper, "The Virginia City Defined," 6 *Virginia Town & City* 10–11 (Feb. 1971).

[3] Norfolk County v. City of Portsmouth, 186 Va. 1032, 45 S.E.2d 136 (1947).

[4] Rush, *The City-County Consolidated* (Los Angeles: The Author, 1941), ch. 21.

tions; a city of the first class had a population of 10,000 or more persons, while a city of the second class had more than 5,000 and less than 10,000 inhabitants. Both first and second class cities were independent of their surrounding counties, although cities of the second class shared the services of certain officials with the county. Both former Virginia Beach and Hampton were cities of the second class, for example, and both shared the services of a court clerk, sheriff, Commonwealth's attorney, and an appointed school division superintendent with their respective surrounding counties. This sharing of certain officials eased somewhat the transition to consolidated city status after the legal merger.

Second, towns in Virginia, that is, municipalities with less than 5,000 inhabitants, are not included in the scheme of city-county separation. Towns are part of the county in which they are located, and town-county relationships conform generally to the city-county relationships in other states. If the population of a town increases to 5,000 inhabitants, it may elect to become a city, at which time it is separated from the county. The transition from town to city status, however, is neither mandatory nor automatic. In 1970 several towns had the requisite population for transition to city status, but because towns share equally in county services, most notably schools, these towns have chosen to retain town status rather than take on the expense of separate city status.

The rapid growth of metropolitan areas in Tidewater and Northern Virginia has caused a breakdown in the traditional urban-rural differentiation between city and county government. Between 1940 and 1960 the General Assembly expanded county powers and functions by both local bills and general law, thereby enabling counties in metropolitan areas to cope with problems brought about by urbanization. Nonetheless, even though metropolitan area counties began to provide limited urban services, in terms of traditional Virginia local government theory the county was still considered to be a rural unit of government. In practical terms this meant, among other things, that the traditional method of adjusting city-county boundaries to accommodate urban growth was left unchanged.

This traditional method in Virginia has been municipal annexation of unincorporated county territory on the urban fringe. Once this territory has been annexed by a city, the application of city-county separation requires that all county jurisdiction and control over the annexed area be surrendered to the city. County jurisdiction ends on the day annexation takes effect.

Annexation and Its Consequences

Annexation in Virginia is a complex process.[5] Essentially, annexation is quasi-judicial in nature and takes the form of an adversary proceeding between the city and county before a special three-judge annexation court. In effect, a city sues the county for a portion of the county's territory that has become urban. The court may enter an order granting the city the area specified in the annexation suit, or it may reduce or add to that territory, or deny completely the city's request. When the formal annexation order is entered, the court may and usually does compel the city to compensate the county for the loss of tax revenue and for permanent improvements that the county has made in the annexed area.

Two aspects of Virginia annexation law and practice should be emphasized. First, the process is entirely in the hands of the annexation court, and no provision is made for a referendum on annexation in the city, the county, or the area proposed to be annexed. Second, annexation cases are decided on the basis of the need for orderly growth and development of the entire area rather than on the wishes of the residents. Whether or not the residents of the proposed annexed area want city government is immaterial; rather, the court bases its decision on whether or not the residents need municipal government because of their urban condition. To determine whether annexation is necessary and expedient, the court considers the extent of urbanization in the area proposed to be annexed, the need for additional services to protect the public, and the probable growth and development of the area.

Annexation proceedings in the past have usually been successful. Chester W. Bain has summed up the results between 1904 and 1965:

By June 30, 1965, a total of 109 proceedings to extend city boundaries had been initiated. Out of the 109 proceedings, 93 were heard on their merits by an annexation court, 8 were withdrawn by the city or the residents initiating the action, 3 were dismissed by the annexation court without a hearing, and 5 were awaiting hearing at mid-1965.

The balance in annexation proceedings has been overwhelmingly in favor of the cities. Of the 93 proceedings heard on their merits, annexation

[5] For a complete discussion of annexation, see Chester W. Bain, *Annexation in Virginia: The Use of the Judicial Process for Readjusting City-County Boundaries* (Charlottesville: Published for the Institute of Government, University of Virginia, by the University Press of Virginia, 1966).

courts granted an extension of the city's boundaries on 86 occasions. In only 7 proceedings have annexation courts after hearing the evidence refused to annex some territory to a city. Appeals from 3 of these unsuccessful proceedings were heard by the Virginia Supreme Court of Appeals. The lower court was affirmed in 2 instances, but in the other case the court entered an order annexing part of the territory requested by the city. In all, then, the extension of Virginia city boundaries has been granted on 87 occasions, representing 94 per cent of the proceedings heard on their merits between 1904 and June 30, 1965.[6]

The Virginia system of annexation is well established and has served to maintain the urban-rural division between city and county government in most of the state. In the nonmetropolitan areas of Virginia annexation proceedings usually involve less than a square mile of county territory and rarely more than five square miles. Such city-county boundary adjustments involving a limited area and population can be made without adversely affecting the operation of either government.

The application of the annexation statutes in a developing metropolitan area, however, has produced an altogether different result. Large areas of a metropolitan county may become urbanized in a relatively brief period of time, with the result that the urbanized area is a legitimate target for any city with expansionist aims. Between 1948 and 1960 in Tidewater, for example, Norfolk County lost approximately thirty three square miles of territory to the cities of South Norfolk, Portsmouth, and Norfolk. Some 110,000 former county residents became city dwellers, and county officials estimated their revenue loss in the form of taxable wealth and other income to be almost $1.9 million per year.[7]

Between 1950 and 1960 increasing urbanization made the actual and prospective loss of area, taxable wealth, and population through annexation the paramount issue for the county governments in the two Tidewater metropolitan areas. Urbanization demanded that the counties undertake minimal but still expensive urban services. Yet annexation of urbanized areas, or the threat thereof, interfered with county attempts to plan, finance, and develop such services. From the counties' view, any investment in urban services would likely be upset by an annexation suit and the

[6] *Ibid.*, pp. 210–11.

[7] These figures were used by the proconsolidationists in the merger campaign involving Norfolk County and South Norfolk and were supplied to the author by Charles Cross, clerk of the circuit court, City of Chesapeake.

subsequent loss of territory to an adjacent city. At the same time, it was impossible for the counties to ignore the service needs of suburban residents if for no other reason than protection of the public health.

One county response to annexation by central cities might have been to promote the incorporation of towns on the urban fringe, encircling those cities that had expansionist aims. Elsewhere in the nation a buffer zone of surrounding small adjacent municipal corporations has served effectively to hem in an aggressive and expansion-minded central city. But this tactic was simply out of the question in Virginia and was never considered. In the first place there was staunch opposition in Virginia to the Balkanization of the state's metropolitan areas for both political and economic reasons. Moreover, from the county viewpoint, the creation of buffer towns was no solution at all. A town, unlike a city, is not immune from annexation by a city. In addition, every such town created is itself a potential city. Towns, like cities, may also engage in annexation, and there is nothing in Virginia law to prevent a town from achieving separate city status by annexing enough county residents to reach the requisite population level. Thus, as far as the counties were concerned, the incorporation of a town simply added to the threat of annexation.

This was the situation confronting the metropolitan Tidewater counties between 1950 and 1960. Virginia annexation law operating in conjunction with the system of city-county separation contributed to three of the four Tidewater mergers—Hampton, Virginia Beach, and Chesapeake. The only way a county could avoid piecemeal annexation was to consolidate with a neighboring municipality and then to incorporate the new consolidated government as a city. Once corporate status was acquired, no part of the new city could be annexed by another city.

Annexation Politics

The general success of municipal annexation impelled the counties to attempt to restrict annexation by legislative action in the Virginia General Assembly. Basically, the counties acted in concert to make the annexation statutes more restrictive, while municipalities struggled for a status quo position or for liberalizing annexation law. The counties tried to modify the annexation law by making it more difficult for a city to enter a suit or to prove the necessity and

expediency of annexation, and by forcing the cities to pay a higher
price following a successful annexation proceeding.[8] At the same
time the cities and towns were usually able to block such changes in
the law and, further, to promote an easing of existing restrictions.
The annexation debate was carried on with intensity during the
period when the Tidewater mergers were initiated and consummated. In fact, it was the legislative struggle over certain aspects of
the state's annexation laws that prompted the Hampton merger in
1952 and brought forth special legislation which permitted former
Warwick County to incorporate as a city of the first class.[9]

In 1938, primarily to protect Elizabeth City County and Warwick
County from annexation by the adjoining City of Newport News,
the General Assembly enacted a law which prohibited the reduction of a county area below sixty square miles by means of annexation.[10] If the annexation court found it to be necessary and expedient to grant annexation in a case which would reduce a county
below sixty square miles, the statute provided that all of the
remaining county was to be annexed to the city. This statute was
the so-called Massenburg Act, named for G. A. Massenburg, a
member of the House of Delegates from Elizabeth City County. In
effect, it protected both Elizabeth City County, with about fifty-
three square miles, and Warwick County, with some sixty-three
square miles, from annexation by Newport News. The stated ra-
tionale underlying this protective legislation was that the reduction
of a county area below sixty square miles would affect taxable
wealth so adversely that effective county government would be impossible.

In 1949 the Virginia Advisory Legislative Council (VALC),

[8] See Virginia Association of Counties [then the League of Virginia Counties],
*Statement Pertaining to Annexation, Consolidation and the Structure of Local
Government in Virginia,* Virginia County Research Report no. 5 (Charlottesville: The Author, 1963). The Association has historically taken the position
that there should be a popular referendum on annexation in affected areas.

[9] The transition by which Warwick County became the City of Warwick in
1952 was the first time in the history of Virginia local government that a county
became a city in one step. Also unique was the incorporation directly by the
General Assembly in 1916 of a portion of Prince George County as the City of
Hopewell. See Bain, *"A Body Incorporate,"* pp. 21–22 and 71.

[10] Virginia Code § 15-152.26 (1950), now § 15.1-1056 (hereafter cited as Code).
The validity of this act was upheld in City of Newport News v. Elizabeth City
County, 189 Va. 825, 55 S.E.2d 56 (1949). Since the mergers, this title of the
Code has been renumbered. When dealing with the law in an historical context,
the Code citation applicable at the time will be used followed by the 1970 Code
citation.

which had been directed to study annexation law and practice, recommended to the 1950 General Assembly that the Massenburg provision be deleted from the Code. Although the underlying reasons for this recommendation are not now wholly clear, the proposed legislation would have reduced the protected area limit from sixty to thirty square miles. Had this recommendation been accepted by the General Assembly, only Arlington County in Northern Virginia, with an area of twenty four square miles, would have enjoyed immunity from annexation.

To counteract the proposal of the VALC, a vigorous and successful campaign was waged by Senator Victor P. Wilson of the Thirtythird District (Warwick County, Elizabeth City County, Hampton, and Newport News) and E. Ralph James, a member of the House of Delegates from Elizabeth City County. In the Senate, Wilson was able to secure retention of the Massenburg provision by an 18–13 vote, but in the House of Delegates a margin of only one vote saved Warwick and Elizabeth City counties from the possibility of being subjected to annexation by Newport News. The closeness of the vote made it apparent to local leaders that the security formerly provided by the Massenburg Act was in jeopardy. As a direct result, Elizabeth City County successfully promoted its merger with the Town of Phoebus and the City of Hampton in 1952, and Warwick County's transition to city status followed in that same year.

To enable the two counties to protect themselves from annexation by acquiring corporate status, it was necessary to obtain special permissive legislation from the General Assembly. Some real doubts existed within the General Assembly as to the wisdom of allowing the two counties to achieve corporate status. Neither of the two proposed county actions, the Hampton merger or the Warwick incorporation, was in keeping with the traditional approaches to local government in Virginia, and both were obviously aimed at blocking any expansion by the City of Newport News. Thus, to ensure passage of the needed permissive legislation assurances had to be given to members from other areas that the matter was indeed local and special in character and could be treated as any other special act or general law of special application. With the support of the local legislative delegation from the affected area, the enabling acts were passed, and merger and transition followed shortly thereafter.

One of the leading promerger leaders explained:

How did it happen? The people did it. They were fired with resentment at the secondary position which Virginia's recently re-enacted annexation law had again relegated counties, as related to cities. They burned with the determination to preserve for themselves the inherent right to choose the form of government under which their majority chose to live. So under dark and threatening clouds of annexation by Newport News, adjacent to both counties, the people pushed their way into the polls and pulled out majorities of five to one and eight to one in Warwick and Elizabeth City, respectively.[11]

On the other side of Hampton Roads, annexation or the threat of annexation was also the issue that initiated both the Virginia Beach and the Chesapeake consolidations in 1962. In these two consolidations, however, the threat to the two former counties of Norfolk and Princess Anne did not emanate from action within the General Assembly but rather from anticipated efforts at annexation by the core cities of Norfolk and Portsmouth. To both Princess Anne and Norfolk counties consolidation and incorporation were a form of self-protection from annexation by Norfolk and Portsmouth. Although these mergers cannot be tied to any overt act on the part of the General Assembly aimed at modifying the state's annexation laws, it can be suggested that failure of the General Assembly to protect the metropolitan county from annexation was a contributing factor to both mergers.

Following the 1950 review of the annexation statutes by the VALC that triggered the Hampton merger, the General Assembly remained deadlocked on annexation policy for the remainder of the decade. Between 1950 and 1960 no significant changes were made either in the theory or practice of annexation. Members of the General Assembly usually viewed proposed exceptions to the annexation law protecting metropolitan area counties against the backdrop of their possible impact upon the nonmetropolitan segment of Virginia. The General Assembly had no inclination to risk upsetting the traditional local government structure, and as a result, nothing substantial was done. Although legislative action was taken to assist the conduct of county government in metropolitan areas, especially in their service functions, the effect of such laws was clearly limited to the urbanized counties and did not threaten the over-all operation of the Virginian system of local government

[11] Stuart M. Gibson, "The Tale of Two Cities," 6 *Virginia and the Virginia County* 7 ff. (Oct. 1952). Gibson was clerk of the circuit court of Elizabeth City County and reputedly engineered the Hampton–Phoebus–Elizabeth City County merger.

in any way. Consequently, counties in metropolitan areas remained targets for cities with expansionist aims.

Had the General Assembly acted to protect the territorial integrity of the rapidly urbanizing counties in Tidewater, it is possible that the consolidated cities of Virginia Beach and Chesapeake would not now exist. However, no important legislative action was taken on annexation until it became clear that the threat of annexation had actually triggered the Virginia Beach and Chesapeake mergers. The General Assembly then responded by declaring a one-year moratorium on annexation and consolidation until the entire matter could be studied in depth. In a subsequent position paper, the issue was well summarized by the Virginia Association of Counties, which officially urged the General Assembly to bring "the annexation and consolidation statutes . . . into relationship with each other so that the threat of annexation may not be used to force consolidation." [12]

Merger and the Law

State laws governing merger were also a significant factor in the development of the Tidewater consolidations. Although the merger process was fundamentally political in character, it was carried on within a legal framework which required that certain actions be taken and that specific conditions be met by the participating parties. The law did not compel merger under any circumstances; rather it provided a method by which two or more local governments might consolidate if they so elected. Provided that differences could be reconciled at the bargaining table, the law established a relatively simple procedure for formalizing such political arrangements.[13]

Merger law in Virginia displays several salient features that deserve special mention. First, and perhaps most important, Virginia laws controlling local government consolidations are clearly intended to promote merger wherever agreement can be reached by

[12] *Statement Pertaining to Annexation,* p. 10.

[13] Statutes permitting merger are constitutional. In Walker v. Massey, 202 Va. 886, 121 S.E.2d 448 (1961), the Virginia Supreme Court pointed out that "there is no distinction between the authority to provide for consolidation of counties, cities, and towns and the authority given to provide for a change in the form of their organization and government."

the local participants through negotiation. The requirements imposed by statutory law are simple, free from burdensome procedural requirements, and flexible. Where a barrier to consolidation has arisen as a result of the law, the General Assembly has usually taken steps to lower that barrier or eliminate it altogether.

Second, the proconsolidation approach to merger adopted by the General Assembly is part of the climate of Virginia government. The specter of local government consolidation does not seem to generate the emotional hostility that often appears in other states. No strong vested political interest against merger exists, and political leaders in Virginia have generally adopted the premise that local government consolidation is inherently worthwhile. Even when the Virginia Beach and Chesapeake mergers encircled and closed off any further territorial expansion through annexation by the core City of Norfolk, an action clearly detrimental to the long-range development of that city, several political leaders in the area expressed the general opinion that "it would all work out" to the benefit of everyone. Indeed, after studying the effect of the Virginia Beach and Chesapeake mergers on the metropolitan area, the General Assembly liberalized the merger statutes even further.

Finally, the local governments themselves have been active participants in shaping merger law. Much of what is now general law applicable statewide developed from special law provisions initiated locally to promote a particular consolidation attempt. After merger talk began in the Newport News–Hampton area about 1940, local governments in Virginia have been increasingly willing to explore merger. This widespread willingness to talk has on several occasions been followed by a good-faith attempt to work out a consolidation agreement. Such explorations have helped to define special problems regarding merger and, further, have brought forth alternative proposals for their solution in the form of proposed law.

Although merger law in Virginia can be traced back to 1910, when the General Assembly employed a special act to permit consolidation of the cities of Richmond and Manchester, the origin of the consolidation statutes in force at the time of the Tidewater mergers dates from 1940.[14] Consideration was given at that time to

[14] For background on the consolidation statutes, the author would like to acknowledge the use of three unpublished reports on town consolidation, city consolidation, and county consolidation prepared for the Virginia Advisory Legislative Council's Committee on Annexation and Consolidation of the 1962 General Assembly. These reports were prepared by George W. Jennings, consultant to the committee, and are in the files of the Institute of Government.

the merger of six local governments in the Lower Peninsula of Virginia, now the Newport News–Hampton SMSA. It was proposed to create a single urban county by merging the existing counties of York, Warwick, and Elizabeth City with the cities of Hampton and Newport News and the Town of Phoebus.[15]

The 1940 proposal was never carried to referendum; yet it was important for two reasons. First, the interest generated by the proposed consolidation brought about additional legislation setting forth many of the legal requirements and procedures that would be used in subsequent consolidations. Second, there was an initial exploration of certain constitutional questions regarding the nature and powers of a consolidated city. One of the more critical questions centered on the construction of section 168 of the Virginia Constitution, which required "uniformity of taxation upon the same class of subjects within the territorial limits of the authority levying the tax." It was recognized that urban and rural areas needed different levels of services, and if a city-county consolidation was to be attractive to all participants, some plan was required that would permit an equitable apportionment of the tax burden to pay for these services. Since the imposition of different tax rates within the corporate limits of the consolidated city might violate section 168,[16] it was concluded that such a taxing system could be worked

[15] See "A Report on a Proposed Metropolitan Peninsula County," mimeographed copy in the files of the Institute of Government, University of Virginia. This report was submitted to the Greater Peninsula Association on Dec. 18, 1940.

[16] A confirming opinion was given by the attorney general of Virginia in 1950. See *Opinions of the Attorney General*, 1949–50 (March 1, 1950), pp. 220–21 (hereafter cited as *O. A. G.*). The attorney general ruled that the proposed charter for the consolidated City of Hampton Roads would be unconstitutional under section 168 if tax rates within the proposed city were not uniform. Quoting Campbell v. Bryant, 104 Va. 509, 52 S.E. 638 (1905), the attorney general noted that "the uniformity extends not only to the rate and mode of assessment but also to the territory to be assessed."

It may be noted at this point that Hampton, Chesapeake, and Virginia Beach either have applied or are currently applying varying tax rates in different boroughs of the cities. Authorization for this action was found under Code § 15-222.3 (9), now § 15.1-1135. To counteract the effect of section 168, the tax levy for schools, police, and general government are uniform throughout the consolidated cities. Other services such as water and sewer service are financed by special levies according to the service rendered in each borough.

In view of the language of section 168, the constitutionality of this procedure was open to question. However, in 1958, the attorney general offered a written opinion which supported the contention that cities may employ special service districts in which the cost of services are borne by residents of the district. See

out only under a county form of government, where special taxing districts could be employed.

In 1940 the General Assembly enacted what was termed a supplemental consolidation statute, providing for the creation of an urban county or a municipal corporation in the Lower Peninsula area.[17] The law was never used in its original form but, when amended, served as the legal base for three of the four subsequent Tidewater consolidations. The exception was the Elizabeth City County–Hampton–Phoebus merger, which was accomplished by means of a separate general law of special application.[18]

The 1940 Act, which subsequently became section 15-220 of the Code, was amended in 1956 to accommodate the merger of the City of Warwick and the City of Newport News. This amendment simply added appropriate population characteristics to existing language so that the act would apply to the two cities. After the Newport News–Warwick merger in 1957, the development of this Code provision took a somewhat curious turn.

In 1958 the General Assembly charged the VALC to study local government consolidation, functions, planning, and zoning. At the time the study began, another prospective merger was under exploration at the local level although the participants, the City of Richmond and Henrico County, did not have authorizing legislation to permit consolidation. In part to accommodate this projected merger, and wishing to avoid use of the population-bracketed general law of local application, the VALC recommended to the 1960 General Assembly that section 15-220 of the Code be made a general law applicable to all counties, cities, and towns in the Commonwealth.[19] This recommendation was subsequently accepted by

---

O. A. G., 1957–58 (April 25, 1958) , pp. 67–68. In 1962, moreover, the constitutionality of such action was upheld in Walker v. City of Virginia Beach: In the Circuit Court of Princess Anne County, Opinion No. 6703 (April 17, 1962) . Judge Wahab noted: "Nothing could be fairer or more equitable than such a flexible tax structure whereby persons pay only for services they actually receive, yet all persons who receive the same service pay the same tax." Differential taxation for consolidated governments is now provided for in art. X, § 1 of the 1971 Virginia Constitution.

[17] *Acts and Joint Resolutions of the General Aseembly of the Commonwealth of Virginia, 1940* (Richmond: Division of Purchase and Printing, 1940) , p. 693 (hereafter cited as *Acts of Assembly*) .

[18] *Ibid.,* 1950, p. 1591.

[19] Virginia Advisory Legislative Council to Study Consolidation of Local Governments and Functions, Planning and Zoning, *Report to the Governor and the General Assembly of Virginia,* House Document 12 (Richmond: Division of Purchase and Printing, 1959) , p. 16; Code § 15-220, now § 15.1-1130.

the General Assembly and enacted with little difficulty. At the time the General Assembly apparently assumed the modification was made solely for the benefit of Richmond and Henrico County, an assumption based on the fact that no other city-county consolidation was even in the discussion stage. But the statutory language of the amendment was not limited to Richmond and Henrico County. The Act states that "any one or more adjoining cities or adjacent counties, or any one or more adjoining or adjacent cities or towns, or any of such counties, cities, or towns, where such counties, cities or towns, as the case may be, adjoin or are adjacent to each other may consolidate into a single county or city . . . ."

The 1960 amendment clearly invited governmental mergers throughout Virginia. Did the VALC really intend to provide Virginia with a general consolidation statute, or was Code, § 15-220 merely an accident of legislative draftmanship? Although many members of the General Assembly plainly did not foresee the potential impact of the amendment, the VALC appears to have been clearly interested in promoting local government consolidation. For example, the committee proposed constructive amendments to sections 168, 170, and 176 of the Virginia Constitution that would have removed all doubts regarding differential tax rates by specifically (1) authorizing the application of different tax rates within a consolidated city and (2) permitting special assessments in consolidated cities on property owners who directly benefited from certain municipal services.[20] In support of these proposed amendments the committee noted that "we feel that these amendments will encourage *consolidations of localities in metropolitan areas.* Counties having both urban and rural areas within their boundaries would not then be inclined to shy away from consolidation because of a fear that inhabitants in the areas not immediately receiving certain services would be subject to taxes as high as land in urban and industrial areas." [21]

The legal requirements and processes for bringing about city-county consolidation were set forth in former sections 15-220-30 of the Code.[22] The law provided for a formal consolidation agreement between the parties with certain mandatory and optional provisions aimed at spelling out the terms and conditions of the merger. It

[20] VALC (Committee to Study Consolidation) , *Report* (1959) , pp. 7–8.

[21] *Ibid.,* p. 8. Emphasis added.

[22] Because the mergers actually took place under these former Code sections, the recodified citations are not employed. The procedure remains basically the same in 1970 and is set forth in Code §§ 15.1-1130–15.1-1144.

also required a referendum on the question of consolidation, and finally, it included certain miscellaneous provisions dealing with the actual transition to a consolidated city or county status.

The mandatory information to be included in any consolidation agreement was brief and simple. The agreement had to show (1) the names of the local governments proposing to consolidate, (2) the name of the new governmental unit or, in lieu of this name, a provision for a referendum to select the name of the new city or county, (3) a statement of the real and personal property belonging to each of the governments proposing to consolidate, (4) a statement of the indebtedness of each unit, and (5) the date upon which the consolidation would become effective.[23] In addition, the agreement had to provide (6) for the disposition of all property or debts due any such county, city, or town and (7) for the assumption by the consolidated city of a just proportion of all other existing debt of the local units to be combined.

The local governments proposing to merge might include, if they so desired, additional provisions within the body of the consolidation agreement. The parties to the merger agreement might (1) provide that no increase be made in assessments for a five-year period in the consolidated city except for permanent improvements, (2) provide that there be no increase in the tax rate on real property for five years, (3) provide that special taxes be levied in certain areas up to a maximum twenty-year period to repay existing bonded indebtedness outstanding at the time of consolidation, (4) establish boroughs within the consolidated city, (5) provide for the establishment of shires if the new governmental unit was to be a county, (6) make provision for an election of new officers of the consolidated city or county, although an election need not be held and other means to select officers could be employed, and (7) stipulate that the council of the consolidated city would have the power to levy a higher tax rate in some areas of the city than in others.[24] Most of these options were exercised in Virginia Beach and Chesapeake, and all have been used at least once except for provision (5). In regard to provision (7), funds raised by special taxation had to be kept segregated, and such taxes could be levied only for services not offered in the whole of the consolidated political subdivision before the consolidation. Specifically prohibited was any special levy for schools, police, or general government services.

[23] Code § 15-221, now § 15.1-1131.
[24] Code § 15-222.3, now § 15.1-1135. The list is selective.

Finally, the consolidating units of government were empowered to include a charter or certain specific charter provisions as an integral part of the consolidation agreement. The law also provided that particular charter sections might be taken from the charter of any city proposing to consolidate or from any other charter for a proposed consolidated city.[25] This provision permitted the merger participants to draft their own charter by borrowing cafeteria-style from other charters, including an optional general law charter which the General Assembly enacted for consolidated cities in 1956.[26] Needless to say, the consolidating units could not include provisions in their proposed charter that were prohibited to other cities by general law or contravened provisions of the Virginia Constitution.

Once the consolidation agreement had been drafted by representatives of the localities proposing to consolidate, it had to be approved by the governing bodies of each county, city, or town that was a party to the merger negotiations. Approval was to be in the form of an ordinance adopted by each participating council or board of supervisors. Next, a copy of the consolidation agreement had to be filed with the circuit court of the county proposing to merge and in the corporation court of each of the involved cities. After these copies were filed, the consolidation agreement had to be published once a week for four successive weeks in a newspaper of general circulation in each of the counties and cities proposing to consolidate.[27]

Upon receipt of the agreement by each of the courts, the respective judges were to order a referendum to be held on the question of consolidation. This referendum could be held either at the time of the regular general election in November or at a special election to be held no sooner than 30 days nor later than 300 days after the agreement was filed with the court. The law specifically required that the referendum on consolidation be held on the same day in each of the localities proposing to merge.[28]

If the referendum results were favorable to consolidation, each circuit court or corporation court judge was required to enter this fact as a matter of record.[29] All elections held on the question of

[25] This provision was added in 1956 for the benefit of Newport News and Warwick.

[26] See Code §§ 15-231.4:1–15-231.4:78 for this charter. These provisions were deleted in a later recodification.

[27] Code § 15-223, now § 15.1-1137.   [28] Code § 15-224, now § 15.1-1138.

[29] Code § 15-226, now § 15.1-1140.

consolidation were to be conducted under the provisions of general law. The voters of each participating local government had to ratify the consolidation agreement for it to become effective.

In the interim between the referendum and the time specified in the consolidation agreement when the new city would come into existence, the law provided that all legal actions against the separate parties should continue as if the consolidation were not to take place.[30] It also stated specifically that senatorial and house districts were to remain the same until changed in accordance with procedures specified by law,[31] and that the jurisdiction of each former county circuit court and city corporation court was to be expanded automatically to include all of the territory within the boundaries of the new city. However, the jurisdiction of the courts could be limited to specific areas of the consolidated city as prescribed by either the consolidation agreement or the new charter for the consolidated city.[32]

The foregoing summary describes the principal features of merger law in Virginia. In sum, at the time of merger the processes by which local governments in Virginia were able to consolidate were basically simple, and the General Assembly had imposed no significant legal barriers to merger.[33] Provided that a consolidation agreement could be reached at the bargaining table and provided further that the voters of each locality were agreeable to consolidation, the law did little more than set forth an orderly and rational method to realize this end.

The Byrd Organization

It is impossible to explore any aspect of Virginia government and politics in the 1950's and early 1960's without touching upon the somewhat nebulous but nonetheless powerful Byrd Organization. At the time of the governmental mergers in Tidewater, Virginia politics was dominated by this organization. To understand the mergers, then, some insight into the organization is necessary, especially as it operated on the local level.

[30] Code § 15-228, now § 15.1-1142.   [31] Code § 15-229, now § 15.1-1143.
[32] Code § 15-230, now § 15.1-1144.

[33] A contrary point of view was offered in 1963 by the Virginia Association of Counties [then the League of Virginia Counties], which characterized the merger process as "too difficult to effect a reasonable and sensible consolidation." See *Statement Pertaining to Consolidation*, p. 10.

The Byrd Organization had long been a political fact of life within the Commonwealth. Somewhat like the United States Senate, it resembled an exclusive club and only its members were fully cognizant of its inner workings. The organization was complex, it rarely talked for publication, and discerning when it was acting as the organization was not always easy. Neither was it always possible to uncover just who constituted the organization or to fix hierarchical levels. As J. Harvie Wilkinson III noted:

The "high command," as the ruling oligarchy was called, included at mid-century E. R. Combs, Bill Tuck, "Blackie" Moore, Congressman Howard Smith, Sidney Kellam, boss of Princess Anne County, and state Senators Garland Gray and Harry Byrd, Jr. A dozen other men hovered on the periphery of the ruling circle whose circumference remained purposely clouded. Yet clearly at the circle's center stood Harry Byrd.[34]

Various writers in the past attempted to describe the inner workings of the Byrd Organization. John Gunther in 1947 provided the following description:

The machine works something like this. Its major instruments are, as always, jobs and patronage, plus the Virginia poll tax. First, through the Democratic National Committee Byrd controls Federal patronage. Next, he pretty well decides the choice not merely of the governor but of most members of the general assembly (legislature). The governor, who in Virginia today cannot be other than a Byrd man, in turn controls the appointment of some thousands of state employees and circuit court judges are chosen—for substantial eight year terms—by the legislature; these in turn appoint the school trustees, county electoral boards, county welfare boards, and trial justices. In each county there is a fixed ring of six or seven machine men. Some county officers like the sheriff and tax assessor are elected but their salaries and expense allotments are, within limits, established by the State Compensation Board, also appointed by the governor under Byrd's control. The pattern makes a full interlocking circle. Nothing could be neater or more complete.[35]

A somewhat different and more elaborate view was provided by V. O. Key, Jr., who came as close as anyone in the late 1940's to understanding the organization. Key correctly observed, for instance, that "dictatorship is hardly the word to apply to the re-

[34] Wilkinson, *Harry Byrd and the Changing Face of Virginia Politics, 1945–1966* (Charlottesville: University Press of Virginia, 1968), pp. 60–61.

[35] Gunther, *Inside U.S.A.* (New York: Harper and Brothers, 1947), p. 709, reprinted by permission of the publisher.

lations between the high command and its local subsidiaries." [36]
Equally important is Key's conclusion that "in essence, Virginia is
governed by a well disciplined and ably managed oligarchy of not
more than a thousand professional politicians, which enjoys the
enthusiastic and almost undivided support of the business community and the well-to-do generally.[37]

Although Wilkinson disagreed with Key in part as to why the
organization received the support of the business community, both
writers discerned that the foundation upon which the organization
rested was local. Key's description of the "outposts" of the Byrd
Organization is especially apt.

County officials usually manage the local outposts of the organization although in some counties a nonofficial person serves as local leader. The
chief elements in each county machine are five elected administrative officers: commonwealth's attorney, treasurer, commissioner of the revenue,
clerk of the circuit court, and sheriff. These officials usually outrank in
political potency the county supervisors who represent subdivisions of the
county. The clerk of the circuit court, perhaps because of his eight-year
tenure of office, often becomes the kingpin of the county organization.
Another figure in the background who sometimes overshadows all these
officials is the circuit judge who possesses important appointing powers. . . . The circuit judge ties into the state organization through his
election by the General Assembly.[38]

Most writers on the Byrd Organization have been concerned with
the operation of the organization on a statewide basis. They have
given attention to the components, the county and city organizations, chiefly for the purpose of exploring the pattern of control, or
the manner by which the organization was held together. This
approach has been unfortunate in so far as it has tended to cast the
local organizations into a single mold. Wilkinson, for example, in
his vignette of the Brunswick County organization, noted that Byrd
candidates were supported overwhelmingly by the county organization and explained:

Similar courthouse support for the Byrd organization throughout the state
caused observers to look for an arm-twisting device enabling the state
hierarchy to keep its local lieutenants in line. What has been overlooked,
however, was the remarkable similarity of viewpoint among organization

[36] Key, *Southern Politics in State and Nation* (New York: copyright 1949 by
Alfred A. Knopf, Inc.) , p. 23; this and succeeding passages are reprinted by
permission of the publisher.
[37] *Ibid.*, p. 26.   [38] *Ibid.*, pp. 21–22.

Tidewater Virginia

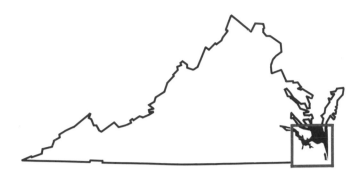

Tidewater

BEFORE MERGER

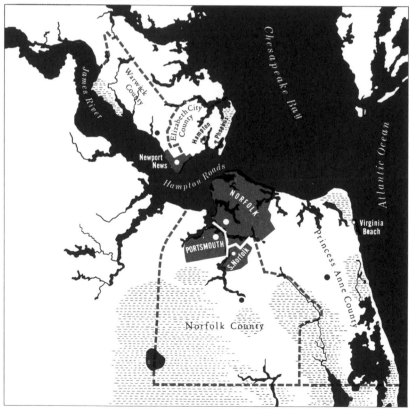

County boundaries
County seat
City hall
City or towns

Virginia

AFTER MERGER

members, which, in the long run, unified them far more effectively and fundamentally than any pressure or patronage tactics ever could have.[39]

While Wilkinson is generally correct in observing that there was a similarity of viewpoint, that viewpoint was by no means monolithic. Moreover, if observers failed to uncover "an arm-twisting device," it was probably because they did not perceive fully the local organization in operation. Machinery did exist at the state level for controlling local officials, but it was employed with significant restraint and apparently only on rare occasions. Overt action emanating from the state level to ensure Byrd control was limited. But, as antiorganization men and mavericks within the organization could testify, significant pressure could be applied locally, both by local officials and private sources. In short, when arm twisting or the threat of arm twisting was necessary, it was often possible to accomplish this internally, unofficially, and locally.

Consideration of the Byrd Organization at the state level has only limited value as far as the Tidewater mergers are concerned. Although the state organization and the "high command" may have been involved in merger at one point, evidence gained by interviews indicates that the Tidewater mergers were to a significant extent in-group arrangements between the local organizations. The existence of the state organization, however, unquestionably helped to facilitate merger.

It is difficult to generalize about the local organizations in Virginia cities and counties, although some appreciation of their more common attributes is essential to understanding the mergers. First, Key is not entirely correct in describing them simply as "local outposts of the [Byrd] organization." Some were more pro-Byrd than others; in a few the alliance with the state organization was barely evident. In some counties and cities local officials avoided identification with the state organization, while some occasionally appeared to be antiorganization. The exact posture assumed by local officials vis-à-vis the state organization depended largely upon local political circumstances and conditions, and realistically, the state organization apparently conceded to such conditions where necessary. Local political relationships with Richmond varied, and although all local organizations necessarily worked through the organization, the local organizations were neither carbon copies of each other nor dominated by the state organization leaders.

[39] *Harry Byrd*, p. 16.

Second, it should not be inferred that the local organizations were created by Senator Byrd or depended solely upon the state organization for survival. Some local organizations predated Byrd's governorship (1926–30), and his contribution was to draw them into the vortex of Richmond. Regardless of the fortunes of the state organization, the leaders of the local organizations were generally politically astute, competent in the duties of public office, and sufficiently attuned to their constituencies to be able to win and maintain political control. Local officials, in sum, did not depend on assistance or leadership from the state organization to keep them in office.

In broad outline Key's description of the local organizations is correct. The circuit court judge was an important political figure, and the arrangement of judicial circuits in the Commonwealth was not without political overtones. The inner core of the local organizations usually consisted of the county or city constitutional officers —the commissioner of the revenue, treasurer, sheriff or city sergeant, attorney for the Commonwealth, clerk of the circuit court, and members of the county board of supervisors or city council. However, not all local officeholders were members of the organization.

As Key observed, the clerk of the circuit court was frequently the head of the county organization.[40] His counterpart in the cities, the clerk of the corporation court, usually exercised less influence. Even so, there were exceptions; the local organization in the City of Norfolk was nominally headed for many years by Clerk W. L. "Billy" Prieur, Jr. The nature of the clerk's office and duties accounted in some measure for his preeminence, although factors such as political ability, personality, and leadership qualities also contributed. Among other assets, the clerk was usually the best paid of the local government officials, and he enjoyed an eight-year term of office, to which he was likely to be reelected. The clerk was keeper of all official records of the city or county and therefore was in an excellent position to assist those whose work required access to public records. He could be especially helpful to lawyers who practiced before the circuit court and to those engaged in real estate transactions. In a number of smaller counties the court clerk served in a dual capacity as clerk to the board of supervisors, and where there was no appointed county administrator, he sometimes assumed ad-

[40] Wilkinson's discussion of Brunswick County also pinpointed the clerk of the circuit court as the local political leader. See *ibid.*, ch. 1.

ministrative duties on his own motion or at the request of the board. In attempting to explain the political potency of the clerk, one local official in Tidewater succinctly summarized the clerk's office: "Officially, he doesn't have to do anything that will make anyone mad."

The local organizations were generally more a cooperative enterprise than a bossed machine. Each of the organization members, especially the elected officers, contributed a measure of individual strength to the group. Policy matters and problems were frequently resolved internally by means of consultation or what may be loosely called "in-group democracy." Although the communication network varied, organization members usually consulted each other on local political questions and issues or on any other matter that had obvious political overtones or consequences. But not all organization members would necessarily be consulted on every issue or question.

At the same time each of the individual officers had a preserve which was something of an individual domain. For example, one local official did not tell another how to run his office or who should be hired. Perhaps the best example of this vested interest, was the individual county supervisor, who, as Key pointed out, was usually less politically powerful within the entire county than were the officials elected county-wide. But in matters affecting his own magisterial district the county supervisor's influence usually expanded immeasurably. In regard to politics or services within his district, custom and usage demanded that the supervisor be consulted, and he often had, in effect, a veto over what could be done.

In the early 1960's both the political unity and the effectiveness of the local organizations varied from county to county and city to city. Some of the local organizations appeared firmly entrenched, and opposition was either nonexistent or ineffectual. In certain other cities and counties factional struggles occurred in the Democratic primary, offices changed hands, and although local affairs were usually the *casus belli,* a split sometimes occurred over personalities or state policies. Even if Democratic organization candidates were unopposed in primary elections at the local level, this was not conclusive evidence of organization solidarity, for most divisions or splits within a particular local organization were latent or subdued, and only on infrequent occasions did these divisions become public.

By and large the local organizations realized that open factional splits endangered their continuance in power. As long as outward solidarity was maintained, the chances were considerably lessened that the organization would fall to an antiorganization movement. With greater frequency than was probably appreciated in Virginia at the time, divisive issues were compromised within the framework of the local organization.

At least four factors contributed to the strength of the local organizations in Virginia. First, the local organizations were usually composed of professional and eminently practical politicians. Members were neither amateurs nor part-time practitioners, and the political hack or incompetent was rare. As full-time professionals they worked hard at the duties of public office, and most worked overtime at the trade of politics. In some local organizations the attention given to political detail, especially to problems of individual constituents, helps to explain why the organizations were able to maintain their power. In every way members of the local organizations took themselves and the duties of office with the utmost seriousness.

Second, the local organizations shunned scandal and corruption. Honesty and integrity in public and private life characterized the Byrd Organization for many years, and these standards were rigorously enforced. For this reason members of a local organization occasionally combined to oust from office one of their number who might become a source of embarrassment. The causes for such action varied, but any threat or tinge of personal or public scandal was usually sufficient to bring about that official's resignation, defeat, or removal. When an elected official was involved, the matter might be resolved by persuading him not to stand for reelection. When a graceful withdrawal was possible, especially if the matter involved a personal problem, this course was encouraged. Publicity was of course avoided whenever possible.

Third, a number of local organizations stressed the assimilation of active or latent opposition, particularly talented opposition, into the ranks of the organization. It is not difficult to discover local officials of long standing and service in Virginia who began their political careers as antiorganization men. However, the practice of assimilating the opposition depended both on the local organization and the individual. There were no hard and fast rules, but the local organizations often absorbed unsuccessful challengers who appeared capable of contributing a measure of strength to the organization and would subsequently give evidence of loyalty and cooperation.

Fourth, most local organizations fostered an image of responsible conservatism in their approach to policy issues and conduct of public affairs. Conservatism was a proved political asset in Virginia;

conservative or moderately conservative candidates almost invariably prevailed over more liberal opposition. The identification
of local organizations with conservatism made them a known quantity to the voters. At the time of the mergers the several local organizations were generally identified with both conservative and honest
government, and accordingly, they had built up an important reservoir of public confidence and trust in their stewardship. In this
manner, at least by indirection, conservatism was an important
factor in the promotion of the mergers. Since the local political
leaders sponsored the mergers and the elected officeholders campaigned openly and directly, the consolidation proposals probably
benefited from the conservative and responsible image of their chief
proponents.

But, obviously, such an image was not the sole contribution of the
local organizations to making the mergers. Because they occupied
responsible policy-making positions, local leaders could and did
speak authoritatively on what consolidation would mean for local
residents. If a question was raised on schools, for instance, an answer
would be given by an authoritative source—a member of the school
board, a member of the city or county governing board, or the school
division superintendent. Moreover, promerger forces enjoyed several
advantages that antimerger proponents lacked. Politically, there
was a ready-made organization with built-in lines of communication
to the electorate. Although special merger organizations were
created, these were not the usual ad hoc citizen groups created to
achieve a particular goal. Finally, local officeholders brought to the
mergers their knowledge of campaign tactics, strategy, and use of
the media of communication, which contributed significantly to the
caliber of the promerger effort.

The Kellam Organization of Virginia Beach

One of the elements that served to make the Tidewater mergers,
then, was the role of the local political official in the merger process.
Of the nine governments involved in the four merger efforts between 1952 and 1963, the local officeholders in no less than seven
governments figured prominently as initiators and/or directors of
these efforts. Only in the case of Warwick, in the Newport News–
Warwick merger, were some local public officials clearly not identified with the promerger cause. And, for differing reasons, former
Newport News was not a stronghold of the Byrd Organization, al-

though there was a local organization and most incumbent officeholders supported merger. Some insight into the structure and capa-
bilities of the local organizations in the politics of merger may be
supplied by an examination of perhaps the strongest and most cohesive of the local organizations at the time of consolidation: the
Kellam organization of former Princess Anne County and Virginia
Beach, whose acknowledged leader and chief spokesman was Sidney
Severn Kellam. Interviews conducted in 1963, as merger became a
reality in Virginia Beach, helped to pinpoint the components of
Kellam's success.

A close-knit organization and continued success at the polls were
the chief ingredients of Kellam power in 1960. For all practical purposes, the Kellam group had not been seriously challenged in an
election since the turbulent early 1950's. Prior to the 1963 consolidation the Kellam organization controlled the politics of both the City
of Virginia Beach and Princess Anne County. At the time of merger,
Kellam forces controlled all the elected posts in the consolidated
City of Virginia Beach. The activists of the Kellam group consisted
primarily of the elected officeholders of the city and former county,
who openly acknowledged Sidney S. Kellam as their leader and
spokesman.[41] The political techniques and tactics employed by the
Kellam organization were not especially novel, but all the persons
interviewed in Virginia Beach in 1963 agreed that they were effective. Matters of political detail were not left to chance, and organization members officially stressed and encouraged personal contact
and precinct work with the voters and residents of the city. As one
Virginia Beach official noted, the officeholders have "an open door
to everybody and are willing to hear everyone's problems." Personal
attention to constituent problems and service by local public officials were recurring themes in all the interviews. As noted by Frank
R. Blackford, a reporter for *The Virginian-Pilot,* in 1965: "In each
of the booming subdivisions of Virginia Beach, there is generally
one resident who is close to the dominant political organization.

[41] No attempt was made in any case to identify all members of a given local
organization, but the existence of the local organizations was incontestable. Officeholders identified themselves with the organization and slates of candidates
openly designated as organization were offered in elections. To the non-Virginian
accustomed to a more amorphous local politics, the very existence of the local
organizations may call forth an attitude of skepticism. To the Virginian, however, the organization was simply a major element in the political system. Moreover, the use of the term *organization* did not necessarily carry a bad or undesirable connotation. Except among antiorganization partisans, the term was
largely neutral and descriptive.

New residents usually receive a call from the organization neighbor who offers help to expedite any services the local government offers." [42]

The exact size and composition of the Kellam group in 1963 could not be determined. There appeared to be something of an inner circle which included the major elective and appointive office-holders. Around this core were located roughly in concentric circles those who might be classed as associates and supporters. The inner group consisted of approximately fifteen persons—at least this appears to have been the case when consolidation was being promoted. At the same time the Kellam organization was supported by a sizable segment of the business community and other influentials.

Sidney S. Kellam was clearly the dominant figure of the organization. Born in 1903 in Princess Anne County, Kellam was one of sixteen children, twelve boys and four girls. As a young man Kellam sold insurance in Princess Anne County, and in the early 1930's he founded the insurance firm of Kellam and Eaton. At that time, also, Kellam was elected treasurer of Princess Anne County, a post he won four additional times, each time running unopposed. In 1950 Governor John S. Battle, whose campaign Kellam had managed, appointed Kellam as director of the Department of Conservation and Economic Development, from which he resigned three years later to return to Princess Anne County. At the time of the merger Kellam held no elective public office but was Democratic Party National Committeeman for Virginia.

The Kellam family has been distinguished in the political and civic affairs of Virginia Beach and Princess Anne County for many years. Kellam's father, Abel E. Kellam, served for twenty years as clerk of the circuit court of Princess Anne County, and it is from him that Sidney reputedly received much of his political education. A brother, the late Floyd E. Kellam, served as judge of the circuit court of Princess Anne County and Richard B. Kellam served as additional judge for the 28th Judicial Circuit. William P. Kellam served in the Virginia State Senate. In addition, the Kellams served in leadership positions in numerous civic associations and on various state boards.

In 1963 Kellam's political and economic assets were apparently diverse. He maintained an office in downtown Virginia Beach at the firm of Kellam and Eaton, which dealt in realty and insurance, and he engaged in other business activities, including the Bank of

[42] Blackford, "A Democrat's Democrat: Sidney Severn Kellam," 87 *Virginia Record* 6 ff. (March 1965).

Virginia Beach, of which he was chairman of the board of directors, and the beachfront Thunderbird Motel. His chief interest, however, was politics, and in 1963 his office at Kellam and Eaton appeared to be one place to conduct political business. "Mr. Sidney," as he seems to have been called by his office staff, was obviously held in high esteem and his political ability was unquestioned by those in Virginia Beach. According to one of his supporters, his political assets included an ability "to define issues and pull divergent factions together." As Democratic Party National Committeeman, he maintained close ties with the Young Democrat clubs; although his exact role in the Byrd Organization was unknown, he was reputed to be highly influential. As national committeeman, however, he openly supported the Democratic Party's presidential nominees, contrary to the "golden silence" posture adopted by other Virginia Democrats.

According to those interviewed in Virginia Beach, the Kellam organization was not a dictatorship. One respondent went so far as to aver that Kellam was sometimes the spokesman for opinions that were not his own. The manner by which the organization obtained consensus on any issue seemed to vary, but the weekly "gabby" was one device frequently used. The gabby was usually a luncheon meeting of Kellam men and was frequently held at the Thunderbird Motel in downtown Virginia Beach. As near as could be learned, there was no order of business, no agenda, and no records were kept. Problems and issues facing the organization and the city government were usually the topics of discussion. Once consensus was reached, however, substantial pressures presumably existed against dissent. As far as could be determined, the institutional gabby managed to escape all public notice in the area newspapers. From all outward appearances, the Kellam group was composed of able and articulate men, it exhibited a high degree of inner cohesion, and it kept in close touch with all events in the political world of Virginia Beach.

Sidney Kellam and the operation of the Kellam organization attained near-legendary proportions in Virginia political circles. Impromptu or informal gatherings of Tidewater public officials often produced at least one Kellam story. Sometimes humerous, and generally apocryphal, the stories added to the image of Kellam's political acumen and strength. On one occasion, for example, it was related that a group of local officials were discussing the manner of ordering candidate names on a ballot—alphabetically by name or according to the date each filed for office. When Kellam was asked how he would list candidates on a ballot, he reportedly retorted: "By preference."

In a like vein, Frank Blackford capsuled effectively the Kellam organization's stress upon personal contact with the voters. As Blackford put it: "Sidney Kellam has a phenomenal memory for names and faces. This is also true of many of his fellow organization men who are great handshakers. This habit has sifted so far down the line that a visitor to City Hall these days usually has his hand pressed by one of the uniformed yardmen who will abandon his grass cutter in order to press a strange palm." [43]

How typical or atypical was the Kellam organization in comparison with other local political organizations in the consolidated cities? In most respects it must be considered atypical, for in 1963 it was perhaps the strongest local organization in the Old Dominion. To paraphrase an outside observer, Kellam was one of the most powerful politicians in Virginia and "even more potent in his home territory than Senator Harry F. Byrd." [44] But if the Kellam organization was atypical, the characteristics that set it apart were to a large extent a matter of degree rather than of kind. It is true that none of the local organizations in the other consolidated cities approached the Kellam organization in cohesiveness and discipline. Nor did the other local organizations necessarily boast a strong leader on the order of Kellam. But there were organizations, in-group consultations, varying measures of internal discipline, and there was usually an acknowledged leader or a two- or three-man board of directors. In most respects the other local organizations displayed many of the features of the Kellam group although their control was less apparent and their tactics were somewhat different.

[43] "Kellam," 87 *ibid.* 6 ff. (March 1965).
[44] Henry Chenault, "Norfolk Threat Sparks Princess Anne Merger," *The Roanoke Times,* Dec. 4, 1961.

CHAPTER III

PREMERGER POLITICS: NEGOTIATION AND PREPARATION

P REMERGER POLITICS includes all the events, arrangements, and activities that occur before the actual legal consummation of a merger and directly or indirectly affect that merger. Involved are those circumstances and conditions in each local jurisdiction that work to promote or deter the merger, the processes and arrangements revolving around the adoption of a formal consolidation agreement and proposed city charter, the referendum campaign in each locality on the merger agreement and the charter, and such other administrative and political arrangements as the transition to a single, unified government requires. The period of premerger politics ends when the participating localities become a single legal entity, on the date and time specified in the consolidation agreement.

Each of the Tidewater mergers was the product of a political environment, and that environment, in turn, was shaped by forces and events that occurred long before consolidation was an active public issue. Thus, the point of beginning must be selected somewhat arbitrarily. With this limitation in mind, this chapter recapitulates certain of the salient features of the premerger negotiations. The negotiations were often delicate, and obviously, any merger proposal hinged on mutual acceptance of a workable consolidation agreement and charter which the leaders of both participating governments could take to their voters. Accordingly, focus here is placed on the process and environment in which negotiation occurred.

Local Premerger Activity

Five phases of premerger activity at the local level can be identified. These are (1) initial explorations and arrangements, (2) the development of a consolidation agreement and a city charter, (3) the referendum campaign on the question of merger, (4) approval of the charters by the Virginia General Assembly, and (5) transitional arrangements required to effectuate consolidation. Because the campaigns (3) and the transitional arrangements (5) constitute a distinct phase of premerger activity, each will be examined in a separate chapter.

A comprehensive and detailed review of each phase of premerger activity in all four consolidated cities is not attempted here. In certain instances this would constitute unnecessary repetition, while in other cases the data needed for the task were simply not available. For example, many of the persons who participated in the Elizabeth City County–Hampton–Phoebus merger in 1952 had left the area, were deceased, or were not available at the time field interviews were conducted.[1] Most of the participants who were interviewed were unable to recall the details of premerger negotiations, the campaign, and the transition. The local newspapers, the *Newport News Times-Herald* and the *Daily Press,* recorded only the major highlights of premerger arrangements, and if memoranda and other documentation were preserved, their existence was not affirmed by a search of records or in interviews. About all that could be determined regarding premerger activity in Hampton was that no one recalled any significant difficulty in the premerger period, although there was apparently some initial reluctance on the part of the former City of Hampton to join the consolidation. Among others, the city manager of former Hampton indicated that he was at the time opposed to Hampton's participation in the consolidation.

Initial Arrangements

With the exception of the Newport News–Warwick consolidation, the first contact between representatives of the governments wishing to discuss merger was usually clandestine and exploratory. Before this contact, however, the county or city official wishing to initiate action had already made some assessment of the consolidation alternative, especially its political feasibility. In the Tidewater mergers, again with the exception of Newport News, this political evaluation

[1] The death of Stuart M. Gibson, clerk of the circuit court of Elizabeth City County, quite likely means that premerger politics in Hampton will never be reconstructed in full detail. Gibson, by all accounts, was both the prime moving force and the chief architect of merger. If he kept any personal papers or memoranda, Mugler Gibson, his son, the deputy clerk of Hampton in 1963, was not aware of their existence.

was made by the established leadership of counties and cities, chiefly the elected officers, although other influential persons were consulted. If, as a result, the assessment was that no obvious barriers to discussions existed, the possibility of an initial meeting with the other side was explored. Arrangements in such cases were usually made informally; in fact, the entire consultative process was deliberately kept informal. No public or other sort of written record seems to have been preserved regarding this first step.

It is difficult to pinpoint just when local premerger negotiations were begun. In the Virginia Beach–Princess Anne County consolidation, one public official indicated that the county leadership was immediately aware of the merger possibility contained in the amendment of Code, § 15-220 by the 1960 General Assembly, which made merger law applicable statewide. Yet the first announcement that merger was being considered was not made until September 21, 1961. In the South Norfolk–Norfolk County consolidation, the initial meeting was held in October 1961, yet the merger prospect was not officially confirmed until mid-December of that year. A responsible source in Chesapeake indicated that the prospects for merger really hinged on the outcome of a councilmanic election in South Norfolk which produced "people with whom the county could deal." Evidence indicates that the Elizabeth City County–Hampton–Phoebus merger was actually begun in 1950 when it was realized that the Massenburg Act which protected Elizabeth City County from annexation might be repealed by the General Assembly. Only in the Warwick–Newport News merger of 1958 is it possible to pinpoint the time of beginning with reasonable certainty.

As a general rule the local newspapers were not made aware that the merger alternative was under consideration, and the preliminary meeting of the parties concerned was essentially a private affair. Except in the Newport News–Warwick merger, initial merger exploration was carried on without the knowledge or involvement of the general public. In Chesapeake, for instance, the major officers of Norfolk County and South Norfolk publicly denied the possibility of merger even after an initial meeting had been held and feasibility had been accepted. Written records show that the first exploratory meeting between representatives of South Norfolk and Norfolk County was held in October 1961 in the Norfolk County Health and Welfare Building. More than a month later *The Virginian-Pilot* reported that one or two informal meetings had been held. In the same article, however, the chairman of the Norfolk County board of supervisors, Colon L. Hall, branded merger as a "rumor," while Councilman H. S. Boyette of the City of South Norfolk stated that merger "wouldn't be considered now." [2]

There is good reason to believe that perhaps the most critical period of premerger activity in each instance fell between the time when the merger alternative came under active consideration and the date that merger exploration was first announced. Interviews with merger leaders indicated that by the time the first public announcement was made, the political leaders on both sides had ascertained that (1) merger was politically and legally feasible, (2) it would not be politically or economically disadvantageous for either party, and (3) it stood a reasonably good chance for success at the polls. Furthermore, some fundamental agreements had been reached as to future strategy and tactics. Undoubtedly, in this exploratory period certain assurances were given on both sides as to respective "vital interests," and there was some discussion of the manner of filling posts in the new government. In short, by the time of the first public announcement, the promerger leadership knew generally where it wanted to go and how it intended to get there. Although in some cases, particularly in the Newport News–Warwick merger, there was subsequent modification of the initial plans, promerger leaders representing both governments were generally able to proceed from a position of established broad lines of agreement.

Newport News–Warwick: The Nonorganization Merger

Of the four Tidewater mergers, the consolidation of the City of Newport News and the City of Warwick stands alone in several respects. First, the consolidation involved two cities rather than a city and a county, so that annexation or the threat thereof was not an issue. Second, the leaders of the merger movement in Warwick were private citizens, not officeholders. Third, premerger politics was somewhat more open to public scrutiny and involvement than in the other Tidewater mergers. Fourth and finally, no reason was readily apparent as to why the two governments would want to merge. From the standpoint of the student of local government, therefore, the Newport News–Warwick merger was perhaps the most intriguing of the four consolidations.

On the surface, this merger may appear to be one of those in-

---

[2] "Norfolk County and South Norfolk May Talk Union," Nov. 30, 1961.

explicable accidents of consolidation by American local governments that have occurred in the past at infrequent intervals. A
closer look at the merger, however, reveals that the consolidation
was anything but accidental. Although the merger was promoted
and led by a citizens' movement, that movement was endowed with
both political talent and muscle.

The Newport News–Warwick merger of 1958 was the direct outgrowth of a consolidation attempt involving the cities of Hampton,
Newport News, and Warwick which was defeated by the voters in a
referendum in 1956. To understand the merger, it is necessary to
return to the year 1952 when Warwick County became the City of
Warwick. The county incorporated as a city of the first class because
of fear that the county might be subjected to annexation by Newport News. The county had already lost territory to Newport News,
the last successful annexation suit having occurred in 1940. However, the attempt to repeal the sixty-square-mile limitation provided
by the Massenburg Act actually stimulated the incorporation movement. Had there been an incorporated place within Warwick
County, a merger would have been necessary, but Warwick County
contained no cities or towns with which to consolidate, and apparently, a merger with Newport News at that time was out of the
question. Thus, Warwick County was transformed into the City of
Warwick.[3] Voters in the referendum on the question of incorporation overwhelmingly supported the move by a vote of 2,516 to 523.

Within three years after becoming a city, Warwick had to face
the issue of a proposed three-way consolidation involving Hampton
and Newport News. An ad hoc but active and influential citizens
group favoring consolidation, composed of business leaders and
other influential people, was established in each of the three cities
in July 1955. A nine-member Joint Executive Committee coordinated activities. J. B. Woodward, Jr., chairman of the Warwick
Citizens Committee for Consolidation, was named chairman of the
Joint Executive Committee. Woodward was chairman of the board
of directors of Newport News Shipbuilding and Drydock Company,
a multimillion dollar corporation and the largest single industry in
Newport News. In response to pressure from the Woodward group
on behalf of a proposed tri-city merger, most Warwick political
leaders took a position bordering on neutrality. Evidence obtained

[3] See, generally, Institute of Government [then the Bureau of Public Adminis-
tration], University of Virginia, "Report on the Problems and Procedures of
Incorporating the Proposed City of Warwick," typescript dated Feb. 11, 1952.
The report included a draft of a proposed city charter.

from Woodward and Warwick officeholders indicates that the latter were generally content to let the Warwick committee for consolidation engage in the promotion of consolidation, although a few did announce publicly in favor of a tri-city merger.

A minor political revolution was in the making in Warwick. The Woodward group had the backing of major business and industrial leaders, and although they were careful to ensure that the merger movement was not identified solely with business interests, the pro-merger leadership was drawn chiefly from business and professional ranks. While the primary concern of this group might be described as "interest in orderly area-wide development," the focus was really on the future of Newport News, the economic hub of the area. In 1955 Newport News was an overcrowded city. Although it contained only 42,000 people, the population was confined to an area of four square miles, and compared with other cities in the United States of more than 25,000 population, Newport News ranked among the top 15 percent in population density. Overcrowded conditions were aggravated even more because substantial tracts of land were occupied by the city's commercial and industrial establishments, including the Newport News Shipbuilding and Drydock Company and the extensive railroad yards and facilities terminating at Hampton Roads.

As several local leaders perceived, moreover, the character of the population was a significant part of the Newport News problem. In the late 1940's middle and upper income white residents began to leave Newport News for the suburbs in the counties of Elizabeth City and Warwick. At the same time the black population of the city increased as blacks began to occupy former white residential areas. This exodus of white residents and the growing black population caused concern among white political leaders and businessmen in Newport News. The 1950 census revealed that the nonwhite population constituted 43 percent of the total population, an increase of 9 percent over the 1940 figure. By 1955 there were definite signs of increased independence among black voters, and black leaders were in a position to challenge the white leadership for seats on city council, appointments to boards and commissions, and control of the Democratic Party. As far as white leaders were concerned, black political control seemed inevitable, especially after the incorporation of adjoining Hampton and Warwick. Newport News could not annex the adjoining white suburban areas belonging to these other cities; the only way to increase the white population of the city was to merge with either Hampton or Warwick or both. Consolidation would recapture white voters and operate essentially to maintain the status quo. Between 1952 and 1957, with sporadic opposition from the Negro community, the efforts of most white political leaders in Newport News focused on consolidation with its neighbors.

Economically and politically, the leaders of the tri-city merger movement were concerned with the growth and development of the Lower Peninsula, in which the role of the core City of Newport News appeared crucial. Business leaders knew in 1955 that a bridge-tunnel link with Norfolk was soon to be authorized, and that it would bring increased economic competition between Norfolk and Newport News–Hampton–Warwick. Because of the physical deterioration of Newport News and the city's unsettled political conditions, the ability of the Lower Peninsula to compete effectively with Norfolk was questioned.

The so-called racial issue in Newport News must be considered against this backdrop to understand its significance and to appreciate the motives of the business and professional community in promoting merger. In sum, at what seemed to be a crucial point in the future development of the Lower Peninsula, business leaders believed that the core City of Newport News might soon fall under domination of its black citizens. Since most of the major business and industrial concerns were located in Newport News, apprehension arose as to the prospective policies that the city government might pursue. In administering taxes and services, a new city council in Newport News responsible to other segments of the community might act contrary to the business community's immediate interests, impede development of the Lower Peninsula, and eventually place that community in a disadvantageous competitive position with Norfolk. Competition within the area was at stake too; the City of Newport News owned and operated the entire water supply system of the Lower Peninsula and thus could exert control over Hampton and Warwick.

The leaders of the merger movement were certainly not white supremacists in the usual racist sense; generally speaking, their racial views were probably quite moderate for that time. The Newport News Shipbuilding and Drydock Company, for example, practiced fair employment and equal opportunity, which, although probably imperfect by present-day standards, was in advance of most Southern businesses in 1955. Perhaps for this reason, the merger campaign never degenerated into vicious race baiting or practiced exploitation of traditional racial fears held by Southern whites. Nevertheless, the proposed merger unquestionably benefited because of racial fears among some whites. Although merger leaders did not emphasize the racial issue, they likewise did nothing to contradict the belief held by voters that continued white control of city government was an issue. To counteract this belief, anti-merger forces, curiously enough, found themselves having to contend openly that white supremacy was not a factor in consolidation. As the Hampton Citizens Committee Against Consolidation wrote:

> The Race Issue in Newport News is Without Fact. Hamptonians are not frightened by a situation that does not exist.
>
> The last election of councilmen in Newport News was a most decisive white victory. (Out of 5618 votes cast, one Negro candidate received 1809 votes and the other 1649. A better than 3 to 2 majority with five white men running.)
>
> There are 8000 white voters in Newport News to only 3400 Negro voters, a better than 2 to 1 majority.
>
> Do not give away the finest city in this state to "save" our neighbor from a "peril" that does not exist.[4]

Fear of a Negro-controlled city government in Newport News and concern for the economic development of the Lower Peninsula were by no means the only motivating factors in the 1956 tri-city merger attempt. In fact, it was suggested in certain interviews that the racial issue was really a false one through which nonresident businessmen with interests in Newport News hoped to extend their influence in the city. The merger leaders in Warwick, at least, did have identifiable economic interests in downtown Newport News. Of the nine-member Warwick Citizens Committee for Consolidation, five members had direct or indirect ties with the Newport News Shipbuilding and Drydock Company, while three others either had a place of business or owned property in Newport News, leaving only one member with no identifiable interests in Newport News.

By the end of 1955 the Joint Citizens Committee had secured councilmanic endorsement from each of the cities to underwrite a study of the probable impact of consolidation upon taxes and services which was subsequently prepared by the Institute of Government of the University of Virginia.[5] In addition, the Joint Citizens Committee drafted a proposed consolidation agreement and

[4] *Daily Press*, Oct. 29, 1956.

[5] See Institute of Government [then the Bureau of Public Administration], University of Virginia, *City Consolidation in the Lower Peninsula* (Charlottesville: The Author, 1956).

charter to be introduced in the 1956 General Assembly in the form of permissive local legislation subject to popular referendum.

The proposed charter and consolidation agreement encountered difficulty in the General Assembly. The Norfolk legislative delegation objected to the proposed name of the new city, Hampton Roads. Although the charter and agreement were in the form of a local bill, to which legislative comity was usually extended, Norfolk won its point and the General Assembly specifically preserved the use of the name Hampton Roads for the harbor. From the standpoint of promerger forces this was unfortunate because the only substitute they could agree on was the uninspired name of Port City. Moreover, this substitution probably influenced a number of votes in Hampton as some residents wished "to preserve Hampton's historic name." A few promerger leaders saw Norfolk's "interference" as a deliberate attempt to scuttle the consolidation and a demonstration of Norfolk's intent to "dominate" the entire area.

The tri-city merger campaign was perhaps the most spirited held on the Lower Peninsula during the decade.[6] Antimergerites generally singled out Newport News as a whipping boy with its "slums, enormous indebtedness, high taxes, and dilapidated schools." Promerger forces stressed improved services and the unity of the region. When the vote was counted following the November 6 referendum, it was found that Hampton voters had defeated the proposal by a margin of 856 votes out of a total of 13,240 votes cast in that city. In Newport News, merger was approved by a vote of 5,385 to 2,058. Nine predominantly white precincts approved consolidation by margins ranging from 10–1 to 18–1, while four predominantly black precincts voted against merger by margins that ranged from 2–1 to 4–1. Warwick voters favored merger by a vote of 5,336 to 3,532. In four Warwick precincts fronting on the James River—Hilton, River, James Brandon, and Riverside—merger carried by a 2–1 margin. These four precincts, composed generally of white middle and upper-middle class residents and termed the "silk stocking precincts" by antimergerites, cast 2,624 ballots for consolidation, a figure which exceeded the total antimerger vote cast city-wide.

After the tri-city merger referendum, six days elapsed before the appearance of any public suggestion that Warwick and Newport News be merged. On November 12, 1956, in a letter to the editor of the *Daily Press,* one Moses Schneider drew the obvious conclusion

---

[6] For a review of the major events of the tri-city merger attempt, see, generally, "Out of the Trenches, Boys—The War's Over," *Daily Press,* Nov. 7, 1956.

from the vote in the two cities, suggesting that such a Newport News–Warwick merger was feasible, and that it should be pursued. This opinion was echoed on November 15 in a letter signed "An Average Citizen," and on November 16 the first "official" word of intent to explore the merger of Newport News and Warwick was published.[7] This was an announcement by J. B. Woodward, Jr., that many of the block and precinct workers active in the tri-city merger campaign desired to begin work to bring about a merger of Newport News and Warwick. On November 27, 1956, the attempt to consolidate the two cities was formally launched by the Woodward group in Warwick and the Newport News Committee for Consolidation, led by Dr. Russell Buxton of that city.

The Consolidation Agreement and Charter:
Toward an Imperfect Union

Following initial contact and agreement among the official parties to explore the merger alternative, the next step entailed drafting a consolidation agreement and charter for the proposed new city. At this point merger proceedings became a part of the public record, for the respective councils and boards of supervisors had to take some official action. Among other things, they usually appointed a committee to draft a consolidation agreement and charter, exchanged letters, or arranged some form of public meeting to consider proceeding with merger.[8] At this time, the matter of merger entered the daily news media. The record was only partially public, however, for the details of committee meetings were not reported in full, and the public was not made privy to all the proceedings. Con-

[7] "Move to Unite Warwick-Newport News in Offing," *ibid.,* Nov. 16, 1956.

[8] Every city approached this step somewhat differently. The council of Warwick appointed a special three-man committee, while the council of the former city of Newport News served ex officio. A convention named the consolidation committee in Virginia Beach and Princess Anne County, and both the council and the board of supervisors subsequently approved the appointment. In South Norfolk and Norfolk County, a special negotiating committee was not formally named; the negotiators consisted of members of the Norfolk County board of supervisors, councilmen from South Norfolk, and others. In Hampton and Elizabeth City County, a draft of the charter submitted to Warwick County by the Institute of Government of the University of Virginia served as the basis for the consolidated city charter. Suggestions of approaches to the study of city-county consolidation may be found in S. J. Makielski, Jr., *City-County Consolidation: A Guide for Virginians* (Charlottesville: Institute of Government, University of Virginia, 1971).

solidation agreement and charter-drafting committees held various meetings in executive session and sometimes issued only summarized statements to the press, and important community interests were on occasion negotiated in secret meetings. At the same time the charter committees usually sought advice from civic associations, the bar association, officeholders, and other individuals, and all the committees retained legal counsel to aid in drafting the consolidation agreement and charter. During this stage, therefore, the public was at least aware that negotiations were underway.

Once the deliberative or advisory body, as the case might be, completed its work, it made a report to each of the governing bodies of the governmental units contemplating merger. If negotiations had been successful, a draft of the consolidation agreement and charter was presented. Each governing board then considered the agreement and charter. If changes were made by one party, the alterations had to be concurred in by the other party; this happened in only two known instances, and in one of these the alterations were minor. Generally, the governing boards had been kept informed during the negotiation process about the status of the negotiations and the emerging contents of the agreement and the charter. After consideration by the governing bodies, a formal motion was made to accept the committee's report, the agreement, and the charter, and if it carried, the proper petitions were submitted to the appropriate courts asking that a date be fixed for holding a referendum.

The issues confronting the various charter-drafting committees were similar, as were many of the responses. These issues included the apportionment of councilmanic seats, the allocation and distribution of future taxes, the services to be rendered, the equalization of assessments, the selection of constitutional officers for the consolidated city during the transition stage, and the location of the seat of government, as well as the blending of the two-court structure.

The response to these issues, generally speaking, was to make as few changes in governmental structure and policy as possible. The promergerites who drafted the charters were not trying to work a political or structural revolution, and they did not wish to be experimental. In Virginia Beach and Chesapeake, for instance, councilmanic apportionment was solved simply by combining the memberships of the former council and board of supervisors.

On the surface, consolidation agreements were prepared and charters drafted with remarkable ease. Even in Newport News and Warwick, where a charter fight developed early in the negotiations, an agreement and charter eventually emerged from a harmonious atmosphere once certain procedural questions were settled and it became apparent that both sides would proceed in good faith. Issues that might otherwise have divided the two governments were compromised in the name of political expediency. Rather than attempt to work out a new and unified court structure, for example, the drafting committee simply renamed the existing courts of Newport News and Warwick and expanded their jurisdictions city-wide. The county agricultural agent was transformed into a newly created municipal Department of Farm and Home Demonstration.[9] Preparing the consolidation agreements and charters presented no real barrier to merger among the Tidewater governments. Indeed, the preparation appeared to be "all within the family."

These agreements or charters did not in any way violate the principles of good government. While they invariably contained special provisions such as those relating to taxes and the provision of services, they were not burdened with cumbersome detail. The frame of government established was simple, administratively well integrated, and conducive to fixing responsibility by the voter. All the city charters, for instance, provided for council-manager government and fixed clear lines of authority from the operating departments to the city manager to council. In brevity, conciseness, and general legal-structural characteristics, the charters did not differ substantially from the Model City Charter of the National Municipal League.

Once the negotiation process was begun, the committees moved with dispatch to produce final drafts of the charters and agreements in time for approval by the governing bodies and the establishment of a tentative referendum date. However, some difficulty was encountered during the Elizabeth City County–Hampton–Phoebus merger and the South Norfolk–Norfolk County consolidation.

The former City of Hampton was not initially a party to the consolidation movement in Elizabeth City County and, according to the former city manager, was something of a "reluctant bride" in the marriage.[10] Although permissive legislation authorizing a merger of the three governments was provided by the General Assembly in 1950,[11] Elizabeth City County was in the process of promoting a

---

[9] See, for example, Charter of the City of Virginia Beach, ch. 15. The consolidation agreement and charter for Virginia Beach are included as Appendixes A and B below.

[10] Interview with L. D. James, July 8, 1968.

[11] *Acts of Assembly*, 1950, p. 1591.

merger with the Town of Phoebus under separate authorizing legislation when Hampton decided it wanted to be included. Although there is conflicting evidence about the reasons for Hampton's decision, some credence may be given to a report that Hampton businessmen and leaders envisioned themselves as surrounded and isolated by an incorporated Elizabeth City County and, accordingly, put pressure on Hampton's council to join in. Reports and past electoral history indicated a favorable Phoebus vote, and it was expected in Hampton that a Phoebus–Elizabeth City County merger would occur in any event. Consequently, in March 1952 Hampton requested that it be included in the proposed merger, and a special joint study committee was established with Stuart M. Gibson, clerk of the circuit court of Elizabeth City County, serving as secretary.[12]

The Hampton–Elizabeth City Study Committee reported a proposed charter and agreement the latter part of April 1952, but the Hampton city council rejected the report.[13] One issue involved preservation of the name Hampton. The City of Hampton was vitally interested in preserving its historical name as well as its claim to being the "oldest continuous Anglo-Saxon settlement in the New World." With the acceptance of Hampton as the name for the new consolidated city, the major difference was resolved. On May 8, 1952, the Hampton city council accepted a revised charter and agreement, and the merger movement was underway.[14]

A similar difficulty with the name for the new consolidated city also arose in the Virginia Beach–Princess Anne merger. Princess Anne had existed as a Virginia county since 1691, and there was considerable public sentiment to retain that name. If a referendum had been held in the consolidated city, it was altogether possible that Princess Anne might have gained a majority over Virginia Beach. But the former City of Virginia Beach was also interested in pre-

[12] There is some discrepancy about the exact date when Hampton first requested that it be admitted to the consolidation. The initial notation appears in the Elizabeth City County Minute Books, March 3, 1952, 15:113, while the City of Hampton, Minutes of Council, 8:90, show the date to be March 13.

[13] Hampton, Minutes of Council, April 24, 1952, 8:97.

[14] Had the Elizabeth City County–Hampton–Phoebus merger failed, the consolidation of Elizabeth City County and Phoebus would have been pursued. In fact, a referendum on this two-way proposal had been scheduled by prior court order for one week after the referendum on the three-way merger. With the success of the three-way proposition, the court order for the two-way consolidation was vacated. However, the fact that Elizabeth City County kept the two-way proposal alive indicates her determination to protect herself from Newport News by means of consolidation. Authority to proceed with this merger came from *Acts of Assembly*, 1952, p. 952.

serving its name, primarily because substantial sums of money had been spent in advertising the beach as a summer resort for tourists. Practical monetary considerations apparently won out over historical affinities. So that the Virginia Beach investment in advertising would not be lost, the consolidation agreement adopted the name of Virginia Beach for the merged city. In order to preserve the name of Princess Anne, however, the former Seaboard Magisterial District of the county was designated as Princess Anne Borough.

The only other crisis for merger at this stage occurred in the South Norfolk–Norfolk County consolidation. This was a "timetable crisis"; verbal consensus on the agreement and charter was reached on December 22, 1961, and the law required that they had to be published in a newspaper of general circulation for four successive weeks prior to the referendum, to be held on February 9, 1962. Moreover, the charter had to be approved by the General Assembly as a special act and there was a filing deadline which provided that charter bills had to be introduced in the General Assembly during the first twenty days of the legislative session. The General Assembly convened on the first Wednesday in January. But with the date of the filing deadline for the court-ordered referendum at hand, the final provisions of the proposed Chesapeake charter had not been settled upon. An official who participated in the drafting indicated that the final draft was done on a conference telephone line with members of the council of South Norfolk and the supervisors of Norfolk County. Each charter provision was read and approved on the telephone. A finished copy was then prepared and rushed by special messenger to the judges of the respective circuit court and corporation court, who had been alerted in advance, so as to meet the legal requirements for filing on that day.[15] To meet the requirement for publication in a newspaper, space had been reserved at an earlier time in *The Virginian-Pilot* under the name of a local automobile dealer. If this had not been done, according to one involved official, a staff member of the newspaper might have notified Norfolk or Portsmouth officials, and they might have tried to delay the required publication.

[15] It is perhaps understandable, then, that parts of Chesapeake's consolidation agreement and charter appear to have relied heavily on the agreement and charter of the consolidated City of Virginia Beach. There was a story told in Virginia Beach, vigorously denied by Chesapeake officials, that when the proposed Chesapeake charter was submitted to the circuit court for purposes of a court-ordered referendum on the question of consolidation, the name Virginia Beach had not been removed in all instances. A direct comparison of the two charters, however, reveals significant differences.

One final problem common to all the mergers was the allocation of jobs in the consolidated city governments. The charter-drafting bodies did not allocate jobs or posts to specific persons, but they had to provide policy guidelines in the consolidation agreements for filling elected and appointive offices. The manner by which these posts were to be filled in three of the four consolidated cities was indeed unique and confirms, in part, the observation that the mergers were promoted from "within the family."

In three of the four mergers, elections were not held immediately before or after the consolidated cities came into being, and the staffing of duplicate elective offices of the consolidated cities was accomplished by the practice of bargaining. The principals holding such offices in the former governments involved in merger bargained between themselves. Even in Newport News, where elections were held for all city posts before the effective date of consolidation, bargaining for office occurred through informal arrangements between certain of the officers. Where a particular office was found in only one government, the office involved was carried over to the consolidated government. The ground rules for bargaining in the three merged cities not holding elections were set forth in their consolidation agreements. For example, Article X, Section 3 of the Consolidation Agreement for the City of South Norfolk and Norfolk County provided:

The attorney for the Commonwealth, the treasurer and the commissioner of the revenue for the Consolidated City shall be determined by agreement between those persons holding such respective offices. In the event that no agreement is reached before the effective date of consolidation, the judges of the court of record shall designate one officer as principal and the other as assistant or deputy.

For employees below the level of appointive department head, the consolidation agreements, again with the partial exception of Newport News, specified that no county or city officer or employee would (1) lose his job, (2) suffer any reduction in salary, or (3) lose any retirement or fringe benefits. Most department heads were also retained, although this was not formalized in the agreements. Of seven city managers and county administrators, two lost their jobs and a third became a department head.

Bargaining for office occurred both before and after the charters were drafted. Major appointive posts such as the city manager and department heads were filled formally by the new council of each consolidated city after the referendum campaign. Understandings regarding elective posts such as commissioner of the revenue, treasurer, Commonwealth's attorney, court clerk, and city sergeant were probably reached prior to publication of the charters although the actual arrangements may not have been completed until after the referendums.

Once the respective elective officials decided between themselves which one should be the principal officer of the consolidated city, practice dictated that the other be appointed chief deputy in that office at no reduction in salary. In Newport News certain understandings were reached that made that city's election something of a formality. There also, in large measure as a result of the failure of the charter-drafting committee to come up with an acceptable alternative solution, Newport News had two clerks of court. F. B. Barham, former clerk of Newport News, became clerk of the corporation court and circuit court while George DeShazor served as clerk of the circuit court, Part II.

Usually, the principal-deputy trade-off provided an equitable, if not especially democratic, solution regarding jobs. One exception was the office of county sheriff which, because of the requirements of the state constitution, could not be duplicated in a city framework. This difficulty was overcome in Chesapeake and Virginia Beach by resurrecting an office that had almost disappeared in Virginia, the position of high constable. This officer, whose duties involved the serving of legal process for the courts not of record, was to be appointed by council. A third elective office, that of city sergeant, tied in with the sheriff–high constable arrangement. The city sergeant, an elective office required of all cities at the time by the state constitution, was an officer of the courts although his chief duty was keeper of the city jail. As specified in the consolidation agreements of both Chesapeake and Virginia Beach, the county sheriff was to complete his unexpired term of office; then there would be an election for the post of city sergeant. The Virginia Beach consolidation agreement provided that the city sergeant of former Virginia Beach would become high constable. In Chesapeake the same result was achieved although the consolidation agreement did not specifically appoint the city sergeant of former South Norfolk to the post of high constable.[16]

A few exceptions were made in the principal-deputy arrangement. In Virginia Beach, for example, the treasurer of former

[16] See the Consolidation Agreement for the City of South Norfolk and Norfolk County and the Consolidation Agreement for the City of Virginia Beach and Princess Anne County, art. X, § 2.

Princess Anne County assumed that same office in the consolidated city. The treasurer of the former City of Virginia Beach apparently declined a deputy treasurer position but was appointed director of public utilities for the consolidated city.

Interviews with the elected officials engaged in the trade-offs uncovered no consistent determinants or criteria for deciding which one would become the principal official in the consolidated city. The issue appears to have been settled by the two contending officers without undue outside interference. In some instances, personal reasons and inclinations were important. Factors such as age and experience were also mentioned by some officials as operating criteria, but this did not mean that an older and more experienced man would necessarily assume the principalship in that office. On the contrary, a younger official might prevail, especially if his counterpart was nearing retirement age and was willing to step down. Although it was not directly revealed in interviews, there may possibly have been an unspoken but "hard-nosed" assessment of who could beat whom if an election were held. And, in a few cases, the officials may have benefited from opinion "within the official family" about which of the two contenders might contribute the most to future politics and government in the merged city.

Through this practice of bargaining, the transitions and mergers were kept in friendly and experienced hands. This had several distinct advantages, especially in that span of time between the date of each merger referendum and the effective legal date of each consolidation. Because elected officials and appointees knew that the responsibility for the new government would be theirs, work could be begun on the transition almost immediately after the approval of merger in the referendum.

The council of the City of Chesapeake, after the merger, authorized a mural to be painted on its chamber's wall immediately behind the council table, facing the audience. The artist chose to depict in somewhat stylized fashion the consolidated City of Chesapeake—industrial South Norfolk joining with agricultural and suburban Norfolk County. Recalling the historic tradition of the area, however, the artist also reproduced as the mural's motto a Revolutionary War quotation from Colonel William Woodford's report following the Battle of Great Bridge, which occurred in former Norfolk County. This was the first Revolutionary War battle fought in Virginia, and one in which the British forces were defeated. The quotation reads: "I have the pleasure to inform you that the victory is complete. . . . This was a second Bunker Hill

affair . . . with this difference, that we kept our posts." No great
sense of humor is required to capture the double meaning that may
be drawn from the mural's motto.

Drafting the Newport News Charter: A Study in Maneuver

On November 16, 1956, slightly more than a week after the defeat
of the tri-city merger proposal, the Warwick Citizens Committee
for Overall Consolidation led by J. B. Woodward, Jr., announced
their intent to pursue a merger of the cities of Warwick and Newport News and fixed January 29, 1957, as the target date for a referendum. The committee proposed further that the general law charter for consolidated cities enacted by the General Assembly in 1956,
commonly called the Hallett Act, should serve as the charter for
the merged city.[17] Petitions were then circulated in both cities requesting that the date of January 29 be fixed for holding the referendum on a proposed Newport News–Warwick consolidation.

By December 4, 1956, opposition in Warwick to the new consolidation attempt had become organized, and opponents raised questions about the constitutionality of certain sections of the Hallett
Act.[18] Warwick's Commonwealth Attorney Henry D. Garnett questioned the provisions that (1) provided for the selection of the
merged city's constitutional officers by lot, (2) determined that
judges of courts of record should settle matters of jurisdiction and
venue sitting as a group, (3) provided that all ordinances of the
two cities should remain in effect after consolidation until new
ordinances were prepared by the council of the consolidated city,
and (4) granted power to the council of the consolidated city to
levy higher taxes in one area than in another according to the services received. Warwick formally requested the chairmen of the
citizens consolidation committees in Warwick and Newport News
to defer further action on merger until a ruling could be obtained
from the attorney general on these sections.[19] At this juncture, State
Senator Stuart E. Hallett, who had sponsored the legislation, inter-

[17] *Acts of Assembly*, 1956, p. 777, and Code §§ 15-231.4.1–78, deleted in recodification. See also "The New Consolidation Move," *Newport News Times-Herald*,
Nov. 28, 1956.

[18] "Group Organizes to Block Merger," *Newport News Times-Herald*, Dec. 4,
1956, and "Anti-Merger Weak Spot," *ibid.*, Dec. 5, 1956.

[19] See "Garnett Questioning Legality of Charter, Asks Delay on Merger," *ibid.*,
Dec. 5, 1956.

vened by requesting Attorney General J. Lindsay Almond, Jr., to render an opinion on the questions raised.[20] By this time the anti-merger forces had mounted a full-scale attack on the provisions of the general law charter,[21] and the City of Warwick had authorized its attorney to contest the validity of the charter if petitions requesting a referendum were filed with the court.

Attorney General Almond ruled on December 13, 1956. He expressed doubt that the officers of the new city could be chosen by lot. On the other hand, he gave a general notation that the practice of differential taxation might be valid under certain conditions and stated that the remaining sections of the Hallett Act seemed constitutionally valid. He observed that the provisions of the general law charter were separable: if a specific section of the Hallett Act charter was found to be unconstitutional, the validity of the merger probably would not be affected. The consolidationists declared themselves satisfied that the Almond opinion upheld the validity of the Hallett Act and announced their intent to proceed with the merger. On December 19, 1956, petitions to hold a referendum were filed in the circuit court of Warwick and the corporation court of Newport News.[22]

Warwick then used the entry of petitions as a basis for challenging the constitutionality of the Hallett Act.[23] Attorney Thomas B. Gay of Richmond was retained to represent Warwick and entered a motion before the circuit court citing five alleged unconstitutional sections of the Hallett Act charter.[24] After a hearing on the Gay motion, Judge Conway H. Sheild, Jr., of the Warwick circuit court on December 28, 1956, deferred the date of the referendum until the second Tuesday in July 1957, which allowed time for an appeal to the Virginia Supreme Court. On January 9 Judge Herbert G. Smith of the Newport News corporation court rescinded his order

[20] See "Almond Will Answer Charter Validity," *ibid.*, Dec. 8, 1956, and "Almond Promises Early Reply on Validity of Merger Charter," *Daily Press*, Dec. 8, 1956.

[21] See "Anti-Merger Speakers Hit City Charter," *Daily Press*, Dec. 11, 1956. George DeShazor, clerk of the circuit court of Warwick, was elected to the anti-merger committee at this meeting.

[22] "4900 Sign Plea for Vote on 2-City Merger," *ibid.*, Dec. 20, 1956.

[23] John Bowen, "Lawyers for Warwick City Council Ask That Petition for Referendum Be Denied," *Newport News Times-Herald*, Dec. 27, 1956.

[24] Gay subsequently withdrew from the Warwick case. See "Withdrawal of Gay from Merger Litigation Is Confirmed; Firm's Other Local Interests Are Cited," *Daily Press*, Jan. 23, 1957.

calling a referendum on consolidation for January 29 and fixed a new date of July 9, 1957.

On the evening of January 8, 1957, the Warwick city council surprised promergerites by passing a formal resolution suggesting the appointment of a committee to draft a consolidated city charter for Warwick and Newport News.[25] The resolution was presented to council by Commonwealth's Attorney Garnett with his recommendation for passage. Garnett noted regarding the Hallett charter:

> As Commonwealth's attorney, I made a study of the proposed charter and came to the conclusion certain sections of the charter were of doubtful constitutionality.
>
> It was my position that if and when the people of Warwick desired to vote the sole concern was to vote on a valid and workable charter. Council has expressed the same view. This council has been criticized unjustly. It has not attempted to thwart a vote, but has acted commendably and in a forthright manner to discharge its duty without favor. If a vote is to be taken, it should be on a good charter.[26]

A new charter, he said, would make it unnecessary to test the validity of the Hallett Act. He noted further that a charter could be drafted in time for the July 9 referendum. Even Vice Mayor Briggs of Warwick, an announced foe of merger, supported the resolution.

In explaining Warwick's seeming about-face, it is only fair to note that several highly responsible persons had doubts about the validity of certain sections of the Hallett Act. Moreover, certain former Warwick officials noted that Warwick had enough registered voters to outvote Newport News in a joint municipal election, and for this reason the provisions of the Hallett Act calling for the selection of officers by lot was especially objectionable. In addition, information obtained from interviews suggests that some Warwick officials concluded that a vote would likely be held on the question of consolidation and that substantial public sentiment favored merger, as evidenced by the 1956 vote on the tri-city merger. These officials might subsequently suffer at the polls if they attempted unduly to block or disrupt the merger attempt. It appears that at this point some Warwick officials attempted to regain the initiative by promoting a charter that would protect Warwick's interests and

[25] "Warwick Council Asks NN to Join in Rewriting Merged Cities Charter," *ibid.*, Jan. 9, 1957.

[26] *Ibid.*

enhance their chances for control of the consolidated city. With the subsequent withdrawal by Attorney Gay from the case challenging the validity of the Hallett Act, moreover, the antimerger forces in Warwick indeed reckoned that their chances for having the Hallett Act charter declared unconstitutional had diminished substantially. Consequently, the tactic to be pursued was to get the best possible consolidation charter for Warwick.

Following Warwick's proposal of January 8 to create a charter-drafting committee, Mayor Robert B. Smith of Newport News issued a guarded statement to the effect that the invitation to draft a new charter would be given "careful consideration." [27] Newport News officials apparently did not take Warwick's about-face seriously. For the most part, they viewed the Warwick proposal to draft a new charter as an action designed to delay even further the scheduled July 9 referendum. Not until the charter was in the process of being drafted did Newport News officials began to perceive that the Warwick offer had been made in good faith. The *Daily Press* showed its suspicion in an editorial entitled "New Charter Proposal a Confusing Device," while the *Newport News Times-Herald* urged, "Don't Upset Merger Applecart!" [28] Smith subsequently stated in an interview that he felt that the Warwick proposal was chiefly a smoke screen designed to delay the referendum.[29] With some reluctance, the council of Newport News accepted Warwick's bid on January 10, 1957, and countered with the proposition that the charter approved by the councils of Hampton, Newport News, and Warwick for the earlier tri-city merger proposal serve as the basis for drafting a charter for the proposed Newport News-Warwick merger.

After an exchange of communications, the Warwick city council proposed on January 23 that a joint meeting of the two councils be scheduled to iron out procedural matters for drafting a charter.[30] The Newport News council agreed, and a joint meeting of the two councils was held on February 5 in the Warwick municipal court-

[27] *Ibid.*

[28] The two editorials appeared on Jan. 10, 1957. Both newspapers are under the same ownership: the *Daily Press* is a morning paper and the *Newport News Times-Herald* appears in the afternoon. Former Mayor of Newport News Robert B. Smith was the editor-in-chief. Throughout the premerger period, both newspapers staunchly advocated merger and, prior to drafting the charter, were generally critical of the actions taken by Warwick's council.

[29] Interview with Robert B. Smith, Aug. 22, 1963.

[30] "Warwick City Council Suggests Meeting with NN Feb. 5 on Charter," *Daily Press*, Jan. 23, 1957.

room. Each council was urged to appoint representatives to a special advisory committee which would meet jointly to draft a consolidation agreement and charter. In accepting this proposal, however, Mayor Smith indicated that he and members of the Newport News council would serve ex officio as the Newport News representatives along with City Attorney Harry Nachman and City Manager Joseph C. Biggins. It was also agreed that the Port City charter that had been utilized in the unsuccessful tri-city merger would serve as the basis for drafting a new charter, although provisions might be taken from the Hallett Act, the so-called Virginia City charter of 1950,[31] and other general charter legislation.[32] The Newport News city council insisted (1) that the first committee meeting be held within one week after the appointment of the Warwick members, and (2) that the committee hold no public hearings since they were only advisory to the councils.

On February 16 the Warwick council appointed a three-member advisory committee to serve as its charter-drafting representatives. Appointed were City Attorney Glenn E. Sparks, Jr.; B. E. Rhodes, a member of the Warwick City Planning Commission and executive vice-president of the Bank of Warwick; and Fred W. Bateman, an attorney.[33] An initial meeting date of February 22, 1957, was fixed for the charter-drafting committee.

Prior to February 22, the Warwick committee caucused on organization, strategy, and tactics. The need for compromise in drafting the agreement and charter was recognized, although Warwick representatives intended to gain as many concessions as possible. At the suggestion of B. E. Rhodes, the Warwick representatives agreed to certain positions that might be employed to protect Warwick's interests. The most important of these was that an at-large plan for electing councilmen would be agreeable, but if compromise was needed either in councilmanic selection or in some other area, Warwick would back a borough or ward system as the means for selecting councilmen. This plan would serve as their "ace in the hole."

Two other decisions were reached at this caucus. First, the War-

[31] *Acts of Assembly*, 1950, p. 1530. The Virginia City charter was prepared for a merger of Warwick and Elizabeth City counties, the cities of Hampton and Newport News, and the Town of Phoebus. This proposed merger never reached the stage of popular referendum.

[32] Al Coates, "Advisory Group to Aid Writing of Merger Agreement, Charter," *Daily Press*, Feb. 6, 1957.

[33] Bateman preserved many of his notes and working papers from the charter-drafting sessions and made them available to the author.

wick representatives decided to invoke the unit rule in deciding on individual charter sections. If two of the three members of the Warwick committee assented to a particular charter provision, then the third member was bound to accept that provision. The right of individual dissent was reserved for the final report to the Warwick city council.

Second, it was decided that Warwick would attempt to take the initiative at the first joint meeting of the charter-drafting committee. This lead to the preparation of a "Statement of Procedure" which was subsequently presented at the February 22 meeting. Specifically, Warwick urged that:

1. The Port City charter of 1956 should serve as an agenda, but the group should be free to bring in provisions from other charters.

2. A decision should be made as to the location of meetings and provision made for the selection of a presiding officer. (It was decided to alternate meetings between Newport News and Warwick and to empower the host city to select the presiding officer.)

3. The Newport News committee, which consisted of seven persons, should establish a quorum able to do business.

4. Special committees or advisors should be appointed to deal with controversial sections of the charter.

5. Committee deliberations should begin by going through the Port City charter in its entirety noting points of agreement while passing over points of disagreement. After the entire charter had been read, the committee would return to a consideration of the points of disagreement.

6. The decision to hold no public meetings should be confirmed. A policy should be fixed regarding news releases and what would be considered public information. Warwick suggested that no statements be given to the press unless approved jointly.

7. A recording secretary should be appointed.

Throughout the course of the committee meetings, held intermittently between February 22 and April 18, 1957, few public statements of record were issued. On March 5 it was announced that a committee representing the Newport News–Warwick Bar Association would assist in drafting charter provisions dealing with the courts and court officers. It was further noted that the charter committee intended to obtain suggestions from judges and other court officers. But for these and a few other terse announcements, committee deliberations were carried on in secret except for an occasional report that "progress was being made," or "the half-way point has been reached."

The charter-drafting committee held its initial meeting on the evening of February 22 at Warwick City Hall in an atmosphere which one participant described as "chilly." The meeting opened with formal prepared statements by both sides, which in effect urged that the committee should work to draft the best charter possible, that is, should neither advocate nor oppose merger, and that it should complete its task as soon as possible, although no deadline was fixed. The remainder of the meeting was devoted largely to deciding procedural matters, including the time and place of future meetings, the length of meetings, the specific use of the Port City charter, the employment of special advisors, and a press release policy. The major substantive recommendation of the evening's deliberations was offered by the Warwick group, which urged that the Newport News–Warwick Bar Association be asked to create a committee to make recommendations regarding consolidation of the judicial systems.

At the next meeting, on February 25, the committee began work in earnest on the charter. Charter language such as that establishing the boundaries of the consolidated city cleared the committee with dispatch; the listing of corporate powers was cleared with only minor changes in the basic Port City charter. The committee passed over elections until a later time and began to consider councilmanic selection and apportionment. Warwick recommended that the number of councilmen be seven, although Warwick representatives agreed to consider a different number. Warwick further suggested that four councilmen ought to be elected from that city and three from Newport News. Newport News indicated that Warwick's plan was unacceptable and countered by offering an at-large system of nomination and election. Various alternative plans were considered without agreement. It was observed that someone would oppose the councilmanic scheme no matter what was done, and the charter committee temporarily passed over the composition and apportionment of council.

Five meetings later, on March 13, 1957, the committee had gone through the Port City charter and had settled a number of difficult matters including councilmanic selection and a merger timetable. If the voters approved merger in the July referendum, a seven-member council would be nominated and elected at large in November 1957. Council could then begin work on transition to a consolidated city. The constitutional officers were to be elected in April 1958, and the new city would begin official operations on July 1, 1958. Although matters such as the court problem, the location of city offices, the meshing of separate budgets, and other important details still had to be settled, the main outline of the charter and consolidation agreement had taken shape.

Delay was encountered regarding the judicial structure for the consolidated city; one member of the charter-drafting committee indicated that this was the single most difficult problem. Although the assistance of the bar association was enlisted, neither the members of the bar nor the council could achieve a satisfactory consensus. After various preliminary reports and discussions, the charter committee drafted the provisions dealing with courts and court officers. No changes were made in the existing court structure except to extend the jurisdiction of the courts of record to cover the entire area of the consolidated city. This meant that the consolidated city had three courts of record, the corporation court of former Newport News and the circuit courts of the former 11th and 14th judicial circuits. The number of courts would be reduced to two in 1960. In addition, the clerk of the corporation court of Newport News and the clerk of the circuit court of Warwick were to be retained in office.

The charter and consolidation agreement also included several provisions for transition to a single city. Besides the election of councilmen in November 1957 and of constitutional officers in April 1958, a referendum was scheduled for September 10, 1957, to select a name for the consolidated city. Other transitional arrangements included retention of both school superintendents in their respective school systems and areas until their terms expired, at which time a single superintendent would be chosen by the consolidated school board. Ordinances of the two cities would remain in effect until the council of the consolidated city prepared a uniform set of ordinances, to be adopted within two years. Election registrars in the two cities would continue in office after consolidation and would be eligible for reappointment. Each city would adopt its own budget as if merger were not to occur, and this joint budget would serve the consolidated city through the first fiscal year.

As a result of the charter negotiations, Warwick gained important concessions. Once Newport News officials became aware that Warwick did not intend to engage in obstructionist tactics, both sides proceeded in a spirit of give and take. The selection of constitutional officers by lot was eliminated, and the seat of the consolidated city government was fixed in Warwick. Council chambers, the city manager's office, all department heads, and all constitutional officers with the exception of the court clerks were to be located at the Warwick facility. Both clerks of court would maintain offices in downtown Newport News, as would the health and welfare departments. The new jail that Newport News had constructed was designated as the jail for the consolidated city. A specific provision was written into the consolidation agreement preserving school bus service for Warwick residents for a four-year period, after which school bus service would be extended city-wide. When the Warwick committee reported the proposed charter to city council, even Vice Mayor Briggs, who continued to be a foe of consolidation, pronounced the result far superior to the Hallett Act charter.

The Newport News consolidation charter displays a number of unique features when compared with the charters drafted by the other merged cities. Although all adopted council-manager government, the three other consolidated cities initially adopted a borough or ward system for selecting councilmen. Elections were not held in the other cities prior to consolidation, either for councilmanic posts or for the constitutional officers, as was the case in Newport News. Finally, Newport News did not make use of the special taxing district for services as did the other three cities. Otherwise, the four city charters were generally similar.

CHAPTER IV

PREMERGER POLITICS: VICTORY IN TIDEWATER AND RICHMOND

ONCE the consolidation agreements had been drafted and approved, the next step was to win voter acceptance at the polls; it is to the several campaigns that this chapter is devoted. Voter approval of the proposed consolidations was a formidable barrier, and the promergerites were not unmindful of the difficulties that confronted them in educating their constituencies for consolidation. Although the consolidation agreements and charters had been drafted with at least one eye to probable voter reactions, promerger leaders were generally aware of the dismal showing that consolidation proposals usually made at the polls. Merger not only had to win at the polls but it probably had to win by substantial majorities, especially in the case of Virginia Beach and Chesapeake. Because the charters of these two cities had to be approved by the General Assembly after the merger referendums, the results at the local level had to be clearly decisive. The promerger leaders now directed their attention toward winning voter acceptance for consolidation.

Campaign and Referendum

Of the four mergers, the best organized campaigns for and against consolidation were conducted in the Newport News–Warwick consolidation.[1] The Virginia Beach and Hampton mergers met with only token opposition, while organized resistance to consolidation was the greatest in Newport News and Chesapeake. The least amount of money spent in the merger campaigns was apparently

[1] This chapter will focus only on the campaigns in Virginia Beach, Chesapeake, and Newport News. As noted previously, it was impossible to reconstruct the Hampton campaign in any detail. The campaign was a rather quiet and localized affair, and there was apparently little or no organized opposition to merger. Merger proponents focused their attention on civic associations, clubs, and other small groups.

in Hampton. Moderate sums were spent by the proconsolidationists in Chesapeake, where a portion of the campaign materials were purchased from the surplus of the successful Virginia Beach campaign.[2] The greatest sum of money spent on campaign paraphernalia and "convincing the electorate" was in Newport News. The Chesapeake campaign involved a near fist fight at one of the consolidation rallies, and the Virginia Beach merger was climaxed by the "great television debate" involving Sidney S. Kellam. A promerger plea by Robert E. Gibson, member of the House of Delegates from South Norfolk, was humorously tagged as "Gibson's Gettysburg Address."

The four consolidation campaigns displayed certain common attributes, and, of these, clearly the most visible was the approach employed. The campaigns were neither public education campaigns nor community service efforts promoting a goal to which it might be assumed that all good people would subscribe. From start to finish they were political campaigns, and promerger leaders approached them as they would have approached any other political campaign.

The proconsolidation campaigns were well planned and well executed, and if uncertainties existed, they were not apparent to the voters. Substantively, the promergerites focused on basic issues and questions related to local autonomy, services, taxes, schools, and citizen access to government. Tactically, the campaigns were carried to the voters on a personal and a small-group basis. Although radio, television, newspaper advertisements, printed flyers, bumper stickers, and other campaign paraphernalia were utilized, promerger leaders relied heavily on a direct personal relationship with the voters.

As a second feature of the campaigns, with the exception of the Newport News merger, elected public officials carried virtually the entire burden of promoting merger. As far as the voters were concerned, there could be no doubt as to who was for each merger. Public officials led the proconsolidation rallies, they were the principal speakers, and they also served as the "authorities" on consolidation. They delivered brief prepared speeches, fielded questions from the audience, and otherwise beat the drum for merger. Because they were well versed in local government, and equally so in the conduct of their particular offices, they were able to spell out

[2] A letter acknowledging the sale of these materials was found among the **Princess Anne** Papers, a term which is described in the Bibliography.

in reasonable detail just what merger would mean for the individual voter. Although the anticonsolidation forces raised several difficult questions during the course of the campaigns, merger leaders were never really entrapped by the uncertainties of the future that consolidated city government might bring.

In the Hampton consolidation the promerger effort was directed by Stuart M. Gibson, clerk of the circuit court of Elizabeth City County. In Virginia Beach campaign strategy was the responsibility of the Kellam organization, with Sidney Kellam as the chief activist. Also prominent in the Virginia Beach campaign was Ivan Mapp, commissioner of the revenue, Princess Anne County, who served as chairman of the Merger Executive Committee. Mapp was assisted by other prominent Kellam organization members, such as John Fentress, clerk of the circuit court, and V. A. "Jack" Etheridge, treasurer, both of Princess Anne County, and R. R. "Buddy" McChesney, city sergeant of Virginia Beach. In Chesapeake the promerger forces were led by Charles Cross, clerk of the circuit court, and Robert "Speedy" Waldo, commissioner of the revenue, both of Norfolk County, and Treasurer N. Duval Flora of South Norfolk.

Other public officials played varying roles in the merger campaigns, including members of the House of Delegates and state senators. County supervisors were effective within their particular magisterial districts, and city councilmen were also active on behalf of consolidation, especially in South Norfolk.

Debate on the question of merger touched upon a variety of subjects and issues. Important issues included the probable impact of merger upon business, industrial development, taxation, debt, and the provision of services. Also, because in three of the mergers the cities had smaller populations than the counties, councilmanic apportionment and representation in the proposed consolidated cities was an active issue. In the participating counties, however, the single overriding issue was the threat of annexation and its probable impact upon county government.

Anticonsolidationists generally pursued the common theme of "things are good as they are now—why change?" Merger was attacked in terms of its probable impact upon taxes, services, and schools, and the need "to keep local government local." Oddly enough, one segment of the antimerger group in all four campaigns argued against consolidation on the ground that it was not in keeping with "a true metro approach." In the Newport News–Hampton area certain of the antis stressed the need to merge Warwick, New-

port News, and Hampton, while across Hampton Roads the antis
pleaded the cause of the core cities of Norfolk and Portsmouth.
Thus there existed the paradox of some antimergerites stressing
the need to keep local government as local as possible, while other
members of the same group argued the undesirability of merger
because of adverse effects upon "real" metropolitan government.

No consistent line-up of social or economic groups among the
antimerger forces was evident. In Virginia Beach opposition seemed
to be tied chiefly to business and political interests in Norfolk and
to long-time opponents of the Kellam organization. A similar situation existed in Chesapeake, reflecting the economic ties of some
Norfolk County residents with the City of Portsmouth, and again,
there was an anti-incumbent political faction. Only in Newport
News and Chesapeake were the antimerger forces supported by any
local public officers. George DeShazor, clerk of the Warwick circuit
court, led the antimerger forces in that city, and the former city
attorney of South Norfolk, Vernon T. Forehand, helped lead the
fight in opposition to the Chesapeake merger.[3] For the most part
the Norfolk County political leaders held firm, as did the officialdom in South Norfolk. Otherwise, in Virginia Beach and Hampton
the antimergerites were few in number and generally ineffective.
Only in Newport News and South Norfolk did the forces in opposition achieve a reasonably effective working organization backed
with sufficient funds and know-how to conduct a sustained campaign.

Schools were a major consideration in merger, and the appointed
school superintendents were called upon in the Virginia Beach and
Chesapeake mergers to pass an official judgment on the impact of
merger upon the schools. Norfolk County school superintendent
E. W. "Ed" Chittum appeared publicly on behalf of merger, while
his counterpart in South Norfolk, E. E. Brickell, opposed it. In
Virginia Beach, Frank W. Cox, superintendent of schools of Princess Anne County, issued the following statement on December 26,
1961:

After careful examination of the proposed Consolidation Agreement between Princess Anne County and the City of Virginia Beach, and having
served as Superintendent of Schools for both the County and the City for
more than twenty years, I am convinced that the proposed Agreement will
have practically no effect on the schools in either the County or the City
except that the transportation of the school children by the County School

---

[3] Forehand resigned his office to campaign against merger.

Board will, under the Consolidation Agreement, be extended to the school children now living within the present City limits. I have studied this very carefully and I am of the opinion that this will not adversely affect our school budget in any way, and the transportation service can be extended to the entire City.[4]

Although no two of the promerger campaigns were exactly alike, there were similarities in both organization and approach. Ivan Mapp, chairman of the Virginia Beach Merger Executive Committee, outlined the manner in which the consolidation was promoted.

When the first step, that of having prepared by competent attorneys a suitable Agreement and Charter to meet the needs of the proposed new City of Virginia Beach, had been completed, we went on to the second step, the campaign itself. We set up a Merger Headquarters office and engaged the services of a full-time secretary. We had an active Speakers Bureau composed of men well versed in our endeavor. We let it be known that all requests for speakers would be taken care of, no matter how large or how small the group, no matter what time of day or evening.

Members of our Speakers Bureau appeared before civic organizations, women's clubs, Church groups, community leagues and, in addition, we ourselves held several public meetings (these usually took place at public school buildings). We made it a point to have a "question and answer" period following each talk, and we believe that this helped considerably because, while our speakers tried to cover the subject thoroughly, we found that almost always intelligent questions were presented which had not been touched upon. Incidentally, our speakers also appeared before high school government classes and before the high school students as a whole in school assemblies. This was done with the thought in mind that these children are our future citizens and voters, and with a subject as widely talked about and of such great importance to our area, it was only fair and right to inform the younger generation of our efforts.

Other means of publicizing our proposed merger was through the use of lapel buttons and automobile bumper stickers proclaiming "Vote Progress, Vote Merger," and through the distribution of brochures which outlined some of the pertinent facts. We had excellent newspaper coverage and, in addition to the general publicity, we ran several informative ads.[5]

Many of the same people who participated in drafting the charters and agreements also joined in the campaigns and, in addition,

---

[4] Copy obtained from the Princess Anne Papers.
[5] *Ibid.*

assumed responsibility for getting the charter bills through the General Assembly. Timing was an important factor in the thinking of promerger leaders, as is evident from the "Suggested Time Schedule" for the Virginia Beach–Princess Anne consolidation, dated October 20, 1961: [6]

Completion of merger agreement and charter in printed form	November 6
Execution of agreement	November 8
Presentation of petition to Circuit Court of Princess Anne County and entry of order of publication	November 8
Newspaper publication dates	November 9, 16, 23, 30
Completion of legal publication	December 6
Entry of order by Circuit Court of Princess Anne County setting date for referendum	December 8
Referendum	January 9
Opening of 1962 session of General Assembly	January 10

This was only a preliminary schedule; it did not correspond in all cases to the actual dates on which particular events occurred. The agreement was approved on Friday, November 10, for example, and the referendum was scheduled for January 4, 1962. However, the fact that such a schedule was prepared indicates the nature of the planning and attention to detail that was a common feature of the campaigns.

Campaign in Virginia Beach

Long before the proposed Virginia Beach merger was announced, the immediate problem confronting the Kellam organization was to divert the City of Norfolk's attention from annexation of Princess Anne County. On January 1, 1959, Norfolk annexed 13.5 square miles of that county, along with approximately 38,000 county residents. This was the first annexation Princess Anne County had suffered, and the Princess Anne leaders clearly recognized that it would not be the last. County territory adjacent to

[6] *Ibid.*

Norfolk was rapidly becoming urban. Norfolk was extending her water lines far into Princess Anne County, and it was not unreasonable to assume that Norfolk's territorial claims would eventually follow her water lines. Since Princess Anne County was dependent upon the City of Norfolk for water, and water was necessary for suburban development, water service was already a source of friction between the two governments. Princess Anne needed water, but on the other hand, the extension of municipal water service supported Norfolk's claim that the territory was urban and therefore subject to annexation.

To protect Princess Anne County from annexation, the Kellam forces and other county leaders unsuccessfully attempted to persuade the 1960 General Assembly to modify the state's annexation law so as to give greater protection to a county's territorial integrity. As one reaction to this effort, the City of Norfolk allegedly delayed any further extension of water service into new or developing residential areas of Princess Anne County. Real estate developers in Princess Anne needed water, and consequently, Kellam negotiated with Norfolk. On April 13, 1960, after extended informal talks with Norfolk officials on water and other problems, he proposed that a study be conducted of a "borough system of metropolitan government for the Norfolk area." In return for backing this metro study, he received an informal pledge from Norfolk for a five-year moratorium on future annexation proceedings against Princess Anne County. At the same time he further agreed not to seek any changes in the state's annexation laws in the General Assembly during that period. Following the Kellam announcement, water service to three new county subdivisions, Pocohontas Village, Point O'Woods, and Curlew Drive, was granted by the City of Norfolk.[7]

Mayor W. F. Duckworth of Norfolk cautiously accepted the Kellam overture regarding metro government in good faith.[8] At a meeting on April 19, 1960, six governments in the area agreed that a study should be made "regarding common interests that might be resolved through a metropolitan approach."[9] Virginia Beach and

[7] See, generally, George M. Kelley, "1st Step Opens Door," *The Virginian-Pilot*, April 13, 1960.

[8] See George M. Kelley, "Metropolitan Plan Greeted Cautiously" and "The Metropolitan Idea," *ibid.*, April 14, 1960.

[9] George M. Kelley, "Committee to Explore Metropolitan System," *ibid.*, April 20, 1960. This meeting was chaired by former Governor Colgate W. Darden, Jr., who had just returned to Norfolk after retiring as president of the University of Virginia. Darden served as temporary chairman and subsequently was ap-

Princess Anne officials issued calls for cooperation, and a special study committee composed of representatives from the six governments was formed. In August the committee selected Sidney Kellam as its permanent chairman.[10]

Although lip service was paid to the metro idea during the ensuing year, this particular metro was dead for all practical purposes. When their intention to study merger was publicly announced by Princess Anne County and Virginia Beach on October 3, 1961, the metro committee chaired by Kellam had not met for more than a year. On October 5, when a reporter from *The Virginian–Pilot* asked when the metro committee might meet, South Norfolk's representative replied, "We leave all that to Sidney." [11] Whether by chance, by a fortuitous combination of circumstances, or by design, the Kellam organization and Princess Anne County had obtained some needed time and diverted Norfolk's attention from annexation.[12] The announcement by Virginia Beach and Princess Anne County of an intent to study merger apparently caught Norfolk city officials by surprise.

Although in 1961 there was no annexation by Norfolk in the immediate offing, the Kellam forces created a "1963 annexation" against which they campaigned. "In 1963," Kellam said, "we will be forced into a bitter annexation fight." [13] "From this annexation struggle," Kellam stated further, "Princess Anne County would lose Kempsville and Bayside magisterial districts. How is the rest of our county to survive if someone carves us up and takes our assessed value? We have a right to live."

Protection from annexation, continued economic progress, appeals to local pride, a chance to tweak the nose of "bully Norfolk,"

---

pointed by Norfolk as their representative on the special metropolitan area study committee. Darden resigned this post within a year. It is interesting to speculate what might have been accomplished by this committee had Darden been appointed its permanent chairman. Among other things, Darden suggested employing the Institute of Government [then the Bureau of Public Administration] of the University of Virginia to make whatever surveys the committee might need.

[10] "First Ripples of a Metro Study," *ibid.*, Aug. 13, 1960. In this editorial, the paper expressed general satisfaction with the appointment of Kellam as permanent chairman.

[11] Adam Clymer, "Metro Future in Doubt," *ibid.*, Oct. 5, 1961.

[12] That Kellam's metro was a deliberate diversion was hinted at by Wayne Woodlief, "Whatever Became of Metro?" 1 *New Norfolk* 7–9 (Feb. 1963).

[13] Frank R. Blackford, "Beach–P.A. Merger Move Expected Monday," *The Virginian-Pilot*, Nov. 4, 1961.

and improvement of the metro possibilities were alternating themes of the Kellam merger campaign. Voters of Princess Anne and Virginia Beach were told that these things might be accomplished without really upsetting the pattern or character of government in either the county or the city.

Curiously enough, the actions of Norfolk city officials provided Kellam with some very effective ammunition in his promotion of the Virginia Beach merger. One case in point was an advertisement in Norfolk's daily newspapers on October 28–29, 1961, addressed to the residents of Princess Anne County and signed by the members of the Norfolk city council. In this statement the council announced its opposition to the proposed merger and stated, in effect, that it could not "approve" of being prevented from attaining normal growth by annexing additional county territory to the city. Through this statement, Kellam's heretofore mythical 1963 annexation suit suddenly became quite real to the residents of Princess Anne County.[14]

In another instance, in early November 1961, Councilman Roy W. Martin of Norfolk publicly suggested to Princess Anne leaders that Norfolk be allowed to join the merger.[15] V. A. Etheridge, treasurer of Princess Anne County, termed this "an 11th hour proposal to confuse the voters." However, Etheridge suggested that Norfolk might prove its sincerity by turning the water utility over to an area-wide authority on the order of the Hampton Roads Sanitation District. Kellam agreed to meet with Norfolk officials to discuss Norfolk's inclusion in the merger.

The meeting was held at the Pine Tree Inn on November 16.[16] Mayor Duckworth of Norfolk read a five-page statement which requested a delay in the referendum scheduled for January 4 so that a study of the entire area might be made. Kellam indirectly rejected Norfolk's plea by stating: "Fortune knocks but once. After that he sends his daughter misfortune."

Norfolk's posture at the Pine Tree Inn meeting was more threat-

[14] Kellam's tactics in this regard are worthy of note. His responses varied from attacking interference to polite dismissal of Norfolk's charges. He repeatedly stated that the people in Princess Anne had nothing but good will for Norfolk while reminding Norfolk officials that the merger was "none of their business." When discussing Norfolk, Kellam almost invariably emphasized that the merger would improve prospects for a subsequent metropolitan area approach.

[15] Frank R. Blackford, "Norfolk Requests to Join Merger," *The Virginian-Pilot*, Nov. 9, 1961.

[16] Frank R. Blackford, "Merger Delay Rejected by Beach, County," *ibid.*, Nov. 17, 1961.

ening than conciliatory. A possible payroll tax by Norfolk was suggested if the merger was passed, and Duckworth stated that competition rather than cooperation would prevail if Norfolk was hemmed in. Kellam responded by recalling that Norfolk Councilman L. L. Layton had recently referred to Princess Anne as a bedroom of Norfolk. "All we want," Kellam stated, "is to come out of the bedroom into the living room."

On December 5 Norfolk's city council by a vote of 5 to 1 publicly threatened to "gun down" the consolidation. If merger was ratified by the voters, the council indicated that city water service to Princess Anne County would be cut off. As Kellam put it, Norfolk was saying "if you don't do what we want we will annex you or cut your water off." Although Mayor Duckworth and city council almost immediately retracted and disavowed the challenge, the damage had been done. The reaction in Princess Anne County was probably well summarized by a representative of the Aragona Village League in Princess Anne County who had stated earlier: "I'm sick and tired of being intimidated by the city of Norfolk. They are squirting a water pistol at us. Let's merge." [17]

The hand of the Norfolk city council was also visible in the formation on December 15 of a citizens committee, composed primarily of business leaders, "to bring to the attention of citizens of Princess Anne county and Virginia Beach the probable effects of their proposed consolidation on taxes, water supply and all levels of governmental services." [18] It was announced that a consulting engineer and a public relations firm had been employed by the committee to collect facts about the proposed consolidation. Mayor Duckworth of Norfolk observed regarding the group: "We feel that such an independent group of outstanding business leaders who obviously have no interest in the political effects of such a consolidation would be received with better grace and be more effective than any efforts that could be made solely by the members of the city council of Norfolk." [19]

Another antimerger group was formed in December, the Committee for Retention of Princess Anne County. This group fired its

[17] Frank R. Blackford, "Beach–P.A. Merger Move Expected Monday," *ibid.*, Nov. 4, 1961. It was estimated in January that organized opposition to the merger in the City of Norfolk spent between $19,000 to $20,000 on advertisements and direct mailing. See William L. Tazewell, "Laughter Greets Cocke," *ibid.*, Jan. 4, 1962.

[18] "Merger Fact Unit Formed," *Richmond Times-Dispatch*, Dec. 16, 1961.

[19] *Ibid.*

broadside on December 28, a scant few days before the January 4 referendum. In a full-page advertisement in the Norfolk *Ledger-Star,* the committee listed twenty-five points against merger in a "Have you been told" format. The advertisement was signed by the Committee for Retention of Princess Anne County, but individual members' names were not listed. Ivan Mapp, chairman of the Merger Executive Committee, returned fire the next day in a similar advertisement. His retaliation was aimed at both refuting the charges made by the Committee for Retention and levying an attack on the City of Norfolk. Whereas the Retention Committee asked Princess Anne residents, "Have you been told that the City of Virginia Beach levies a utilities tax of 10 percent," Mapp noted that the City of Norfolk levied a 15 percent tax. He also attacked the "secretive" nature of the committee's membership.

One admitted member of the Committee for Retention was Littleton B. Walker, a long-time Kellam foe and a defeated candidate for county treasurer in 1955. Walker denied that he represented the old opposition of the 1955 campaign against Kellam, but the committee apparently did include former Kellam enemies. That the committee was led by the usual opposition, or at least was cast in that image, did little to enhance its influence.

In a final attempt to delay the referendum, Walker entered a suit on December 28 in the circuit court of Princess Anne County challenging the constitutionality of the merger.[20] His brief raised numerous questions about the charter provisions, most notably the creation of special taxing districts and "special" expenditure of county monies for purposes such as advertising the beach proper. Kellam replied on December 29 with a statement to WBOF radio and the Norfolk *Ledger-Star.*

I am sure anyone who has read the suit filed by Mr. Walker will admit that there never has been such a political propaganda filed under the guise of a legal suit. Some of the questions raised are not even worthy of the consideration of a Justice of the Peace much less taking the time of the Court of Record. I am sure that if the attorneys were not so involved they would be the first ones to admit this.

I am confident if the people of Princess Anne County and the City of Virginia Beach vote for the consolidation next Thursday the suit will be withdrawn. I am sure that if Mr. Walker thought he had any legal standing he and his unknown committee would not be spending hundreds of

20 Walker v. City of Virginia Beach and County of Princess Anne: In the Circuit Court of Princess Anne, Opinion No. 6703, Opinion and Decree of Dismissal entered April 17, 1962.

dollars to run newspaper ads in an effort to confuse the people. I am also sure that had he and his attorneys thought that they had any legal standing they would have brought this suit some time back so that it could have been determined before the election.[21]

The case was not decided until April 17, 1962, well after the voters had indicated their preference for merger. At that time, Judge Robert S. Wahab, Jr., entered an opinion and a decree of dismissal of the Walker suit, and no appeal was taken to a higher court.

The running debate with the City of Norfolk on merger and water should not obscure the well-planned and executed campaign that Kellam and the Merger Executive Committee conducted in Virginia Beach and Princess Anne County. From its inception, on October 4, 1961, a day after the intention to study merger was announced, an eleven-man study committee composed of businessmen and other notables was formed with Kellam as one of the cochairmen.[22] This committee held its initial working session on October 11. After Kellam made his opening remarks, a working copy of the consolidation agreement was distributed, and matters relating to the expenses incurred by the committee were discussed briefly. The bulk of the meeting was devoted to discussing the steps required to develop a final consolidation agreement and the legal requirements for bringing the consolidated city into being. The advisability of merger had been settled. The study being conducted by the committee was "how to do it." As Kellam noted: "I'm confident Princess Anne County is going to find some way to become a city." [23]

By October 20 the committee had settled upon the name of Virginia Beach for the new city, as well as the details of councilmanic representation and special taxing districts. Although taxing districts were to correspond to magisterial district lines, the opinion was expressed that the districts might be drawn up to suit any need. The Virginia Beach Erosion Commission was to continue unchanged and to remain separate from the consolidated city. The operation of the convention center was to continue without change. It was recognized that a study of roads would be needed.

By October 30 attorneys had submitted a working charter and a

---

[21] Copy from the Princess Anne Papers.

[22] A summary account of developments was printed in "TV Debate Ends Merger Drive," *Virginia Beach Sun-News*, Jan. 4, 1962, and, also, William L. Tazewell, "Consolidation Study Committee Appointed," *The Virginian-Pilot*, Oct. 5, 1961.

[23] William L. Tazewell, "Consolidation Study Committee Appointed," *The Virginian-Pilot*, Oct. 5, 1961.

consolidation agreement to the committee, which had been meeting in closed session.[24] In order to preserve the name of Princess Anne, the committee decided to change the name of the Seaboard Magisterial District to Princess Anne Borough. Finally, it agreed that the principal seat of government would be located at Princess Anne courthouse, some thirteen miles from the existing City of Virginia Beach. On November 3 the public was given its first glimpse of the charter, and on the same day the Virginia Beach Chamber of Commerce endorsed the committee's study. On November 10 the city council and the board of supervisors accepted the agreement and charter, and the matter was turned over to Mapp's Merger Executive Committee to carry through on the referendum.

Mapp's committee met on November 15 and held about twenty meetings between that time and the January 4 referendum. Approximately 200 people took part in the promerger campaign, including members of the committee, the speakers bureau, and workers. They raised funds, purchased materials, circulated petitions supporting merger, and broadcast minute spot announcements over WBOF.[25] But the bulk of the campaigning focused on taking the merger issue directly to the people. For the remainder of November and throughout December, with Kellam as the most prominent member, promerger leaders plugged away for consolidation in meeting after meeting. Newspaper and other reports indicate that virtually every organized group in Princess Anne County and Virginia Beach heard a merger speaker. In addition, meetings were scheduled throughout the county for the general public, and individual workers were active at the precinct level. A summary of one week of speeches by the promergerites in late November indicates the burden assumed by public officials on behalf of consolidation.

> Sidney S. Kellam . . . spoke to a group of about 500 . . . residents Monday night at Linkhorn Park School.
> Appearing with Kellam on the stage were Frank W. Cox, Superintendent of Schools, who introduced the speaker, J. W. Wood, Kellam's co-chairman on the study group, and County Treasurer Jack Etheridge. . . .
> In a speech Tuesday noon before the Norfolk Civitan Club, Kellam predicted that South Norfolk and Norfolk County may follow suit and also consider a merger. . . .[26]

[24] See Frank R. Blackford, "Merger Study Called November 6," *ibid.,* Oct. 31, 1961.

[25] A public appeal for funds was made on November 16.

[26] No public announcement regarding the impending South Norfolk–Norfolk County merger attempt had been made. Although Kellam stressed that his

Kellam also spoke to the Princess Anne Jaycees at 7 p.m. Tuesday and at Princess Anne Court House at 8 p.m. Wednesday night he spoke to the Virginia Beach Fraternal Order of Police.

Other officials have also had a heavy schedule of speaking engagements on behalf of the proposed merger. John Fentress, clerk of the Princess Anne Circuit Court, appeared before the Carolanne Farm Civic League Tuesday night at Kempsville Meadows School. Ivan D. Mapp, county commissioner of the revenue, spoke at St. Gregory's Catholic Church Tuesday night and will speak at the Charity Methodist Men's Club tonight.

Mapp and V. Alfred (Jack) Etheridge, county treasurer, will appear together Friday before the Baylake Pines Civic League at our Savior's Lutheran Church.[27]

Poll workers reported satisfactory progress on December 28, and at the same time the merger committee stated that an imposing list of civic associations endorsing merger had been assembled.[28] The North Virginia Beach Improvement League in a telegram to Kellam "dissented" from the haste of the merger and asked for a delay.[29] Along with the Cavalier Bay Park Civic League, these two groups were apparently the only dissenters among the civic and benevolent associations.

If the outcome of the referendum was ever really in doubt, no one bothered to record it. As the final gesture of the merger campaign, however, Kellam debated merger with attorney Dudley DuBois Cocke on WTAR radio and television the night before the referendum. Departing from his prepared remarks, Kellam turned the debate into a promerger rally.[30] The auditorium of Princess Anne High School was decorated with promerger banners, and Kellam had the crowd of about 1,000 people whooping it up almost from the start. Cocke was greeted with loud laughter when he asserted

---

sources were unofficial, he in fact tipped off the public about the Chesapeake merger in this speech.

[27] "Meetings Give People Answers on Merger Plan," *Virginia Beach Sun-News,* Nov. 30, 1961.

[28] Included were the Virginia Beach Chamber of Commerce; the Virginia Beach Hotel, Motel, and Cottage Association; the Cavalier Yacht and Country Club; the Council of Civic Organizations of Princess Anne County; the Princess Anne Ruritan Club; the Princess Anne–Virginia Beach Young Democrats; the Virginia Beach–Princess Anne Real Estate Board; the Virginia Beach Fraternal Order of Police; the Virginia Beach Bar Association; and numerous other civic associations, men's clubs, women's clubs, and volunteer fire departments.

[29] The telegram is in the Princess Anne Papers.

[30] No record was kept as to what Kellam actually said. A copy of a prepared text is in the Princess Anne Papers, but all accounts seem to indicate that this draft was discarded early in the meeting.

that "I don't think annexation even enters into this thing." [31] Kellam countered by waving newspaper advertisements for the TV viewers and criticized Norfolk officials for interference. "This is our problem," Kellam is reported to have said. "You stay out of it." [32] Most everyone agreed that Kellam "stole the show."

The *Virginia Beach Sun-News* appeared on January 4 with a lead editorial entitled "The Hour of Decision" which summarized the promerger case.

Today is the hour of decision for Princess Anne County and the City of Virginia Beach. This is the day the citizens of the county and the city will be given an opportunity, probably for the last time, to decide for themselves whether or not they want to preserve the area of the county and the city as it now exists. Whether or not they want to keep the government of the county and city in their hands. Whether or not they want to keep the same basic type of government under which they have lived for many years, or whether they prefer to be carved up, a large portion of the county annexed to Norfolk City, and have the remaining portion in such a financially weak condition that the tax burden on the remaining citizens may be more than they could bear.

Both Princess Anne County and Virginia Beach responded overwhelmingly for merger. Over 11,000 votes were cast, and the Kellam forces won in every precinct. The proposition carried the county by 7,476 to 1,759 and Virginia Beach by 1,539 to 242 votes.[33] The lowest margin of victory for the promerger forces was in Cape Henry Precinct where more than a 3-2 margin (375 to 215 votes) was achieved.

At merger headquarters on election night in downtown Virginia Beach, the campaigners jubilantly cerebrated their victory, congratulated each other, and toasted the new city. Commonwealth's Attorney Robert L. Simpson exclaimed: "Did you ever see a vote like that?"

A man said: "Not outside the Iron Curtain."

"You couldn't get a vote like that if you ran Santa Claus for election at Christmas," Simpson replied.[34]

[31] William L. Tazewell, "Laughs Greet Cocke," *The Virginian-Pilot*, Jan. 4, 1962.

[32] *Ibid.*

[33] The author would like to thank John V. Fentress, clerk of the circuit court of the City of Virginia Beach, for providing photostatic copies of the official returns as well as a precinct-by-precinct breakdown of the vote.

[34] Robert C. Ramage, "Beach–P.A. Merger Wins by Sweeping 5–1 Margin," *The Virginian-Pilot*, Jan. 5, 1962.

Somewhat earlier in the festivities, two election workers had entered campaign headquarters carrying a stretcher with a bandaged and bloodied effigy bearing the placard "Duckworth," for the City of Norfolk's Mayor W. F. Duckworth. Kellam entered the room, saw the effigy, and reacted visibly. "I wouldn't do that," Kellam said. "I wouldn't do that." The effigy was quickly hustled out of the room.[35] The Princess Anne–Virginia Beach merger campaign was over.

Campaign in Chesapeake

The Chesapeake campaign differed in several respects from that of Virginia Beach. Merger was not so easily promoted; there was significant opposition in both the county and city; and the organizations promoting consolidation were not so cohesive, unified, or disciplined as the Kellam group. In Norfolk County several of the local political leaders had only recently come to office, while politics in South Norfolk was historically a topsy-turvy affair; power exchanges were relatively common, and no one faction had been able to gain ascendancy for a prolonged period of time. Some measure of political stability had been achieved in Norfolk County by virtue of the long-term service of county supervisors such as G. A. "Beef" Treakle and Colon L. Hall, but the board of supervisors operated as if the county were divided into individual fiefdoms—one result of the district system of electing board members. Each supervisor looked after the affairs and interests of his own magisterial district; this practice was to have important ramifications in the postmerger period.

It was not necessary for Norfolk County officials to create a mythical annexation on which to base their merger campaign. There had been four annexations since 1948 with the county losing 33 square miles, approximately 110,000 people, and an estimated annual revenue of $1,881,000.[36] The County had spent $247,000 on defense against these annexation suits by Norfolk, Portsmouth, and South Norfolk. Moreover, in December the Portsmouth city council voted 5 to 1 to enter another annexation suit claiming 44.77 square miles of Norfolk County.[37] This area represented about 13 percent of Nor-

[35] *Ibid.*

[36] These figures were used in the merger campaign and were supplied by Charles Cross, clerk of the circuit court, Chesapeake.

[37] Don Hill, "Portsmouth Votes for Annexing, 5–1," *The Virginian-Pilot.* Dec. 6, 1961.

folk County's land and contained some 10,600 people. The Portsmouth annexation suit, passed as an emergency ordinance by city council, was apparently a response to leaks in the merger talks then underway between Norfolk County and South Norfolk.

The annexation proceeding by Portsmouth was not the primary cause of the Chesapeake merger, but it certainly contributed to the urgency of the situation.[38] Also, at an earlier time, when it became relatively clear to political observers in Tidewater that Virginia Beach and Princess Anne County would consolidate, speculation arose that Norfolk might soon turn its annexing attention to Norfolk County. If and when the Virginia Beach merger was consummated, thereby blocking all eastward expansion by Norfolk, it was apparent that Norfolk County would then constitute the city's only remaining avenue for territorial expansion. As Lloyd H. Lewis described the situation: "Under Virginia annexation laws, this left Norfolk with no direction to expand except into Norfolk County. County officials immediately had visions of Norfolk sprinting down the east shore of the Elizabeth River's southern branch, with Portsmouth matching pace down the west bank." [39]

Although the merger talks were not confirmed until December 4, and intent to bring the proposed merger to referendum was not announced publicly until mid-December 1961, consolidation discussions had been quietly taking place since October.[40] On December 11 a local industrialist, George T. McLean, suggested publicly to officials of Portsmouth, South Norfolk, and Norfolk County that a three-way consolidation be considered in lieu of a Norfolk County–South Norfolk merger. Although Portsmouth's Mayor R. Irvine Smith indicated a willingness to talk, the McLean proposal was received noncommittally by Norfolk County and South Norfolk. When the charter and the consolidation agreement between South Norfolk and Norfolk County were made public, the announcement brought forth a storm of protest in both the county and the city. In Norfolk

---

[38] The annexation suit was filed on Dec. 9, 1961.

[39] "Give and Take Spirit Winner," *Ledger-Star*, Jan. 1, 1963.

[40] See, for example, "Norfolk County and South Norfolk May Talk Union," *The Virginian-Pilot*, Nov. 30, 1961, and "Annex-Merger Battles Erupt Through the State," *ibid.*, Dec. 4, 1961. The first official press release of the group, dated December 4, 1961, read:

"A meeting was held between the governing bodies of the City of South Norfolk along with the County of Norfolk, along with their Constitutional Officers and discussed the question of a possible merger of the respective communities.

"The meeting was harmonious and it was decided that further discussions would be held, the time and date to be determined later."

County, for example, an active group opposing merger came into being on December 27, 1961, a scant few days after the county board of supervisors signed the agreement. This group was composed of citizens of the Western Branch Magisterial District who opposed merger or were moderately in favor of annexation by the City of Portsmouth. In part because the City of Portsmouth divided the Western Branch District from the remainder of Norfolk County, some residents of the district had closer ties with Portsmouth than with South Norfolk or, for that matter, even Norfolk County. In its initial statement the group set forth its purpose.

The immediate interest of the association will be the prevention of any merger between Norfolk County and the City of South Norfolk which would include the Western Branch District. The citizens of the Western Branch hold in highest esteem the people of the other districts of Norfolk County as well as the people of South Norfolk. *However, our members are convinced that the proposed merger is economically unfeasible and politically inequitable for the Western Branch District.*[41]

Antimerger forces then attacked on a broad front in both South Norfolk and Norfolk County. They stressed the haste and secrecy of the merger forces, the lack of a feasibility study, increased taxes and debt, and the adverse impact of merger on schools and services. The Western Branch Citizens Association subsequently proposed that the Western Branch District be separated from Norfolk County and be allowed to merge with Portsmouth, a plea that was rejected by the county board of supervisors.[42] In the City of South Norfolk it was argued that the city was being sacrificed in order to bail the county out of debt.[43] In Norfolk County opponents pointed to the fact that the county would have only equal representation on the consolidated council even though the county population was two and a half times greater than that of South Norfolk.[44]

Schools were a major issue in the consolidation campaign. Opponents in both South Norfolk and Norfolk County charged that the proposed merger would adversely affect the school system in each of the governments. Members of the South Norfolk school board and its superintendent of public instruction, E. E. Brickell,

[41] A copy of this statement was obtained from Charles Cross, clerk of the circuit court, Chesapeake. The emphasis is theirs.

[42] See "County Kills Merger Plea," *The Virginian-Pilot,* Jan. 10, 1962.

[43] A copy of an antimerger flyer to this effect was obtained from Charles Cross.

[44] Robert R. Barber, "Merger 'Haste' Deplored," *The Virginian-Pilot,* Jan. 4, 1962.

openly attacked the consolidation proposal. On January 8, 1962, the school board passed a resolution condemning the merger "until such time as a scientific, well-planned study be made of all the implications thereof, and such facts presented to the public over a period of time commensurate with public understanding." A copy of this resolution with a covering letter signed by W. Roy Britton, chairman of the school board, was mailed to school patrons.[45] An antimerger broadside entitled "Kill Merger—NOT SOUTH NOR-FOLK," addressed to South Norfolk residents, warned:

> What will happen to the plans for our new schools if we merge? A new school for the Portlock area. New junior high schools. New facilities at Holly Street. Three new facilities for our colored children. Will the 51,000 people of Norfolk County vote to build schools in South Norfolk? The answer is NO. THINK IT OVER.
>
> A $6,000,000 school bond issue has just been passed in Norfolk County. If this merger takes place, South Norfolk will have to pay for their schools. According to a pamphlet issued by Norfolk County, "New buildings and facilities proposed (for Norfolk County) will be provided according to plans." This means—$6,000,000 will be spent in Norfolk County—nothing in South Norfolk. THINK IT OVER.
>
> Free bus transportation has been promised Norfolk County school children. Not one word has been mentioned about South Norfolk students. THINK IT OVER.[46]

In what was supposed to be a peacemaking session between the South Norfolk city council and South Norfolk school officials, Superintendent Brickell registered strenuous dissent from statements about South Norfolk schools allegedly made by Norfolk County officers. Brickell stated:

> I'll stack our school system up against theirs any time they want. As a school man I resent what's coming out over there.
>
> We have better administration—and I can prove it.
>
> We have more certified teachers—and I can prove it.
>
> Our graduates do better in college—and I can prove it.
>
> Some people judge a school system on the basis of per-pupil cost. We're better there—and I can prove it.[47]

Brickell went on to complain that Robert E. Gibson, a member of the House of Delegates and a promergerite, had applied political pressure on a principal of a South Norfolk school regarding the

---

[45] Undated copy from Charles Cross.

[46] Undated and unsigned broadside, copy from Charles Cross.

[47] William L. Tazewell, "School Board and Council Clash on County Merger," *The Virginian-Pilot*, Jan. 13, 1962.

consolidation. "I told him fun is fun and politics is politics," Brickell said.[48]

The South Norfolk Anti-Merger Committee led by former Mayor Clarence E. Forehand took up the school debate with a broadside comparing South Norfolk's schools to those of Norfolk County.[49] It characterized Norfolk County schools as overcrowded and anticipating split shifts. Comparisons of teacher salaries, per pupil expenditures, and administrative costs all proved favorable to South Norfolk.

Two sidelights to the South Norfolk–Norfolk County school controversy are noteworthy. First, much of the rancor that surrounded the controversy was generated by an announcement in Norfolk County well in advance of the referendum about the appointment of the school superintendent for the consolidated city. Although his move was perhaps ill-timed, merger leader Charles Cross felt it necessary to assure the voters of Norfolk County before the referendum that E. W. "Ed" Chittum, superintendent of schools of Norfolk County, would be appointed the new superintendent.[50] This likely offended the South Norfolk school board, and it obviously offended Superintendent Brickell. Brickell noted, quite correctly, that Cross, clerk of the circuit court, had nothing to do legally with the appointment of school superintendents; this was the duty of the school boards. However, many persons both in and out of Norfolk County regarded Chittum as one of the finest school superintendents in the Commonwealth, and if he were to be deposed, the merger probably would have lost votes in Norfolk County.

A second outgrowth of the school controversy was that the chairman of the South Norfolk school board, W. Roy Britton, became a merger casualty.[51] He had been a member of the school board for fifteen years and had served most of those years as chairman of the board. In January 1962 he acknowledged that he did not expect to be reappointed because of his opposition to the merger, and prior to consolidation but after the referendum, the council of South Norfolk refused to reappoint Britton to the school board.

Throughout the school debate the Western Branch Citizens Association of Norfolk County continued to attack the proposed con-

---

[48] *Ibid.* This statement was vigorously denied by Gibson. See "Brickell Slants Merger Talk Facts: Gibson," *ibid.,* Jan. 15, 1962.

[49] Copy from Charles Cross.

[50] Cross stated at the time that he knew of one member of the South Norfolk school board who would vote for Chittum, thereby making the necessary majority for Chittum's subsequent appointment.

[51] See "A Casualty of the Merger," *The Virginian-Pilot,* June 24, 1962.

solidation. The debate was at times acrimonious and emotional, and a promerger rally in Churchland in the Western Branch District produced a flare of tempers with a momentary scuffle. Order was quickly restored but the discussion remained heated. Certain of the questions raised by the citizens association seem to have been well taken, especially those points dealing with the allocation of state road funds for maintenance of streets in the consolidated city and the fact that county sanitary district law would not apply within the consolidated city after merger.[52]

In South Norfolk antimerger forces used a "save our city" approach in conjunction with "a parade of horrors" that would result from consolidation. An antimerger flyer in South Norfolk noted the following:

Stop and think what Norfolk County has to offer us. The answer is *nothing*. Nothing but making us a dumping ground for anything and everything. Nothing but higher taxes and less services. Nothing but taking us over and making us do exactly what they say.

Your present office-holders have sold you out for promises of bigger salaries and nice jobs. Don't be fooled by the pictures of paradise they will try to paint for you. . . .

Our Council made many promises to us while they were campaigning, but they, too, have sold out. They promised to put the City on a sound financial basis, and now they are handing us over to Norfolk County. . . .

We are told that we need to become bigger—bigger with what? Bigger with the Dismal Swamp of Norfolk County? Fit for nothing but snakes and bears?

Did you know that there are 51,000 people in Norfolk County and only 21,000 in South Norfolk? Who do you think is going to rule?

Read the proposed charter carefully. Remember that by 1967 there will be five Councilmen from Norfolk County and two from South Norfolk. Where will we be then? . . .

Certainly Norfolk County wants to merge. They want the $250,000 we get from the Bridge Commission every year. They want political rule over all of us. They want to take us over. We must stop this now or forever live to regret it. They want our factories. They want our low bonded indebtedness.[53]

The promergerites held approximately 100 meetings between the time of the merger announcement and the date of the referendum.

[52] Letter from William H. Oast, Jr., Louis Brenner, and E. S. Everhart, Western Branch Citizens Association, to the Chairman and Members of the Board of Supervisors of Norfolk County, undated, copy from Charles Cross.

[53] Undated and unsigned flyer, photostatic copy from Charles Cross.

At major advertised rallies in Norfolk County, Court Clerk Cross usually presided and led the discussion, backed up by other county political leaders. At a rally at Great Bridge on January 8, 1962, for instance, those speaking included Cross, Delegate W. H. Hodges, Jr., Commonwealth's Attorney Peter M. Axson, Sheriff J. A. Hodges, Commissioner of the Revenue Robert Waldo, State Senator Gordon F. Marsh, Supervisors E. P. Wadsworth and G. A. Treakle, and School Superintendent Chittum.

The promerger leaders in Norfolk County pointed to annexation and its disruptive effects on county finances and planning. "Our future holds nothing for us but one annexation after another," Cross stated. "This [merger] is the only way we can give you the right to vote on your future." [54] T. Ray Hassell, a supervisor from the Butts Road District, termed the annexation suit by Portsmouth "another stab in the back" and attacked "the selfish millionaires who don't sit in the seats of government but tell them what to do." [55] State Senator Marsh called for an end to annexation, "which sets brother against brother and friend against friend." [56] "Let us enter an era of order," he stated, "something we haven't had in 20 years."

As might be expected, promergerites targeted in on the Portsmouth annexation suit against Norfolk County although, in balance, the Chesapeake merger campaign was not as fully "anti-Portsmouth" in tone as the Virginia Beach campaign was "anti-Norfolk." However, Portsmouth did come under fire, and the antiannexation theme was apparently well received by county voters. As one spectator from Norfolk County put it at a public meeting, he had been annexed three times by Portsmouth "and now it looks like they're going to chase me clear to Carolina." [57] Cross drew applause for his antiannexation stand: "We have come to the end of our rope. It's merger versus annexation. It's not merger versus stay-as-you are. They won't let us stay as you are." [58]

In addition to the annexation issue, promerger forces in the county emphasized that consolidation would not bring tax increases and would permit "each borough . . . to decide its character, individuality, and its services, have a vote as to its taxation, and elect

[54] William L. Tazewell, "County Officers Claim Merger Is Only Hope," *The Virginian-Pilot*, Jan. 5, 1962.

[55] *Ibid.*

[56] "Senator Marsh Urges End Annexation—Vote Merger," *The Virginia-Carolina News*, Jan. 11, 1962.

[57] "S. Norfolk Merger Challenged," *The Virginian-Pilot*, Jan. 10, 1962.

[58] *Ibid.*

its representative." [59] They also stressed the advantages of a balanced industrial, agricultural, and residential community. Norfolk County should consolidate, Robert E. Gibson stated,

because it needs a stable industrial economy. We here in South Norfolk have what the County needs and as a team presents perhaps the greatest natural self-supporting economy of any city on the Atlantic Seaboard, barring none. We then as a city will have farm areas, residential areas, commercial areas and finally industrial areas, all with unlimited resources and a low inviting tax rate. In fact the lowest in our area, and likely the lowest for any city of our size in Virginia.[60]

The emotional appeal to the future was also made in both the city and county. As Gibson put it:

Finally, it has been said we are too hasty. Yet, emergencies have always been necessary to progress. It was darkness that produced the lamp. It was fog that produced the compass. It was hunger that drove us to exploration and it took a depression to teach us the value of a job. Now we are faced with a great emergency; will our leaders consider themselves only and not the children of tomorrow? Will they stumble and fall over political personalities and let the greatest opportunity of the century pass us by?

It's not the political factions that are at stake; it's not the job of one man or another that is important; it is the future growth and happiness of your children that is at stake; the future growth and development of your city that is at stake.

Victor Hugo once said if God had intended that a man should go backward he would have given him eyes in the back of his head. I don't know how any person young or old realizing the challenge to the tidewater area today could hesitate in support of this program.

Finally, it's not what South Norfolk will do to Western Branch or what Western Branch will do to us. It's what each will do for the greatest city of tomorrow. It's what the greater city can and will do for a greater tidewater community.

If our forefathers had waited, they would have missed the boat, they would still be in England. If our grandfathers would have waited most of us would still be in North Carolina. We owe it to them to have the courage to go forward, to greater progress for future generations.[61]

The promerger emphasis was somewhat different in South Norfolk, where annexation was not a factor and there was significant

_____

[59] Broadside entitled "A Historic Past—A Promising Future," copy from Charles Cross.
[60] Speech by Robert E. Gibson, Jan. 8, 1962, copy from Charles Cross.
[61] *Ibid.*

opposition to consolidation. Promerger leaders brought up the problems that would result from encirclement as a consequence of annexations around South Norfolk by the cities of Norfolk and Portsmouth. Also, an open letter signed by three South Norfolk councilmen indicated that the city had financial problems and that consolidation would be one way to alleviate them. For the budget year 1961–62 in South Norfolk, there was a revenue deficiency of $400,000, which had been made up by selling two mortgaged sewer lines to the Hampton Roads Sanitation District for $455,000. But, as the councilmen pointed out:

The point is very simple. That $455,000 was used to balance the budget this year. When the City prepares its next budget in June, we won't have that $455,000 to use again. One of two things must then be done. Either new tax revenues must be found equal to this amount or the budget must be cut by $455,000. This sum represents ⅕ of all our local revenue so it won't be easy to replace. If replaced by a raise in real estate taxes, it will require a 55% increase.

The financial situation of our City will also be affected in the near future by the construction of the interstate spur to highway 64. This highway will be cut through the City taking 158 acres of land and 232 houses. More than $21,000 per year will be cut from our tax revenue. Where will new revenue be found to replace it? [62]

The councilmen concluded by noting that the existing budget did nothing but keep South Norfolk as it was. No provisions had been made for public improvements, new schools, or salary raises. At the same time, they noted that Norfolk County had surplus funds, a better financial rating, lower taxes by one-third than in South Norfolk, and an expanding tax base as a result of industrial development.

The promerger group in South Norfolk stressed the history the city shared with Norfolk County, their cultural and social ties, and the existing cooperative arrangements for fire protection, jails, law enforcement, and public welfare. Finally, as a result of attacks levied by the South Norfolk antimergerites against Norfolk County, those promoting merger in South Norfolk spent a good deal of time explaining and defending the financial operation in the county and reassuring the voters that the county was financially sound.

As in Virginia Beach, the opposition entered suits (1) attempting

[62] "Open Letter to the Citizens of South Norfolk," Jan. 29, 1962, signed by Councilmen Allen, Boyette, and McPherson, copy from Charles Cross.

to delay the date of the referendum [63] and (2) questioning the constitutionality of the merger.[64] The primary points at issue were the tax differentials projected for the merged city and the selection of constitutional officers by agreement. Charles Cross labeled the suit "a desperate attempt by desperate men to prevent the people of the county from being able to vote on their future government." [65] The only concrete result of this legal maneuvering was to postpone the date of the merger referendum from February 9 to February 13. A final order of March 20, 1962, resulted in dismissal of the suit.

Victory for merger in Norfolk County was achieved by a vote of 2 to 1.[66] Of 6,875 votes cast, 4,839 approved. Majorities of 3 to 1 or better were recorded in all magisterial districts except Western Branch, but even in that district the proconsolidationists carried the day by a total vote of 1,383 to 1,163. Over one-half of the total opposition vote in the county came from the Western Branch District. In Churchland Precinct No. 2 of Western Branch the defeat of the merger proposal by a vote of 641 to 530 undoubtedly reflected the sentiment of the Western Branch Citizens Association.

In South Norfolk the voters opted for consolidation by a margin of 433 votes, 1,809 to 1,376. In the six precincts of South Norfolk, however, the proposal was defeated in two, and carried by less than 20 votes each in two others. Only in the second precincts of the first and third wards did merger pass by a comfortable margin. Thus, while there was no doubt that the margin of victory was decisive, the vote also indicated strong localized antimerger sentiment in South Norfolk. It soon became quite clear that even though merger had been approved by the voters, there remained a real problem in developing a city-wide approach to governmental services.

Campaign in Newport News

As has been noted, the direction of the Newport News–Warwick merger attempt was in the hands of two citizens committees—the

[63] In re Consolidation of the City of South Norfolk and Norfolk County, Virginia: In the Circuit Court of Norfolk. See Order of Jan. 22, 1962.

[64] Western Branch Citizens Association v. Board of Supervisors: In the Circuit Court of Norfolk County, Bill of Complaint filed Jan. 15, 1962; Final Order made on March 20, 1962.

[65] See "County Merger Foes Petition Circuit Court," *The Virginian-Pilot,* Jan. 16, 1962.

[66] The author would like to express appreciation to Charles Cross, clerk of the Chesapeake circuit court, for supplying photostatic copies of the merger vote on a precinct-by-precinct basis.

Newport News Citizens Committee for Consolidation led by Dr. Russell V. Buxton and its counterpart organization in Warwick under the chairmanship of J. B. Woodward, Jr. Following the defeat of the tri-city merger attempt on November 6, 1956, there remained the well-organized Warwick Committee, which had successfully carried Warwick for the tri-city merger and still had unspent campaign funds.[67] The committee was in good shape for another campaign, its prestige had been enhanced by the recent electoral victory, and the Woodward group was dedicated to promoting merger.

Public officials played a mixed role in the Newport News–Warwick merger. The constitutional officers of the two cities were not active leaders in the campaign, with the notable exception of George DeShazor, clerk of the circut court of Warwick, who led the anti-mergerites in that city. Members of the respective city councils likewise were not particularly active although it is plain that the citizens committee had the full backing of the Newport News council and a majority of the members of the Warwick council. A few public officials announced in favor of merger, including Lewis A. McMurran, Jr., a member of the House of Delegates, and George Abernathy, a former councilman and mayor of the City of Warwick.[68]

Judging by the volume of the promerger literature, the number of advertisements, and their use of communncations media, the promerger forces did not lack financial support. Those in opposition were obviously less well financed, but they were able to buy limited advertising space in the local newspapers, to publish three issues of a four-page paper entitled *The Issue*, which made liberal use of cartoons depicting how Warwick was being "taken in," [69] to prepare and mail letters to businessmen and other citizens regarding the consolidation issue, [70] and to utilize other campaign methods. One such method was a comparison of real estate taxes using existing assessments and rates in Warwick and projected ones in a consolidated government. Notices were sent to individual taxpayers

[67] The author would like to acknowledge the cooperation of the late Mr. Woodward, who allowed the author access to selected files and papers relating to the consolidation.

[68] See, for example, "2 City Merger Benefits Cited by Abernathy," *Daily Press*, July 10, 1957.

[69] Published in May, June, and July of 1957. Also included besides cartoons were two or three articles in each issue on some phase of the consolidation. Copies of *The Issue* were provided by George DeShazor, clerk of the Newport News circuit court, from his personal files.

[70] Copies of these letters were provided by George DeShazor.

computing that person's tax before and after merger. Finally, the antimerger forces were able to attain some semblance of a working precinct organization and formed a speakers bureau to provide persons who would speak against consolidation. But, according to DeShazor, the antimerger campaign was not much above the level of a weak protest when compared with the promerger effort. The antimergerites undoubtedly suffered from the enthusiastic support of consolidation by the two daily newspapers of the area, the *Newport News Times-Herald* and the *Daily Press*.

The antimerger campaign centered almost entirely in Warwick, where the best hope existed to defeat consolidation. Increased taxes were cited as the chief reason for opposing merger, and a projected real estate tax increase of $353,000 was envisoned. Warwick taxpayers, it was argued, would bear the increased costs resulting from consolidation. Antimerger forces also charged Warwick's school system would be endangered, school bus service would be jeopardized, the people of Warwick would lose control of their affairs, and that Warwick "would lose its proud name." Consolidation, according to the antimergerites, would not "create a single teacher, policeman, or fireman, build a single inch of street, overpass, or fire station, nor provide any extra recreational facilities." [71] Thriving Warwick was compared unfavorably with static Newport News. Antimerger forces also made occasional references to the "silk stocking" interests who resided in Warwick, primarily the Newport News shipyard executives.

No special efforts were made by promerger leaders to exploit the issue of probable black control of the then existing City of Newport News, although promerger forces did inject it into the campaign at a relatively early stage, knowing it would have to be faced. No Negroes served on either of the promerger committees, and this worked to fix the white character of the movement. The exclusion of blacks was a deliberate move by promerger leaders, who admittedly felt that the presence of a black citizen might work to alienate more white voters than it would win black voters. But from a practical standpoint promerger leaders saw no real need to exploit the issue of black control of Newport News. Those whites who would vote for merger because of probable black control were already convinced; promerger forces knew they could win Newport News without carrying black precincts, and consequently, the Negro vote was

[71] Warwick Citizens Committee Against Consolidation, "Warwick: Our City with a Future," *Daily Press*, July 14, 1957.

generally conceded in advance to the antimergerites. However, promerger forces did go through the motions of campaigning in black
precincts in Newport News and were frankly surprised at the favorable results achieved. The vote was much closer than promerger
leaders had anticipated, and in fact, merger carried in three of four
predominately black precincts by narrow margins.

Antimerger forces concentrating on Warwick attempted to use
the racial situation in Newport News to win white voters in Warwick. Newport News was under a court order to desegregate its public schools, and the antimergerites contended that the court order
would apply to Warwick if consolidation were to occur. Although
its effect is difficult to gauge, this gambit probably frightened a
number of white Warwick voters and therefore hurt the promerger
cause in Warwick. At the same time, the manner in which the antimerger committee presented the issue probably helped the promerger cause in the black precincts of Newport News.

In balance, the public school situation in Warwick probably did
more damage to the antimerger cause than to the promergerites.
While antimerger forces stressed the issue of local control of public schools, the *Newport News Times-Herald* called attention to the
poor quality of public education in Warwick.[72] According to the
1957–58 budgets Warwick spent $219.22 per pupil for the year as
against $269.04 spent in Newport News. On a per-pupil expenditure
basis Warwick ranged 32nd among the then 32 Virginia cities as
compared with a ranking of 18 for Newport News.

Throughout the campaign promerger forces hammered away at a
single theme, namely, that the boundary line between Newport
News and Warwick was an artificial one. In a series of newspaper
advertisements and in public meetings, promergerites stressed the
common interests of the two communities. Industrial Newport
News, it was said, complemented residential Warwick, and Warwick's future was bound to a flourishing Newport News.

Promerger forces also focused on the level of public services provided by Warwick and on Warwick's needs. They emphasized that
Warwick had been deficient in providing an adequate level of
municipal services and that eventually these service needs would
have to be met. In "Consolidation Corner," a daily column appearing in the *Newport News Times-Herald,* the Warwick Committee
stated:

[72] John Bowen, "Warwick's Local Effort Is Low," *Newport News Times-Herald,*
July 11, 1957.

Let us consider Warwick's needs—whether we consolidate or not. We need many things if we do not consolidate—namely, schools, overpasses, curbs, gutters, sewers, parks, playgrounds, street repairs, health and welfare services, recreational facilities, a new jail, a juvenile home, and others. If we do consolidate, the jail, juvenile home and recreational buildings in Newport News will be shared by us and perhaps immediate construction of these will not be necessary in Warwick. If we do NOT consolidate, we must bear the cost of all of these items out of our own funds. Our taxes are bound to jump to pay for these needs. On the other hand, there is no pressing need in Newport News for most of these items and, therefore, if we consolidate it is very clear that Newport News will assist in paying for Warwick's needs. It is that simple. Analyze it and you will see that we can provide our needs in Warwick easier and cheaper if we consolidate.[73]

The promergerites took some care to avoid two issues that had had adverse effects on prior consolidation attempts. These were (1) identification of the promerger effort with a single or a limited number of economic interests and (2) promised reduction in governmental expenditures that would allegedly result from consolidation. Regarding the second point, the promerger forces recognized that taxes would likely go up even if a merger were consummated; therefore, they adopted the position that an increase in taxes would occur regardless of what happened. Moreover, the promerger forces had experienced some disenchantment with the economy theme in the prior tri-city merger attempt. That greater efficiency and economy would result from consolidation was impossible to prove conclusively, and there was good cause to believe that no immediate economies would result at all. The objective report on the effects of consolidation prepared for the tri-city merger attempt by the University of Virginia's Institute of Government, in fact, had supplied as much ammunition for antimergerites as it had for the promerger group. Since promergerites had not gained any significant partisan advantage from either the report or the economy and efficiency issue, it was decided simply to forego the issue except in broad general terms. Thus, while it was claimed that greater economy and efficiency in government would result from merger, dollar and cents figures that might be challenged were avoided.

A fire helped, however. On July 1, 1957, fifteen days before the referendum, a fire destroyed Rich's supermarket in Warwick. The

[73] "Consolidation Corner," *ibid.*, July 2, 1957. This series of columns, sponsored by the Warwick Citizens Committee for Consolidation, covered a different issue of merger each day.

Warwick Fire Department and volunteers answered the call, but help had to be requested from Newport News, which responded with an aerial truck and two pumpers. The aerial truck was credited with preventing the fire from spreading, although the supermarket burned to the ground. The *Daily Press* drew the obvious conclusion regarding "the increased efficiency, and fire-fighting power, which would result in ONE COMBINED FIRE DEPARTMENT working even more closely to meet any possible emergency." [74] From that point on, promerger speakers usually managed to refer to the supermarket fire.

Promerger electoral organization stressed the neighborhood and precinct approach with door-to-door campaigning.[75] A few rallies were held, and promerger speakers appeared before civic groups, clubs, and other public gatherings. In part because the promerger forces felt that victory was at hand, they turned down a proposal by the antimergerites to debate consolidation on television. Promerger and antimerger speakers did appear on the same platform in certain of the public meetings.

The vote in Newport News was overwhelmingly in favor of merger, 4,398 to 873 for a total of 5,271 valid votes. Only the 5th Precinct of the Third Ward, predominantly black, voted against the proposition by a vote of 246 to 133. In the 4th Precinct of the Third Ward, a white precinct, the promerger vote was 48 to 1.

The vote in Warwick was much closer, in part a tribute to the effectiveness of the antimerger group. Merger was approved by a vote of 3,938 to 3,253 for a total of 7,191 valid votes. Of the twelve precincts in Warwick, however, antimerger forces won in five. In Stanley Precinct the vote against merger was 87 to 7; in Denbigh Precinct, 253 to 89, and in Jefferson Park Precinct, 295 to 50. On the proconsolidation side, the "silk stocking" River Precinct provided the largest margin for merger in ratifying the proposal by a vote of 484 to 169.

The next morning the *Newport News Times-Herald* hailed the favorable vote as setting the stage for growth and progress.[76] At the same time, residents of Warwick driving to Newport News along busy Route 60 through antimerger Denbigh Precinct noted a banner stretched across the highway bearing the legend "Denbigh Secedes."

[74] "Two Cities—and Fires," July 2, 1957 (emphasis theirs).

[75] Insight regarding this organization is provided by "Merger Forces Select Neighborhood Teams," *Newport News Times-Herald*, July 3, 1957.

[76] "Historic Vote for Progress," *ibid.*, July 17, 1957.

Officials of the Peninsula Shipbuilders' Association issued a statement that "it is hoped that the citizens of both fine cities will forget any differences that might have existed and work in unity toward a common goal—progress and a greater area." [77] Action was initiated shortly thereafter for a referendum to select a name for the consolidated city.

Merger and the General Assembly: The Charters

By tradition and practice, each of Virginia's cities and towns has its own particular charter enacted by the General Assembly in the form of a special law. Prepared locally, charter bills and amendments to existing charters are usually noncontroversial items on the legislative calendar; they are introduced by members of the legislative delegation representing the city or town; and they are usually enacted without debate under an unwritten rule of legislative comity. As the system works in practice, moreover, the General Assembly has granted substantial leeway to the cities and towns of the state in drafting their charters.[78]

Because the charter bills for the consolidated cites of Hampton, Virginia Beach, and Chesapeake worked to seal off expansion by the core cities of their respective metropolitan areas, however, they were clearly not in the routine tradition of the Virginia municipal charter. These bills, especially those of Virginia Beach and Chesapeake, raised several important questions regarding their possible effect on Virginia local government.

First, the consolidated cities were obvious affronts to the theoretical urban-rural division between city and county government. At the time of consolidation, none of the merged cities qualified as completely urban, even in a loose sense of the term. Second, the consolidated cities established a precedent which other urban centers viewed as inherently dangerous. Cities such as Richmond and Roanoke, for example, envisioned themselves in the position of Norfolk and Portsmouth—cut off from expansion through the merger and/or incorporation of their surrounding counties. The formation of the consolidated cities of Virginia Beach and Chesapeake was

[77] "P. S. A. Cites Consolidation," 1 *The Shipbuilder* 1 (July 1957). At the time, this was the official organ of the Peninsula Shipbuilders' Association.

[78] See Weldon Cooper, "The Charter and Virginia Local Government," 45 *University of Virginia News Letter* 29–32 (April 15, 1969).

therefore viewed as a device to circumvent the operation of the state's annexation laws. The basic presumption of the Virginia system of annexation was that "cities have a right to grow," a right that obviously would be denied to Norfolk and Portsmouth if merger became a reality.

What might have been a major legislative debate on the nature and operation of Virginia local government never materialized. The questions were raised, but the debate did not ensue. The legislative delegations representing Norfolk and Portsmouth registered protests, but they were ignored. Outwardly the charter bills were handled in a routine fashion, and they passed through the General Assembly with only a mere handful of dissenting votes, chiefly those from the Norfolk and Portsmouth legislators.

One of the most difficult questions to answer is why, in 1962, the General Assembly thus saw fit to enclose the state's largest and third largest cities, respectively, with the two consolidated cities of Virginia Beach and Chesapeake. On what grounds did the General Assembly enact into law the two charters that, in effect, denied, alone among Virginian cities, any further hopes for territorial expansion to Norfolk and Portsmouth?

An ex post facto assessment of the reasons and motives of individual legislators suggests that various factors contributed to the decision. Certain obvious circumstances and events in 1962 helped the charter bills along, and although each cannot be accurately weighed one against the other, collectively they explain why the General Assembly acted as it did.

First, the consolidations appeared to some to be local in nature. Interviews conducted in Tidewater in 1963 suggested that this was a factor of some importance in legislative thinking. Second, the local referendums, which had been highly favorable to merger, undoubtedly swayed legislative opinion in so far as legitimacy was concerned. Third, as the proconsolidationists argued in both Virginia Beach and Chesapeake, the mergers were not intended to be barriers to future metropolitan cooperation. In fact, the promergerites declared that the mergers enhanced the climate for a true metropolitan area-wide approach to common problems. Fourth, the charter bills benefited from expert lobbying by leading Virginia Beach and Chesapeake officials, both through their local legislators and by men such as former State Senator V. A. Etheridge, treasurer of Virginia Beach, who took up temporary residence in the Hotel Richmond adjoining the capitol grounds to help see the Virginia Beach charter bill through. Fifth, the charter bills benefited to some extent from annexation politics played in the 1962 General Assembly. In this regard, the tactics adopted by the Norfolk and Portsmouth legislative delegations may have alienated other legislators. For a sixth and final reason, however, it is necessary to recount briefly the nature of Byrd Organization politics in the waning years of the 1950's and early 1960's. At that time the organization was under severe internal stress, and its much-vaunted unity was deteriorating.

In the latter part of the 1950's Virginia politics was dominated by one overriding statewide issue—the continuation of segregation by race in Virginia's public schools and, more specifically, the Byrd Organization's program of "massive resistance" to racial integration. Clearly, massive resistance in no way "made the mergers," but the circumstances and events surrounding the abandonment of massive resistance contributed to the political climate in which the charter bills were approved.

The 1954 decision of the United States Supreme Court in the *Brown* case had a far greater impact upon the Byrd Organization than was commonly realized or understood at the time.[79] Within the organization, the *Brown* case resulted in a division between those who were willing to adopt a moderate state policy which would promote gradualism in integration in compliance with the Supreme Court's decision, and those who were unalterably opposed to any racial integration in the public schools. Tension within the organization began to increase when initial pronouncements by Byrd leaders indicated that Virginia would comply with the law, albeit reluctantly. Southside Virginia, with its high concentration of blacks, was especially restless over the prospects of any racial integration. Southside, that is, the area stretching from Nansemond County on the east adjacent to the Norfolk-Portsmouth SMSA to Prince Edward County on the west, was the core of organization strength, and its disaffection would have constituted a serious blow to Byrd power. On the other hand, it appeared that a policy of massive resistance would satisfy Southside and might be acceptable in the remainder of the state. Moreover, although some leaders in Virginia at the

[79] When this manuscript was completed in the form of a Ph.D. dissertation in 1965, the impact of massive resistance on the Byrd Organization had not become apparent. By far the best general treatment of this subject is to be found in J. Harvie Wilkinson III, *Harry Byrd and the Changing Face of Virginia Politics, 1945–1966* (Charlottesville: University Press of Virginia, 1968). More than any other writer, Wilkinson has effectively capsuled the dilemma of the Byrd Organization regarding massive resistance.

time advocated compliance with the *Brown* decision, believing that
obedience should be given to the decision regardless of its distaste-
ful effects, no leader in the white community was openly advocating
racial integration. With these factors in mind, in a special session in
1955 the General Assembly enacted massive resistance into law and
provided, among other things, that any and all public schools would
be closed if such action were necessary to avoid racial integration.

In Norfolk the local organization headed by Court Clerk W. L.
Prieur, Jr., followed the Byrd line of massive resistance. In this decision Prieur was joined generally by Mayor W. F. Duckworth, the
city council, and the remaining constitutional officers. Nonetheless,
opposition to massive resistance was expressed by *The Virginian-
Pilot,* the Norfolk school board, and eventually the Norfolk Committee for Public Schools. When Norfolk public schools were subsequently closed to prevent racial integration, white and black
citizen dissatisfaction with massive resistance increased, and the
committee's numbers grew in strength. It was this committee, in
fact, which initiated the legal suit that was eventually to topple
massive resistance as a lawful response to the *Brown* decision. Benjamin Muse has described the circumstances.

In the meantime, the Norfolk Committee for Public Schools had taken
a step of fateful portent for massive resistance. Consideration had been
given to several forms of legal action in federal court to force the reopening
of the city's closed schools. Attorneys for the seventeen Negro pupils who
had been ordered enrolled with white pupils withdrew an earlier petition
for this relief, when Federal District Judge Walter E. Hoffman informed
them that they were proceeding against the wrong parties in naming the
members of the school board only, and filed suit, naming Governor Almond
as a defendant. The parents of a single white pupil also filed suit.

But the litigation which was to be followed through was one promoted
and financed by the Norfolk Committee for Public Schools. In this suit,
filed October 27, twenty-six white Norfolk residents, including eleven children, challenged the school-closing law.[80]

Massive resistance came to an end on January 28, 1959, when
Governor J. Lindsay Almond, Jr., speaking to a special session of
the General Assembly, requested the enactment of new legislation
that would permit the reopening of Virginia's schools. This was a
break with the hard-line organization policy of statewide massive
resistance, and Almond had acted without the approval of Senator

[80] Muse, *Virginia's Massive Resistance* (Bloomington, Ind.: Indiana University Press, 1961), pp. 93-94.

Byrd. A split emerged within the Byrd Organization, dividing political leaders essentially along pro-Almond and anti-Almond lines.
State Senators Edward L. Breeden, Jr., of Norfolk and William B.
Spong of Portsmouth followed the governor's lead and supported
the enactment in March 1959 of local option legislation for racial
integration of the public schools. Even though massive resistance
was clearly dead, the legislative margins for local option were slim;
in the Senate the core of the governor's program was saved by one
vote. The conflict left political scars, and the split within the organization had not been healed.

During this period the local organization in Norfolk found itself
in a difficult political situation vis-à-vis the state organization. Most
of the city's leaders had no wish to sever the ties that bound them
to Byrd and Richmond. Yet it became apparent that the local officeholders could neither safely nor conscientiously become identified
with any resurrection of massive resistance. School integration in
Norfolk had been effected without serious incident, and there was
decided citizen opposition to reverting to the status quo ante
bellum. Court Clerk Prieur and other local officials found themselves challenged by the antiorganization Citizens for Democratic
Government in the 1961 Democratic Party primary; the major issue
was their stand on massive resistance. Prieur was endorsed by *The
Virginian-Pilot* on the basis of his experience in office and the fact
that he was personally not a "massive resister." [81] Of a total of 24,502
votes, Prieur won by a margin of 1,352 votes, and by different
margins, the remaining local organization candidates were also
victorious.

The crucial point of the 1961 primary was that members of the
Norfolk and Portsmouth organizations did not support the state
organization designees for governor and lieutenant governor. The
organization candidate for governor, Albertis S. Harrison, Jr., was
acceptable locally and was, in fact, endorsed by *The Virginian-Pilot*.
But there was strong objection to the organization candidate for
lieutenant governor, Mills E. Godwin, Jr., who had been a leading
force in the promotion and defense of massive resistance while
serving in the Virginia State Senate. As a result, the Norfolk leadership individually chose either to sit out the primary campaign or to
give informal support to A. E. S. Stephens, the opposition guberna-
torial candidate. For example, Colgate W. Darden, Jr., Prieur's

[81] "The 1961 Primary: Norfolk's Clerkship," *The Virginian-Pilot*, July 7, 1961.

campaign manager, endorsed Stephens, as did the state senators, Breeden of Norfolk and Spong of Portsmouth.

This action by Norfolk and Portsmouth leaders hurt whatever chances the Norfolk-Portsmouth legislative delegation might have had to block the Virginia Beach and Chesapeake consolidations in the organization-dominated 1962 General Assembly. Not only had the Norfolk people supported Governor Almond in the abandonment of massive resistance, but they also failed to rally to the organization banner in an important election. The Harrison and Godwin ticket, moreover, failed to carry Norfolk and Portsmouth, yet won by a comfortable margin in the total statewide vote. With this victory, there was no sympathetic ear for Norfolk or Portsmouth when the Chesapeake and Virginia Beach charter bills came before the General Assembly. As Lloyd H. Lewis, the city hall reporter of Chesapeake, wrote in the Norfolk *Ledger-Star* regarding the Virginia Beach and Chesapeake charters:

> There remained the business of getting a charter from the General Assembly.
> Happily officials of the two communities had prepared for this by (a) Concluding that the state organization would win the fall gubernatorial election, (b) Backing the organization candidate to the hilt and (c) Rolling up organization majorities at the polls.
> Equally happily for the fortunes of the merger, the voters of Norfolk and Portsmouth had done just the opposite.
> When the General Assembly convened in January, therefore, it was simply a matter of collecting their reward while watching the big city opponents suffer. Of such is politics in Virginia—or anywhere else for that matter.[82]

In what measure, then, was the enactment of the charters a product of Byrd Organization politics and massive resistance? Unfortunately, it is impossible to answer this question with precision. Some reluctance to talk about this phase of the mergers in detail was encountered during interviews in 1963, although the outline of the story was clear. One local official perhaps phrased it best when he justified the legislative action by responding that "Norfolk had gotten too big for its britches."

At the same time the promergerites clearly had to play the politics of legislative maneuver in the General Assembly, a necessity which

---

[82] "Give and Take Spirit Winner," Jan. 1, 1963.

indicated that enactment of the charter bills was far from being a foregone conclusion. Virginia Beach, in particular, began to lobby for its charter well in advance of the session, and there can be no doubt that Norfolk and Portsmouth legislators tried desperately to block the passage of both bills.

Legislators from Norfolk and Portsmouth had two courses of action open to them. First, because the charter bills required a two-thirds majority of the total membership of each body for enactment, there was a faint hope that 37 members of the 100-member House of Delegates, especially those representing cities, might be persuaded to vote against the Virginia Beach charter, which was to be considered first. However, in part because of their advance lobbying, promerger leaders felt they could reasonably count on 80 votes in the House of Delegates; so this approach was soon abandoned by Portsmouth and Norfolk legislators.

As a second alternative, Norfolk and Portsmouth legislators threatened to cast their votes with the counties in support of strict antiannexation laws if the charter bills were passed.[83] Because the legislative margin on the annexation issue was narrow, there was some likelihood that strict antiannexation laws could have been enacted with Norfolk and Portsmouth's support. This would have affected all cities in Virginia adversely.

In this manner the sizable Richmond legislative delegation, as one writer put it, was "swept unwittingly into the middle of a waterfront free-for-all fight between sailors and longshoremen." [84] Richmond had a pending annexation suit against Henrico County which was very much at stake in the annexation-charter controversy. If the Richmond delegation voted for the charters, there was a real possibility that Norfolk and Portsmouth might make good on their threat. If the Richmond delegates voted against the charters, Princess Anne forces indicated that they would get behind a strong anti-annexation bill.

Eventually, the Richmond legislative delegation voted for the charters. After additional legislative maneuvering and consultation, the word was apparently passed from the governor's office that Governor Harrison would, if necessary, veto any changes in the state's annexation laws passed during that session of the General Assembly, and this settled the issue. Curiously enough, one on-site

[83] See, generally, James Latimer, "Foes of Annexation May Get Big Boost," *Richmond Times-Dispatch*, Feb. 1, 1962.
[84] *Ibid.*

participant indicated that certain leaders of one of the consolidated cities had a secret commitment to vote with the counties for changes in the annexation law in return for broad county support of the charter bill. In any event, that commitment never had to be honored.

Outwardly, then, the General Assembly acted in routine fashion. No legislative hearings were held on either of the charter bills despite the efforts of both Norfolk and Portsmouth legislators. The position taken by the promerger leadership and adopted by the General Assembly was that "the people had spoken and hearings were unnecessary." [85] Despite pleas such as that voiced by Portsmouth's Senator Spong that the consolidated City of Chesapeake would have a population of only 198 persons per square mile "not counting the bear and deer population of Dismal Swamp," both charter bills cleared the House of Delegates and the Senate with ease.

[85] Certain newspaper accounts of the legislative history of the charter bills provide much insight as to the reasons for the failure of the Norfolk and Portsmouth efforts. See, especially, George M. Kelley, "Beach Charter Gains," *The Virginian-Pilot*, Jan. 31, 1962; Kelley, "P. A.–Beach Charter Passes House, 85–9," *ibid.*, Feb. 2; 1962; "Second City Charter Advances," *ibid.*, Feb. 28, 1962; and "2nd Merger Charter Approved by Senate," *ibid.*, March 2, 1962.

CHAPTER V

TRANSITION

O NE common characteristic of the Tidewater consolidations was that the primary goal of merger was retention of the political status quo in so far as possible. Even in the Newport News–Warwick merger, where annexation was not a factor, maintaining control of the government of Newport News was an important goal. Elsewhere, city and county voters were assured and reassured by promerger leaders that government after consolidation would be much the same as before. While it was recognized that certain administrative, structural, and legal changes would occur, it was felt that the basic relationship between the citizen and his government would remain unaffected. Or as Sidney Kellam reportedly summed it up for the voters of Princess Anne County, "About all we're going to do is take down the county sign and put up the city sign."

Throughout the campaigns that preceded the referendums, promerger leaders pointed to the positive benefits that would accrue from consolidation. Merger would bring stability and protection from annexation, the tax base would be broadened, and future development would occur on an orderly and planned basis. At the same time, no one really asked how all this would be brought about. The specifics of transition to a single governmental entity were never developed in the merger campaigns, nor did anyone consider in any depth the effects that the differences between county and city government might have on the merger process. In part for this reason, the transition to consolidated city government is one of the more fascinating aspects of the Tidewater mergers.

Transition is defined narrowly here to include those acts and events that occurred locally between the date of the referendum on merger and the effective legal date of merger specified in the consolidation agreement. The transition period in each of the consolidated cities encompassed about one year.

The political leaders of all the merging governments realized the need for an orderly transition. Although these leaders had won approval of merger from the voters and had expended significant energies during the campaigns, they recognized early that much remained to be done in order to begin operations under a consolidated city government. In fact, they were faced with the problem of organizing a completely new government. The consolidation agreements did not contain specific instructions on what should be done, when it should be done, and how it should be done. Some precedents existed for Virginia Beach and Chesapeake from the Hampton and Newport News consolidations, and Virginia Beach sought ideas from Newport News on effecting the transition. But because of the special circumstances of the Newport News–Warwick merger, most notably that it involved cities only, it had only limited application.[1] State statutes controlling merger provided neither details nor insight into the actual formation of a single working government. And, finally, there was no body of literature containing suggestions on how to proceed.

As a result, each of the merged cities approached the matter of transition somewhat differently, and with varying degrees of success. Undoubtedly the transitions were not as smooth as they might have been. But, in balance, what was truly impressive was how well the transitions were carried out. With no expert guidance and pressed by the deadline for the effective legal date of consolidation, each of the consolidated governments was a going concern when merger became a legal reality. If there was some slippage in the process, it was not discernible to the average citizen.

The exact time after the referendum when official thoughts turned actively to the matter of transition varied. In the Chesapeake and Virginia Beach mergers, for instance, the leadership was preoccupied with getting the charter bills through the General Assembly, and concentrated attention to transition seems to have been held in abeyance until the spring of 1962. Once begun, however, activity continued through the summer, and by October an increase in the tempo of work was obviously looking to the effective date of merger, January 1, 1963. In Newport News the transition was carried on against a backdrop of elections which intermittently occupied local leaders. Transition in Newport News was not formally begun until after the election of councilmen for the consolidated city in November 1957, with merger set for July 1, 1958. In

[1] A copy of the suggestions offered by Newport News was found in the Princess Anne Papers. The request for advice emanated from the Virginia Beach–Princess Anne Merger Executive Committee.

Hampton, a beginning seems to have been made within a short time after the completion of the merger referendum campaign.

There are no adequate criteria for comparing the transitional arrangements of the four consolidated cities. From a subjective standpoint, it appears that the smoothest transition occurred in Virginia Beach, where there was a history of shared functions and where the Kellam organization in both the former county and the former city provided a unified framework for working out transitional details. In Hampton there were apparently last-minute difficulties with transition brought on by two governing bodies which committed most of the funds remaining in their local treasuries to strictly local projects. The Newport News transition was carried out with little difficulty. Transitional arrangements in Chesapeake, and the process by which transition was effected, seem to have paralleled generally the arrangements made in Virginia Beach. If anything, transitional arrangements in Chesapeake were carried on in a more formal context and atmosphere than was the case in Virginia Beach.

Unfortunately, there is a gap at this point in the public records of Hampton, Virginia Beach, and Chesapeake, and newspaper coverage of the transitions can be best described as sparse, perhaps because the transitions did not seem to contain the element of political drama, and in part because the process was more deliberative in nature. Meetings were held by officials and records were kept, but neither the full nature of the process nor the records were publicized to any appreciable extent. Newport News was something of an exception, for the entire transition was reasonably well covered by the daily newspapers serving that city.

Much in the way of detail had to be settled or explored before the effective legal date of consolidation. There were such matters as getting mail delivered to the new city, renaming and renumbering the streets and houses, and installing additional telephone lines between the former city hall and county courthouse. Petitions had to be entered requesting certain changes in utility rates and fees. In Hampton, Virginia Beach, and Chesapeake a new city street department had to be established almost from scratch. Former counties found they would no longer be provided forest fire protection by the State Division of Forestry. The Virginia State Police was to cease policing county highways on the effective date of merger. Office space had to be found, subordinate officers and administrative and advisory boards appointed, a scheme of departmental organization established, equalization of assessments arranged, a taxing policy formulated, a consolidated budget prepared, the nature and

scope of services surveyed, equipment inventoried, and new ordinances prepared. While tending to these matters, each of the governments involved had to conduct business as usual.

Some of the actions that were taken may have been extralegal
since there was no clear-cut statutory authority for such actions. For
example, the governing bodies of the governments to be merged
held joint meetings and decided many of the details and policies
of the new consolidated governments under charters that were not
yet legally effective. Whenever possible, the results of these meetings
were formalized by the respective governing bodies meeting in their
separate chambers, but for reasons which included the lack of statutory authority to act, much was not formalized until the effective
date of merger. The basic questions to be explored here, however,
do not involve the legality or extralegality of these acts. Rather,
the purpose is to consider transition from the standpoint of what
was done and how it was done. By what processes, by what devices,
and to what extent were the consolidated governments ready on the
day when the merged cities became legal operating units?

Selecting a Name

The first task confronting the voters of South Norfolk–Norfolk
County and Newport News–Warwick after the merger referendums
was the selection of names for the new consolidated cities. In Hampton and Virginia Beach this question had been decided prior to the
time of the referendums, and the names of the two new cities had
been specified in the consolidation agreements.

On July 31, 1957, in Newport News, pursuant to the provisions
of the consolidation agreement signed by the two cities, the judges
of the courts of record entered an order for a referendum to be held
on September 10 to select a name for the consolidated city. Three
names were listed in the consolidation agreement for inclusion on
the ballot: Newport News, Warwick, and Newport News–Warwick.[2]
No additions to the list were permitted, and if none of the three
names received a majority of the vote in the referendum, a second
referendum was to be held with the two names receiving the most
votes on the ballot.

The selection of a name for the city was approached in an obvi-

[2] See "A Name That Tells Something," *Newport News Times-Herald,* July 31,
1957.

ously earnest manner. The historical origins of the names of Newport News and Warwick were explored and publicized by Cerinda
W. Evans, librarian emeritus of the Mariners' Museum.[3] Both
names could be traced in Virginia history back to the seventeenth
century, although the precise origin of Newport News was rather
obscure. To a number of people, Warwick was "prettier," but Newport News's shipbuilding and maritime enterprises made that city's
name more widely known. Business interests seemed to favor Newport News, which, like Virginia Beach, had invested money in
advertising the city and its port facilities. The *Newport News
Times-Herald* characterized Newport News as "practical," and Warwick as the "emotional favorite."[4] The *Daily Press* endorsed the
name of Newport News, citing the fame of the port, the promotion
of the former City of Newport News by the Chesapeake and Ohio
Railway, and the desirability of identifying the Newport News Shipbuilding and Drydock Company with the city.[5]

The name Newport News received an overwhelming majority of
the votes cast in the referendum. Of 4,258 votes cast in the former
City of Newport News, 4,107 voters opted for the retention of Newport News. Even Warwick residents provided a clear-cut majority
for Newport News. Of 4,475 ballots cast in Warwick, the name
Newport News was favored by 2,873 votes. As Newport News had
received a majority of the total vote, a second referendum was not
necessary.

In the case of Chesapeake, no names were mentioned specifically
in the consolidation agreement, and the proposal of names was left
entirely to the voters. When the deadline for the entry of petitions
had been reached, a total of twelve names had qualified for a place
on the ballot. These included Bridgeport, Chesapeake, Churchland,
Glendale, Glennville, Gosport, Great Bridge, Norcova, Port Elizabeth, Sunray City, Virginia City, and Woodford. Other suggestions
had been offered from time to time, such as Sonoco (South Norfolk
County), but these failed to gain enough signatures to appear on
the ballot.[6] Lloyd H. Lewis of the *Ledger-Star* provided a thumb-
nail description of the campaign to select a name.

[3] See "Views of Our Readers," letter by Cerinda W. Evans, *Daily Press,* Aug.
24, 1957.

[4] "Tuesday's N-Day at Polls; Newport News Is Practical, Warwick Emotional
Favorite," Sept. 7, 1957.

[5] See "Voters Make Name Choice Tuesday," Sept. 8, 1957.

[6] Raymond L. Bancroft, "Mergerites Play Name Game," *The Virginian-Pilot,*
March 3, 1962.

Then came the problem of picking a name for the new city. "Chesapeake" had been an early favorite among the planners, but it had disadvantages, and the leadership vaguely hoped that someone would come up with a real zinger.

But no one did. And when it became apparent that no one would, an attempt was made to regroup behind "Chesapeake." This brought on the first split.

A small but powerful group of county officeholders were for ditching "Chesapeake" and grouping behind "Great Bridge." Their reasons were simple: They lived in or near Great Bridge, and they liked the place.

The question was put to the people, and "Great Bridge" came close to grabbing the county vote. But "Chesapeake" prevailed, and South Norfolk came storming in to give it a clear majority over, not only "Great Bridge," but 10 other contenders.[7]

Once the vote had been tabulated and the name Chesapeake designated as the voters' choice, political leaders were embarrassed to discover that there was already a Chesapeake in Virginia—a rural postal station of the Cape Charles Post Office located on the Eastern Shore. Postal officials ruled initially that all mail addressed to Chesapeake would continue to be routed to the Eastern Shore station. However, after brief negotiations between officers of the Post Office Department and Chesapeake officialdom, the Post Office Department extended official recognition to the consolidated city.

Although Chesapeake was the overwhelming choice of those casting ballots, voter disinterest in the matter of choosing a name was evident as only 1,662 persons went to the polls. Of these, Chesapeake was the preference of 1,274 voters, followed by Great Bridge, which received 171 votes. A few names barely placed in the balloting—Gosport received one vote, Woodford two, and Glennville three.

Because of historical and other ties, there was a measure of voter sentiment regarding the name of the city. Since the issue had emotional overtones, it was important to the transition that the matter be settled calmly. The selection of a name might have generated a factional division within the consolidated cities which would have had an impact upon subsequent transitional arrangements. Yet such a split did not occur, and the selection of a name did not present a significant barrier to merger, nor did it upset the essential harmony that was to characterize the transitions.

[7] "Give-and-Take-Spirit Winner," Jan. 1, 1963.

The Councilmanic Election in Newport News

Newport News was the only consolidated city to elect a full slate of new city officers before the effective date of merger. Actually, within a span of twelve months, the voters of consolidated Newport News participated in four separate elections. There was (1) the referendum on the question of merger, (2) the referendum to name the new city, (3) the general election of November 1957 for councilmen, and (4) the special election of constitutional officers for the city in April 1958. Thus, between the date of the merger referendum on July 16, 1957, and July 1, 1958, the effective date of consolidation, the voters were fully occupied with political matters and elections.

Councilmanic elections coincided with the general election of November 1957, with seven councilmen to be chosen by the voters on a nonpartisan and at-large basis as provided in the consolidated city charter.[8] A plurality of the votes was sufficient for election, and the new council was to meet and begin work on the transition immediately after the election.

Almost from its inception, the councilmanic election was marked by confusion. There was uncertainty regarding the requirements and procedures for filing by candidates; it was decided that candidates had to file with the electoral boards in each city and also with the State Board of Elections. Filing was accomplished through the presentation of nominating petitions signed by at least fifty qualified voters accompanied by a formal declaration of candidacy filed in each city. Later, additional uncertainty arose about the deadline date for filing, as the consolidation agreement provisions conflicted with state election law. The consolidation agreement provided that candidates had to file for office sixty days before the election; yet the election was classed as a special election and state law fixed the deadline date for filing as being thirty days prior to the date of election. Finally, there was no agreement between Warwick and Newport News on the order of the names of the candidates as they would appear on the ballot. As a result, Warwick listed the candidates alphabetically, while Newport News used the date of filing to determine the location of the candidate's name on the ballot.

Speculation about the composition of the council for the consolidated city began in early August 1957 when it was announced that

[8] Charter of the City of Newport News, sec. 3.01. For the Newport News charter, see *Acts of Assembly*, 1958, p. 147.

a committee of representatives from both Warwick and Newport News "to seek the best candidates for city council" had been formed.[9] This committee, apparently self-appointed, proposed that a mass meeting be held to identify and recommend qualified candidates to the voters. At the scheduled mass meeting on August 12, at which press estimates recorded seventy-five persons in attendance, it was announced only that the group had not yet reached a point where suggestions might be offered. By this date, three persons from Warwick and two from Newport News had already filed.

Meanwhile, the *Daily Press* expressed editorial sentiment that both Warwick and Newport News ought to be represented on the council, and that the new city would benefit if a considerable proportion of the new council included members from the existing city councils of Warwick and Newport News.[10] Both of the area newspapers pursued this editorial line throughout the course of the campaign.

The committee that had sponsored the first meeting scheduled another meeting on August 22 for the purpose of recommending candidates. By the time of the meeting, seven candidates had filed, including Mayor H. M. Hussey and Councilwoman Mrs. Joel M. Williams of Warwick. Some difficulty was encountered during the course of the meeting, and an attempt to endorse a slate resulted in the members being nearly outvoted by apparent outsiders.[11] Control of the meeting was retained by a narrow margin, and a tentative slate of eight candidates was offered for consideration by the voters. The names of Mayor Hussey and Councilwoman Williams were not included on the list.

By September 1 the number of entries for the seven council seats had grown significantly, and seven of the ten incumbent councilmen of the two cities had filed petitions and declarations. A last-minute rush occurred at the sixty-day deadline date for filing, and when the deadline had passed twenty-eight candidates had filed. Of these twenty-one were Warwick residents and seven were from Newport News. Because uncertainty continued to exist about the deadline date for filing, it was announced that the clerks would accept petitions and declarations of candidacy until October 5. In the interim, no additional candidates entered the race.

[9] "Committee Seeks 7 Candidates for New City Council," *Daily Press*, Aug. 6, 1957.

[10] "The City Will Need a Council," *ibid.*, Aug. 6, 1957.

[11] Al Coates, "Warwick Citizens Rally on Councilmanic Slate Balked by Late Comers," *ibid.*, Aug. 23, 1957.

The councilmanic campaign was described by the area news-papers as "lackadasical." Candidates placed great emphasis upon personal campaigning, although there was one rally to which all candidates were invited, introduced, and given five minutes each to speak. Alliances were formed, and an obvious dependence was placed on "slating." Debate on issues by the candidates was virtually nonexistent, nor was there any sign of the activity that had charac-terized the merger referendum campaign.

Prior to the merger, Warwick had used the ward sytem, but New-port News had elected councilmen on an at-large basis and had followed the practice of "slating" candidates. In this councilmanic election for the consolidated city, several groups proposed slates, including the Citizens for Massive Resistance, the Ex-Service Politi-cal Club, and a slate for Negro voters. In addition, special organi-zations were formed for the sole purpose of considering the candi-dates and suggesting a slate to the voters. Of these, the most widely publicized and perhaps the most influential was the Association for a Greater City.

The chief excitement of an otherwise dull campaign came on November 1, four days before the election, when the area news-papers reported the formation of the Association for a Greater City.[12] There were strong suspicions that it was a resurrected ver-sion of the Woodward Citizens Committee for Consolidation, which had officially disbanded in August. However, the Association's founders and sponsors were described simply as a group of citizens from Warwick and Newport News, and Woodward's name was not connected directly with the group. Although the stated purpose of the Association was to conduct "a nonpolitical investigation and survey to ascertain the best fitted candidates . . . for council," the speed of its deliberations cast some doubt on its impartiality. On November 3, only two days after the announcement of the group's formation, the Association endorsed ten candidates for council in a full-page advertisement appearing in the *Daily Press*. These candi-dates were three members of the Newport News city council, Vice Mayor Paul S. Ward of Warwick, and six other residents of War-wick. Of the ten endorsed candidates, five were subsequently elected.

The late Association endorsements generated a measure of appre-hension from certain other candidates. On November 3, for in-

---

[12] See Al Coates, "Association for a Greater City Is Formed to Pick 'Best Fit-ted' Candidates for Seats on Council," *ibid.*, Nov. 1, 1957.

stance, candidate E. Alton Parrish, Sr., who had not received an endorsement, lashed out at the Association.[13] Describing candidates endorsed by the Association as the "gilded bloc," Parrish contended that the group was dominated entirely by business and professional interests. He charged that the ticket was drawn up for the purpose of carrying several weak candidates who otherwise "could not stand alone and face the voters." This blast had no obvious impact upon the outcome of the election, nor did it help Parrish, who was defeated on November 5.

Precinct returns from the 1957 councilmanic election tend to support the charge that the Association was, in fact, the resurrected Citizens Committee for Consolidation. In Warwick, for instance, promerger strength was based on the four precincts fronting on the James River. These were River, Riverside, James Brandon, and Hilton, which had supplied significant majorities for merger and represented 45 percent of the total Warwick vote in the referendum. These precincts voted for seven Association-endorsed candidates, including the three incumbent Newport News councilmen. Morrison Precinct of Warwick was the only other precinct in both cities to vote for seven Association-endorsed candidates. All the remaining Warwick precincts gave strong support to Warwick's two councilmen, Hussey and Williams, who were not on the Association slate.

Generally speaking, as Table 5 shows, Newport News strongly supported candidates from that city. The chief exception was O. J. Brittingham, Jr., of Warwick, who appeared on almost everyone's slate and led all candidates in total votes. Except for Brittingham, Newport News voters supported five local candidates.

On the Warwick side, the effect of the Association endorsement was clearly visible in the votes for Marvin M. Murchison, Jr., and Robert B. Smith of Newport News; Murchison won more votes in Warwick than he did in his home city while Smith's vote was nearly equal in the two cities. Their excellent showing in Warwick may be contrasted with that of J. Fred Christie of Newport News, who did not receive Association endorsement and ran eighteenth in Warwick. Christie, however, was on the slate of candidates endorsed by black leader W. Hale Thompson and received nearly one-third of his vote in four black precincts in Newport News. Councilman William C. Bowen of Newport News, on the other hand, who was endorsed by the Association, barely managed fifteenth place in War-

[13] "Parrish Flays Association's 'Gilded Bloc,' " *ibid.*, Nov. 4, 1957.

Table 5. Winners of the 1957 councilmanic election in consolidated Newport News

Councilman	Place of residence	Association-endorsed	Total vote (12,270)	Newport News Vote (5,856)	Newport News Rank	Warwick Vote (7,414)	Warwick Rank
Brittingham	Warwick	Yes	7,791	3,625	2	4,346	1
Monfalcone *	Newport News	No	5,796	3,644	1	2,152	8
Murchiscn *	Newport News	Yes	5,536	2,687	4	2,849	3
Smith *	Newport News	Yes	5,332	2,681	5	2,651	4
Christie	Newport News	No	4,348	2,823	3	1,525	18
Ward *	Warwick	Yes	4,005	1,413	12	2,592	5
Bowen *	Newport News	Yes	3,944	2,045	6	1,899	15

SOURCE: The voting figures were supplied by the Newport News and Warwick clerks of the circuit courts.
* Incumbent councilmen in former cities.

wick. Bowen's over-all victory, however, was attributable to the fact that he won in three of the Warwick precincts fronting on the James River.

The Negro vote was important in the 1957 councilmanic election. Only the votes that they won in Warwick enabled Murchison, Smith, and Bowen, all incumbent councilmen in Newport News, to overcome a black bloc vote which went to another slate that included winners Brittingham, Alfred M. Monfalcone, and Christie, who were the top vote-getters in Newport News in that order. In five predominantly black precincts of Newport News that cast a total of 2,174 votes, Murchison, Smith, and Bowen received only 229, 207, and 174 votes, respectively. Councilman Christie, on the other hand, won 1,607 votes in these precincts. In Warwick the predominantly black precinct of Jefferson Park, which cast 435 votes, gave 356 votes to Christie and only 13, 8, and 12 votes, respectively, to Murchison, Smith, and Bowen. Thus, there is some reason to suggest that Association endorsement worked to offset a Negro bloc vote which might otherwise have resulted in the defeat of the three incumbent Newport News councilmen. Councilman Bowen's victory over Mayor Hussey of Warwick, for example, was by a narrow margin of 50 votes. Mayor Hussey's name appeared on the slate of candidates suggested for blacks, but he was not endorsed by the Association. Thus, while Murchison, Smith, and Bowen would have won in former Newport News without Negro support, their over-all election depended on offsetting lost black votes with votes from white Warwick.

Warwick's vote was diluted among its twenty-one candidates, who seem to have fallen victim to a determined effort to elect Bowen, Murchison, and Smith. Candidates Monfalcone and Christie won by carrying Newport News, including its Negro precincts, but they were helped also by a divided Warwick vote. Warwick's diluted vote was the key to success for Newport News candidates predicated upon their ability to carry their own city. Even though Warwick outvoted Newport News, a predictable Warwick victory was turned into a defeat for Warwick candidates.

Only one candidate among the seven winners had a majority of the total vote cast. One of the winners polled less than 30 percent of the total vote. Warwick outvoted Newport News by 7,414 to 5,856, but five candidates, including four members of the council of that city, were elected from Newport News and only two from Warwick. Mayor Hussey of Warwick was among the top seven candidates in only four of the twelve precincts in his home city and thereby failed to win election. Mayor Smith of Newport News, on the other hand, was among the top seven in eight Warwick precincts and was elected. Mayor Smith received 2,651 votes in Warwick as against 2,074 for Mayor Hussey. Only one incumbent member of Warwick's five-member city council was elected.

Several different interpretations of the 1957 councilmanic election were given during interviews in Newport News in 1963. Some respondents suggested that the entry of twenty-one candidates from Warwick into the race resulted from a leadership vacuum created by the ineffectiveness of the DeShazor group in Warwick and the disbanding of the Citizens Committee for Consolidation. As a result of this vacuum, some respondents argued, one candidate's chances for election were as good as those of any other candidate. Because none of the candidates really had a consolidated city-wide electoral base, this interpretation is highly plausible.

At the same time, a few respondents suggested that the entry of twenty-one Warwick candidates into the race was a deliberate attempt to dilute the Warwick vote and thus gain control of the council for Newport News. This was essentially a "devil theory" which focused on particular Warwick residents with economic interests in Newport News. Contradicting this view, however, were those who held that the Association for a Greater City was set up because there were so many Warwick candidates in the race. Any deliberate attempt to dilute Warwick's vote risked the chance that a black bloc vote would decide the outcome of the election. Indeed, some respondents indicated that the Association for a Greater City was activated precisely to prevent this possibility from taking place; Association endorsement was chiefly a counterforce against a black bloc vote. However, all that can be concluded with certainty is that Warwick's vote was diluted by its twenty-one candidates and that this helped Newport News candidates to win control of the consolidated city council.

The lessons of the 1957 councilmanic election were reviewed by Warwick officials, and by the time of the April election for constitutional officers, they were able to present a semblance of a united front. In that election Warwick outvoted Newport News by a margin of 1,400 votes, and Warwick candidates were elected to the offices of Commonwealth's attorney, commissioner of the revenue, and treasurer. In a three-man race for the office of city sergeant, a Newport News candidate won by a margin of 411 votes over two Warwick candidates. It was agreed by political observers that the two Warwick candidates for city sergeant had once again split the vote.

Transition in Newport News

The transition to consolidated city government in the Newport News–Warwick merger began shortly after the referendum. In early August 1957 the Warwick City Planning Commission extended an invitation to its counterpart in Newport News to hold joint meetings with regard to planning in the consolidated city. The city council of Newport News, meanwhile, authorized Mayor Smith to seek a conference with Warwick officials on municipal projects and plans for that period of time before merger was officially consummated. The *Newport News Times-Herald* expressed approval in an editorial entitled "Planning's the Place to Start." [14]

A joint meeting of the two city councils was held on August 14, 1957. The construction of municipal facilities in the two cities was the major item of business, with special attention being given to housing the new government. Warwick councilmen expressed the view that Newport News ought to continue with its million-dollar waterworks expansion plan. Councilmen from Newport News offered to make that city's fire-fighting equipment available to Warwick immediately, as well as the use of its jail and prison farm. The school boards were to meet for a joint discussion of problems and to coordinate school construction projects.

Blending the two school systems was to be a source of some difficulty in consolidated Newport News. Operating problems were compounded by population pressures in Warwick and the obsolescence of the plant in Newport News. Both white and black schools had classroom shortages, and racial integration was a problem that remained to be faced.[15] A teacher shortage existed, and officials suggested the use of such alternatives as teacher's aides and classroom television. Since each school system was supposed to operate separately until the effective legal date of consolidation, the

---

[14] Aug. 7, 1957.

[15] These problems were highlighted in a series of articles written by John B. Greiff which appeared in the *Daily Press* shortly after the successful merger referendum. See especially "Problems in School Merger Are Varied," Aug. 11, 1957; "Classroom Shortage for Whites, Negroes Facing Merged City," Aug. 12, 1957; and "Merged City May Seek New Teaching Methods to Meet School Needs," Aug. 13, 1957.

preparation of capital and operating budgets also presented a problem. Among other things, it was urged that a director of personnel
be hired for both systems to recruit new teachers for the consolidated system.

As is customary in Virginia, the city school board was to be appointed by council. The appointments to the consolidated school
board, however, generated some friction. Only three members of
the two former boards were appointed to the consolidated school
board. Among those rejected was Dr. C. Waldo Scott, a Negro
member of the Newport News school board. Although the appointments did produce some rancor, it cannot be said that they unduly
upset the transition.

Meshing the fiscal years of the two cities also presented a problem. Warwick's fiscal year began on July 1; that of Newport News
on January 1. Under the terms of the consolidation agreement the
consolidated city's fiscal year was to begin on January 1. Consolidation was to occur on July 1, 1958, and thus the first consolidated
city budget had to be a six-month budget running from July 1, 1958,
to December 31, 1958. In order to prepare the 1959 consolidated
city budget, estimates had to be based on the six-month budgetary
experience between July and December, a period too brief to reflect fully the city's financial situation. Samuel P. Hoyle, director
of finance for the consolidated city, described the situation:

It became evident that a calendar year fiscal year was the one way to prevent the new city from starting off with a deficit in its first year. The next
order of business, after setting the fiscal year to begin January 1st, was the
preparation of a six-month budget for the new city. With the revenue
fixed, the main problem was to make a half-year budget for the last half of
1958 that would be adequate but one that would set the expenditure level
at a rate that could be maintained in 1959 and subsequent years. A budget
made by combining the two city budgets into one proved to be inadequate.
There were too many areas in which the differences in procedure between
the two cities were so great that an entirely new annual budget had to be
made.[16]

The charter for the consolidated city provided that the newly
elected council might meet in the interim between councilmanic

[16] Hoyle, "Fiscal Problems Arising When Two Cities Consolidate," 31 *Municipal Finance* 144 148, 144 (May 1959). Among other things, this article cata-
logues the financial ordinances required to bring about the transition and dis-
cusses the problem of equalizing assessments, a problem common to all four
consolidated cities.

elections and the effective date of consolidation. Acting under this authority, the first meeting of the consolidated council was scheduled for November 19, 1957, to consider matters relating to the transition. In all, some thirty public meetings and, in addition, a number of executive sessions were held prior to the effective date of merger. At the November 19 meeting the first action of the consolidated council, to no one's surprise, was to name Joseph C. Biggins as the new city manager. Biggins announced that he would begin work immediately on financial problems, governmental reorganization, and the preparation of a budget.

The first note of serious discord was struck in regard to a pension plan for the consolidated city. The question was whether to adopt the Newport News or the Warwick plan. The problem was broached on December 3, 1957, but it was not until March 4, 1958, that a decision was finally reached.[17] As the *Daily Press* explained,

The pension talks dragged on over a period of nearly three months, with the present Newport News plan coordinated with social security being adopted. Representatives of a 10-member Committee for Efficient-Economical Government, an organization whose prime aim appears to have been the supporting of the Virginia Supplemental Retirement System rather than the Newport News plan, and city forces helped to liven up the retirement plan discussion.[18]

City Manager Biggins raised a crucial question on November 25 when he inquired whether the city manager had the authority to appoint his department heads before the legal date of merger. On December 6 this question was answered in the affirmative although the appointments were held not to be legally binding until the consolidated council was properly installed. Manager Biggins's appointment policy caused some minor irritation among councilmen. According to newspaper reports, Biggins had indicated that a reduction in force would occur with consolidation and that this would be necessary from the standpoint of both efficiency of operation and budgeting. However, Councilman Monfalcone stated that Biggins had told him that every present city employee would be needed in the new city, while Councilman Christie insisted that

[17] See Elmer Curran, "Newport News Pension Plan Said More Beneficial for All Workers," *Daily Press,* Dec. 4, 1957, and Elmer Curran, "Council-Elect Adopts Pension Plan with 30-Year Retirement," *ibid.,* March 5, 1958.

[18] Elmer Curran, "Council Elect Okays $7,160,866 Half-Year Budget for New City," *ibid.,* May 20, 1958.

Biggins had said it would be impossible to keep everyone and some employees would have to go. The actual reduction in force proved to be small, and Biggins subsequently expressed an opinion in a 1963 interview that elimination of duplication of effort was not one of the main benefits of merger.

By May 20, 1958, preparation for the new city were complete. A half-year budget of slightly over $7 million had been approved, officers had been appointed, and some twenty-eight ordinances had been enacted. Conflicts had been relatively few and most of the actions taken by council had been unanimous. Some appointments remained to be made, such as a board of zoning appeals and a board of assessors, but the city was ready. As its final act before merger, the council-elect voted to give itself a one-week vacation!

Transition in Virginia Beach

Two circumstances helped to promote a smooth transition in the Princess Anne–Virginia Beach merger. First, the unified Kellam organization was able to approach the transition in much the same manner and with the same single-mindedness as it had approached and carried on the merger campaign. Second, the former City of Virginia Beach, as a city of the second class, was carrying on certain functions jointly with the county at the time of merger, and in addition, the city and county shared certain officers. Joint functions included schools, health, welfare, library service, and mosquito control. The city and the county shared the school superintendent, clerk of the circuit court, and Commonwealth's attorney. It was the unanimous opinion of these officials that merger had virtually no impact in these particular areas.

Responsibility for bringing about the transition in Virginia Beach was essentially a group effort, and committees were utilized extensively. The primary executive and coordinating committee was the existing Merger Executive Committee chaired by the county commissioner of the revenue and including, among others, the county clerk of the circuit court, county treasurer, city treasurer, city commissioner of revenue, and city sergeant.

A number of special committees were appointed to study particular phases of the consolidation and to make recommendations to the council and board of supervisors. In most cases the special committees employed an interlocking directorate organization; one member of the Merger Executive Committee was usually appointed to serve on one or more of the special committees. Ivan Mapp, for example, in addition to serving as chairman of the Merger Executive Committee, was also a member of the Committee on Street Names and Numbers, the Committee on Equalization of Tax Assessments, the Committee to Study Merchants' License Fees, the Transportation Committee, and the Water Committee. The Merger Executive Committee served ex officio as the Committee on Needed Office Space. Other special subject matter committees included the Committee to Study Garage Facilities, the Committee to Work on Ordinances, the Committee to Decide Office Locations, the Committee to Negotiate for the Purchase of Land, the Committee to Set Up a Water and Sewer Department, the Committee on Opening a Road Through Camp Pendleton, and the City Seal Committee.[19]

One of the first moves of the Merger Executive Committee was to request reports from city and county officials on the operations of their respective departments or offices. These reports served to identify problems merger would bring and provided recommendations for the establishment and operation of the several departments of the consolidated city. On April 26, 1962, for example, County Treasurer V. A. Etheridge observed that the local auto tags issued by the two governments did not run consecutively, and that real estate taxes were being collected quarterly in the city and annually in the county. Another problem was the application of the Virginia Beach business license tax throughout the new city. Other reports dealt with the offices of high constable, city sergeant, and city manager. A report on the department of finance was filed by Giles Dodd, county comptroller, who was to become director of finance for the consolidated city.

Dodd's report provides some insight into what the several reports were intended to accomplish as well as their general nature and scope. His report attempted to delineate the functions and responsibilities of the department of finance as provided for in the consolidated city charter and projected a department encompassing the functions of accounting, purchasing, and payroll preparation. The report noted that merger would likely result in an increased work load for the staff, but it recommended no increase in the number of personnel for the time being. It estimated that 1,850

[19] These committees were appointed at different times between March and November 1962 at joint sessions of the Merger Executive Committee, the city council, and the board of supervisors.

square feet of office space would be required by the new department as against the existing 650 square feet. Further, it proposed that the department be consolidated at Princess Anne courthouse, and that no branch offices be maintained at the city hall of former Virginia Beach. Finally, it noted that Princess Anne County paid all county employees on a monthly basis while Virginia Beach employees, with the exception of public school teachers, were paid twice a month. It suggested that all employees of the consolidated city be paid twice a month with the exception of the teachers, who would continue to be paid monthly.

A committee report on police protection recommended the establishment of six police districts in the consolidated city, the retention of the police and trial board, a salary increase for policemen, and the retention of the services of the Virginia State Police for highway patrol within the former county for a six-month transitional period following the effective date of merger. A report on fire protection focused on the operation of the thirteen volunteer fire companies of Princess Anne County and their relationships with the full-time fire department of Virginia Beach. Other reports were submitted on parks and recreation, tourism, planning and economic development, and highways. The last-named report urged the retention of the state highway employees since they were familiar with the state-maintained county roads and would be better able to care for them when the roads became city streets after merger.

These reports helped to get the transition underway and to stimulate some hard thinking about certain problems the new city government would face. Joint meetings of the Merger Executive Committee, the city council, and the county board of supervisors were held to consider the specific proposals contained in the several reports. Meanwhile, additional reports from the special functional committees began to come in during the summer of 1962. On July 13, 1962, for example, the Committee on Street Names and Numbers offered its recommendations to the council and the board of supervisors. Among other things, the committee recommended that the joint planning commissions present detailed plans for naming and numbering streets, that an inventory be made of everything within the public rights of way, and that an appropriation be made to finance these surveys.

By September 1962 Ivan Mapp, reporting for the Merger Executive Committee in a joint session with the council and the board of supervisors, was able to observe that a new phase of merger was beginning. Most of the problems and problem areas had been identified; it was time to begin work on the actual establishment of the new government. Although some policy issues facing the consolidated city government had already been decided, the pace of transitional activity and decision making was accelerated in September.

By the end of October 1962 significant progress was evident. Final plans had been completed for the operation of the offices of commissioner of the revenue, treasurer, and high constable. A city-wide tax on cigarettes of two cents per package was agreed upon, as well as continuation of the special tax on amusements, food, and lodging in Virginia Beach Borough, the former City of Virginia Beach. It was also agreed that the Virginia Beach Advertising Board would be continued after merger, and an appropriation was made for this purpose. A legal publishing firm was engaged to prepare a code for the consolidated city, and the salary of the city manager was fixed. Numerous appointments were announced between September 1 and the end of October, including the city engineer, superintendents of sanitation and streets and bridges, directors of personnel, public welfare, public utilities, and public health, and the agricultural agent. Tentative plans for establishing a central city garage were submitted, initial arrangements were made for a radio tower building, and it was agreed to advertise for bids for additions to the police station and the offices of the treasurer and the commissioner of the revenue. Miscellaneous transition matters considered at this time included adoption of the slogan "World's Largest Resort City," a report on the progress of the city seal campaign, fixing the bond for plumbers in the consolidated city, and a report that ten members of the Virginia State Police would continue to serve the consolidated city for a period of six months after the effective date of merger.

The Merger Executive Committee, the council, and the board of supervisors held six meetings, largely policy and appointment sessions, between November 1, 1962, and the end of the year. In November, for example, they adopted the changes in street names recommended by the planning commission, and decided the composition of various administrative and examining boards. Among these were the planning commission, board of electrical examiners, plumbing board, welfare board, advertising board, and police and fire pension board. They agreed to place all city employees under the Virginia Supplemental Retirement System. Certain codes were adopted for the consolidated city, such as the Southern Builders Code, the electrical code of the former city, and the plumbing code of the former county. Agreement was reached that the consolidated city council would meet twice monthly and would operate under the rules of procedure of the former city council. Speed limits were fixed within the merged city, and the city planning commission was requested to make all zoning designations uniform. State rules and regulations pertaining to health and sewage disposal were adopted, and the county's trailer ordinance and leash law for dogs were extended city-wide. The need for additional telephone lines between Princess Anne courthouse and Virginia Beach Borough was explored, as was the matter of obtaining new city letterhead stationery. The ordinances of former Virginia Beach pertaining to the regulation of restaurants and food establishments were extended city-wide.

Other business coming before the joint merger body included discussions with the power company on the utility tax and a meeting with representatives of the bus company to explore the possibility of extending bus service within the city. A committee was appointed to meet with a counterpart committee from Chesapeake to explore the policy for hiring state highway workers to form a joint bridge crew. The salaries of the mayor and councilmen were fixed, and a salary schedule was adopted for city employees. At the final meeting, the working hours of city employees were established, and a tentative outline of the council's first docket was presented.

The first formal council meeting was set for January 1, 1963, and the last meeting of the two governing boards and the Merger Executive Committee took place on December 28, 1962. At that time, speaking for the Merger Executive Committee, Mapp reported that there would "be no pressing problems" after the December 28 meeting. On January 1 the council adopted twenty-seven ordinances and formally appointed the city manager, clerk, city attorney, welfare board, advertising board, and police and fire trials board. Mayor Frank Dusch accepted a bronze plaque of the new city seal from Captain Joseph W. Crawford, Jr., of the Navy repair ship *Amphion*, and the meeting was adjourned.[20] By the time it was all over, the

[20] See "New Council in Speedy Session in First Meeting," *Virginia Beach Sun-News,* Jan. 3, 1963. See, also, "Former Volunteer Firemen Named to New City Force," *ibid.,* Jan. 3, 1963. The latter article is especially instructive insofar as it covers the events of the last joint meeting of the Merger Executive Committee, the council, and the board of supervisors—the December 28 meeting. The gist of the article is that the appointments were made by the Merger Executive Committee. The article covers the appointment of the firemen, the supervisor of weights and measures, and the adoption of the Virginia Supplemental Retirement System. A record of this meeting found in the Princess Anne Papers shows that 18 items were discussed, of which 4 are related to the above points.

political leaders of Virginia Beach knew that they had done much more than merely "take down the county sign and put up the city sign."

Transition in Chesapeake

In several respects transition in the South Norfolk–Norfolk County merger was the most difficult and complex but also perhaps the most interesting of the Tidewater mergers. To begin with, the City of South Norfolk and Norfolk County were almost totally dissimilar in every respect. South Norfolk was predominantly industrial and largely populated by workers and craftsmen. Its politics was characterized by a frequent turnover of councilmen and city managers. South Norfolk was primarily a city of lower and middle-income residents, its business district was small, and, in most respects, it appeared to be an "across the river" extension of the cities of Norfolk and Portsmouth.

Norfolk County, on the other hand, was a mixture of rural and suburban residents. Prosperity abounded on the fringes of Portsmouth, South Norfolk, and Norfolk, and the county included a number of upper-middle-class residential areas, especially in the Western Branch Magisterial District. Politics in Norfolk County was factionalized to some extent, but the pattern of rapid turnover that characterized South Norfolk was not present. Norfolk County utilized the traditional form of county government under which each supervisor was responsible for the affairs of his own magisterial district according to an unwritten rule of comity which prohibited interference in another man's district. At the time of merger, there was no organization equal in strength or unity to the Kellam group in Virginia Beach, and while there was some history of cooperation between Norfolk County and South Norfolk prior to the merger, it was not comparable to that between Virginia Beach and Princess Anne County. Since South Norfolk was a city of the first class, it shared no officers and few functions with Norfolk County.

The first joint meeting of the governing bodies of Norfolk County and South Norfolk was held on March 20, 1962, and resulted in a recitation of the ground rules for subsequent meetings and the approval of a "Statement of Purpose," which declared:

This mandate of the people must now be translated into action.
A great deal of study and planning must be done in the next nine

months in order that the transition from a city and a county government to a single consolidated government may be accomplished smoothly and efficiently. To this end the Council of the City of South Norfolk had the Board of Supervisors of Norfolk County propose to hold joint sessions to provide for the orderly integration of the services now being provided by the two communities. It will be the primary purpose of these sessions to provide for the continued efficiency of present services and to achieve added efficiency and scope when the combined services are instituted.[21]

The rules of procedure indicate that the approach to transition in Chesapeake was conducted more formally than was the case in Virginia Beach. This was apparently due to the lack of significant prior rapport between the two governments and, also, to the fact that there was no counterpart of the Kellam organization. There was no body akin to the Virginia Beach–Princess Anne Merger Executive Committee. The following list, much like the rules of the charter-drafting committee in the Newport News–Warwick merger, represents highlights of the rules adopted by the supervisors and councilmen in their first joint session.

1. Joint meetings were to be held on the third Tuesday of each month alternating between the board room and the council chamber.

2. The chairman of joint sessions was to be determined by the meeting place. The chairman of the board of supervisors was to serve when meetings were held in South Norfolk and the mayor of South Norfolk was to preside when meetings were held in Norfolk County.

3. Roberts Rules of Order were to be followed.

4. Majority assent of each governing body was to be required for adoption of an act.

5. A quorum was to be not less than three members from each of of the governing bodies.

6. The press and public were to be excluded. Invitations to attend joint sessions were to be extended to the constitutional officers and members of the legislature.

It was also agreed at this meeting that means would be provided to facilitate the interchange of information between the various boards, commissions, authorities, and departments of the two governments and that copies of the ordinances of both governments would be exchanged.

[21] Copy in the Chesapeake Papers. See Bibliography for a description of the Chesapeake Papers.

Chesapeake did not pattern its use of committees after the Virginia Beach practice. In Virginia Beach the committees were generally ad hoc in nature, but Chesapeake set up standing committees in such broad areas as finance, public safety, public works, welfare, and retirement. Like those in Virginia Beach, however, the committees were on the order of interlocking directorates, with the constitutional officers serving as members.

It is also important to note that there were background figures of some influence in the Chesapeake transition. For example, M. L. Carnifax, who served as Norfolk County's auditor, seems to have played a significant role in the determination of financial issues. A number of officials interviewed in Norfolk County attributed "financial wizardry" to Carnifax; he was usually consulted by the board of supervisors on financial matters; and he enjoyed the reputation in the county of almost always being "able to come up with needed money." If good advice in Virginia Beach was to "see Sidney," equally good advice in Norfolk County regarding financial affairs was "check it with Carnifax."

One of the first reports presented to the joint body, dealing with health services, introduced a common problem in city-county consolidation, namely, the location and maintenance of branch offices. In this particular case, it was recommended that both the health department clinic and departmental headquarters be maintained at Great Bridge, the site of the city hall for the consolidated city. However, it was also proposed that the South Norfolk health center, some twelve miles from Great Bridge, serve as a branch office and clinic.

The reasons for establishing branch offices varied in the four consolidations. In every case except Hampton, city officials were confronted with problems of distance, and branch offices seemed a reasonable administrative solution. Second, residents of the former city and county were accustomed to certain office locations; retaining them preserved an element of convenience for the citizen and likely prevented upsetting routines. Third, and perhaps most important, branch offices were politically significant. If, for example, all branch offices in South Norfolk had been abolished for the sake of full-scale centralization of all functions and services at Great Bridge, credence would have been given to the charge of a "take over" by Norfolk County and there would have been political repercussions. On the other hand, the use of branch offices had several inherent disadvantages, to be covered more fully in the next chapter.

One of the more interesting reports presented to the joint merger body dealt with the disposition of certain positions and offices. This document, among the first such reports submitted, noted:

At the request of the City Sergeant of South Norfolk and the Sheriff of Norfolk County, your Committee discussed the division of duties to be performed by these two officers after the consolidation. The consolidation agreement provides for the interim performance of their duties by these two officers. Your Committee recommends that the position of High Constable of the consolidated city be activated by the Council of the consolidated city at the earliest practicable date in accordance with the charter. The present City Sergeant of South Norfolk and the Sheriff of Norfolk County (both of whom are members of this Committee) advised us that if this office were activated on or about January 1st, 1963, they would be agreeable to having the present Sergeant of the City of South Norfolk fill the office of High Constable and the present Sheriff of Norfolk County fill the office of Sergeant for the consolidated city.

The Committee recommends that the position of City Attorney for the consolidated city be activated at the earliest practicable date. Your Committee has been requested by the Commonwealth's Attorney of Norfolk County and the Commonwealth's Attorney of South Norfolk to advise the Council of the consolidated city that upon activation of the office of City Attorney, the Commonwealth's Attorney of Norfolk County is agreeable to assuming the duties of the Commonwealth's Attorney for the consolidated city, should the Council and Board of Supervisors see fit to appoint the present Commonwealth's Attorney to the post of City Attorney for the consolidated city.[22]

Proceeding in much the same manner as Virginia Beach was at that time, the county board and city council began establishing a working government. In June it was decided to employ Phillip Davis, city manager of South Norfolk, as the new manager for the consolidated city, and Davis began work immediately on a position classification plan. It was also decided to operate the two housing authorities separately because the Norfolk County authority dealt only with housing while its counterpart in South Norfolk was responsible for an urban redevelopment project. By October most of the posts of the new city had been filled, and the joint body concerned itself with finance and taxation. It was also decided at that time that real estate taxes were to be collected semiannually, but it was not until December 18 that the utility consumer's tax rate was fixed at 10 percent and a local motor vehicle license tax was approved. A minimum housing standards board was established along

22 *Ibid.*

with a recreation board and a ten-member industrial commission. Considerable time was spent on the problem of obtaining needed road equipment, while other reports noted a need for eleven new cars, twenty-four additional policemen, and two clerks. It was decided to purchase three cars and hire fifteen additional policemen and one clerk.

The general atmosphere of the transition in Chesapeake differed somewhat from that in Virginia Beach. On the one hand, it cannot be said that there was a lack of cooperation. Neither did any evidence from records or interviews reveal that the meetings were plagued with disharmony. Plans were made by the school board, interdepartmental cooperation and an exchange of information did occur, and all was done that likely could have been done. But there were things that could not be agreed upon, such as planning and zoning, and these were to plague the consolidated council after merger.

The problems of the Chesapeake transition are difficult to characterize. It appears that such problems were partly attitudinal. For example, the members of the county board of supervisors wanted a consolidated city and recognized that certain prerogatives regarding their magisterial districts would probably have to be surrendered. But it also seems that they did not appreciate the nature of council-manager government, planning, or centralized administration and control. At the same time, its seems clear that South Norfolk officials did not understand the manner in which government had been carried on in Norfolk County. On the county side, there was the belief that merger was not supposed to bring about change, and that somehow Norfolk County would go on being Norfolk County. The new government was ready at the time of the effective legal date of merger, but it was an admixture of county and city government, and there was friction. After merger, City Manager Davis found himself in difficulty with his council for presenting a budget deemed by former Norfolk County supervisors to be "unrealistic," and he resigned six months after the date of merger. One former county official mentioned that in preparing the budget the city manager had obviously not "checked with Carnifax."

No One Best Way

All the merging governments recognized that policy, program, and personnel adjustments were necessary to effect merger, and all took steps to make the transitions as orderly as possible. The approach employed was necessarily ad hoc, in part because no two mergers were alike and in part because there are no established guidelines for creating a single government out of two or more established and distinct local governmental units. The simple fact is that no one has really bothered to examine the process by which merger is to be accomplished, or the things that need to be done after the voters have approved consolidation. In view of the Tidewater experience, it would seem that the definition of tasks to be accomplished before actual merger is itself a problem of no small proportions.

With the possible exception of the Newport News–Warwick merger, the transitional arrangements seem to have been accepted by the public and the news media as if they were routine in nature. Yet a review of the policy decisions of the transitional period suggests that transition was anything but routine. In actual practice, a nonlegal council and administration were formulating policy and establishing a new government without the usual restraints of public accountability, and frequently in closed sessions. Much like the premerger negotiations, the transitions were approached as if they were "all within the family." Had this not been the case, however, and had the skills and knowledge of public officials not been utilized to the fullest, there is good reason to believe that the transitions would not have been so smooth as they were.

Transition is a highly critical phase of merger. The myriad of policy decisions needed in the building of a consolidated government cannot be spelled out in advance of the referendum, and yet the resolution of many of these details must be accomplished prior to the actual merger. Moreover, where the character, style, and legal base of the governments differ, the resolution of such policy questions and issues becomes exceedingly difficult.

None of the four merged cities discovered the one best way for effecting a transition. Each approach was in part the product of a political environment existing in a particular community as modified by the need to compromise. Those who were responsible for the transition, moreover, were essentially practical people, and their primary concern was not in the theoretical realm. They were interested in making the new government work, and they drew on their accumulated knowledge and skills to do so. If the transition process must be characterized generally, the best descriptive term perhaps is expediency.

Even though significant policy decisions were made during the transition periods, they were made by promerger leaders who had deliberately cast the mergers in a conservative image. The promerger leaders, in fact, were the product of an essentially conservative constituency, and that constituency was assured that no major political or economic upheaval was being contemplated or would occur through consolidation. In this sense, the transitions and specific transitional arrangements were developed with an eye to their impact on former constituencies. Each change that had to be made was considered in light of its probable political impact in each of the communities.

This approach to the transitional stage of merger raises a number of value-laden questions. For example, should the transitional arrangements be left to the elected officials of the former units of government? What happens to administrative and political responsibility during the transition period? What should be the role of the citizen during transition? Or, at what point and on what questions should the citizen be consulted or at least given an opportunity to express his views? These questions imply no general condemnation of transitional arrangements in Tidewater. The essential point is that such questions were never asked at the time, let alone answered.

The fact is that in the transition stage, even though consolidated city decisions were being made, there was no consolidated city political base. Practically speaking, in the three cities where no elections were held before consolidation, the political bases upon which the new governments were to rest existed in limbo during the transition. Whatever political inputs influenced those responsible for the transitions reflected former community ties and alliances. These former associations, however, do not necessarily reflect the relative economic, social, or political make-up of the consolidated political community. Indeed, there is some evidence to support a belief that the approach to the transition employed in three of the four cities gave undue weight to certain constituencies without regard to the relative strength those constituencies would have in the consolidated cities.

Which transition was best? If elections before merger and open meetings serve as the standard, then the choice would likely be that of Newport News. If, on the other hand, assuring access and representation to existing political and economic interests or ensuring the full utilization of the skills of incumbent officials during the transition seems more important, then the approach adopted by Chesapeake, Hampton, and Virgina Beach is to be recommended. The results, in any case, do not show any clear-cut superiority of one approach to transition over another.

Finally, those who were responsible for effecting the transitions were confronted with the problem of striking a balance between democratic practice and the fact that merger was never intended initially to bring about political, social, or economic change. Some measure of criticism may be made that the political leadership was, at times, perhaps unduly concerned with finding middle ground or protecting the status quo. But in no case was reform ever a stated goal of merger in Tidewater, nor did anyone on the proconsolidation side ever concede that merger might alter significantly the existing political relationships between the citizen and his government.

CHAPTER VI

THE POSTMERGER PERIOD: PROBLEMS AND POLITICS

EIGHT MONTHS after the effective date of merger, on August 13, 1963, to be exact, the city council of Chesapeake was preparing to meet in regular session. At 7:30 P.M., with the meeting still thirty minutes away, the parking lot adjacent to the courthouse–council chamber was nearly filled with cars. The weather that evening was warm, and as people ambled from their cars to the entrance door, many paused outside to admire the modern civic center complex that housed Chesapeake's government at Great Bridge.

Inside the courthouse, the council chamber was crowded. Most of the available 109 seats were taken, and late arrivals crowded at the double entrance doors where they had to remain standing. A few minutes before 8:00 P.M. the city clerk, city attorney, and acting city manager assumed their places at a table facing council. The spectators conversed in subdued tones, rustled newspapers apprehensively, and consulted the mimeographed councilmanic agenda that had been handed out at the door. The audience was overwhelmingly male.

A few minutes after 8:00 P.M. the door to the anteroom opened and the ten-member council filed in and took their places. All members of council were present. After a moment's pause to survey the crowd, Mayor Colon L. Hall called the meeting to order. The spectators became quiet as council turned to its agenda.

There could be no doubt as to why the crowd was present. The conversation and discussion among the audience before the council's appearance had centered on Agenda Item 3-F, a proposed ordinance to prohibit hunting with rifles in the City of Chesapeake east of Route 17, which bisects the city on a north-south line. Most hunter-spectators in attendance had turned out to oppose what they viewed as councilmanic infringement on their sport.[1]

---

[1] Persons knowledgeable in the politics of former Norfolk County had indicated to the author earlier in the day that Agenda Item 3-F was controversial. It was recalled that an attempt in Norfolk County to change hunting seasons had

The council proceeded through its agenda in a businesslike fashion and disposed of routine matters in short order. The crowd watched politely but with an attitude of obvious impatience. Finally, Item 3-F was next on the agenda. Before the issue could be joined, however, the city attorney arose to announce that (1) an adequate draft of the proposed ordinance was not ready, and (2) doubt had been expressed about its legality and the adequacy of notice. Accordingly, council decided to defer action until a later date. One of the hunter-spectators cried, "We're ready now!" Still another, obviously impatient with the decision to delay action, arose to inquire just when the matter would be considered and, further, to assure council that the assembled group augmented by still other interested parties would return when this occurred. Mayor Hall reassured the hunter that he would be welcome and stated that adequate preliminary notice would be given before any councilmanic action. At this point, in recognition of the crowd's size and purpose, the council declared a ten-minute recess to permit spectators to leave before the usual order of business was resumed. The crowd, satisfied that no further action would be taken on the rifle ordinance that evening, filed out, leaving a near-deserted council chamber. After the recess council returned to consideration of its agenda. Long before the hunting season had opened, the citizen-hunters of Chesapeake could boast that they had "bagged" one proposed ordinance.

Item 3-F on Chesapeake's councilmanic agenda serves to underscore one major point, namely, that the operation and focus of government in the consolidated cities were significantly different from that of other cities in Virginia or, for that matter, in the United States. A city is not usually a place where hunting and fresh-water fishing rank high among the prime attractions. Yet in 1962 hunters had killed an estimated 1,200 deer within the corporate limits of the City of Chesapeake. In fact, deer, bears, foxes, squirrels, rabbits, and doves were hunted extensively in both Chesapeake and Virginia Beach, while Virginia Beach, especially, was noted throughout the state for its superlative duck hunting. In Chesapeake it was altogether possible to travel a city street and see a bear

---

necessitated a special meeting in a school auditorium to accommodate the crowd. Some observers subsequently guessed that council's decision to defer action resulted from a hurried but accurate assessment of the temper of the crowd. For a newspaper account of this incident, see Lloyd H. Lewis, "No Target Set Up for Riflemen," *Ledger-Star,* Aug. 14, 1963.

on one side and a deer on the other.[2] For this reason, both cities obtained special legislation from the 1962 General Assembly to permit hunting and fishing within their corporate limits. These laws were patterned after similar statutes that governed hunting and fishing in the merged cities of Hampton and Newport News.

In considering politics and problems in the immediate post-merger period, it is important to keep in mind that the single most salient feature of the consolidated cities was their rural character. In 1952, when it incorporated as a city of the first class, the City of Warwick had 146 farms with a total farm area of 12 square miles. Virginia Beach, on the date of merger, could boast 417 farms, which included 37 percent of the total acreage of the consolidated city. At the time of merger, in fact, the farms of Virginia Beach ranked over all the counties in the state in yield per acre of corn and wheat and third in the value of vegetables sold. Chesapeake at the time of consolidation had 500 operating farms in addition to its 100,000 acres of commercial forest and the vast areas of the Great Dismal Swamp.

The Problem of Comparison

The fact that the consolidated cities were different from other cities in Virginia need not be unduly belabored. That such differences existed will be evident from the discussion of postmerger politics and problems, so it is enough to say here that the cities were not compact urban places with high population densities. For this reason, any strict comparison between the consolidated cities and other Virginia cities is not possible. Nor is it always possible to select a premerger phase of one of the governments and compare it with its postmerger counterpart. Either of these processes would be a comparison of two dissimilar things.

To select one example, the ad hoc Virginia Beach Advertising Commission might be compared in terms of its powers, structure, and operations to similar bodies in other Virginia cities. Before its merger with Princess Anne County, the City of Virginia Beach had an advertising commission which had been established to advertise the beachfront and promote tourism for the city. During the course of the consolidation negotiations it was decided that the commission

[2] E. E. Edgar, "Deer, Bear, Ducks, Fish, Flourish in New Cities," *ibid.*, Jan. 1, 1963.

should be continued in the consolidated city and should have an expanded membership, jurisdiction, and budget. Outwardly, therefore, the commission following merger might be compared with its predecessor or with a like body in another Virginia city. One fact, however, clouds any strict comparison. Just prior to merger, apparently as part of the price tag for continuation of the commission, it was agreed that certain energies and sums of money had to be devoted to advertising agriculture. This move was an apparent concession to rural Princess Anne County residents, whose tax dollars, after merger, would help to make up the commission's budget. But the fact that it engaged in advertising agriculture made the Virginia Beach Advertising Commission unique, to say the least, and, in the view of selected respondents, introduced a new problem for the commission. To paraphrase the observation of one respondent, "Just how does one go about advertising agriculture—what is there to advertise?"

Exploration of the nature and scope of postmerger politics and problems must necessarily differ from that of premerger politics. In premerger politics there was the recognized goal of winning voter acceptance of consolidation, and it was relatively easy to retrace the steps leading to that goal. But in postmerger politics no such goal is present in obvious form. The provision of services, planning, and conduct of administration are but a few of the municipal activities that never come to an end. In broad outline, then, postmerger politics is best characterized as the day-to-day process of adjustment to the legal fact of merger, centering around the evolution (or lack of evolution) of policies and programs that reflect the current realities and needs of the consolidated city.

This chapter focuses on selected broad problem areas that point up the difficulties of implementing merger in what may be termed the immediate postmerger period, that is, the first year after merger. Certain fundamental problems common to all of the merged cities influenced the course of postmerger politics and policy development; other circumstances, conditions, and events had an impact in each particular city. At the conclusion of one year, significant adjustments had been made to consolidated status, although the full impact of these adjustments may not have been visible until a later time.

The full adjustment process appeared to require about four years before policies, programs, outlook, and individual attitudes came to accept consolidation completely. The primary manifestation of complete consolidation seemed to occur when leaders adopted, either consciously or unconsciously, a city-wide approach to current political, social, and economic issues. When this city-wide approach had clearly supplanted former loyalties and ties, it can be said that consolidation had occurred in fact as well as in name. This process was not marked by any one dramatic event, but by the end of four years in all of the consolidated cities, the city-wide approach to issues and problems had generally prevailed over the particularism that characterized the immediate postmerger period.

Fundamental Problems of Consolidated Government

Four general problems face the decision makers in consolidated city government, add complexity to the conduct of postmerger politics, affect policy and program development, and cast consolidated city politics in a unique mold. These are problems that (1) stem from a large geographic area or size with a low population density, (2) arise from applying corporate organization to a semiurban city, (3) center around the adaptation of council-manager government to the consolidated entity, and (4) are attributable to blending two formerly distinct political communities into a single entity.

Size

It is customary to think of cities as large or small in terms of their population. Moreover, it is usually assumed, by definition, that this population is concentrated in a reasonably compact urban area with a definable core, and with most economic and political activities centering around that core. However, in the immediate postmerger period none of these factors was present in the consolidated cities. Newport News displayed many characteristics of a strip city with sizable rural areas. Hampton was likewise a strip city, and if there was an economic core, it was downtown Newport News. Virginia Beach and Chesapeake did not really fit any known classification, but they might probably be best described as semiurban cities. A brief description of a journey from the business district of Virginia Beach to its city hall in 1963 may assist in visualizing the city at that time.

From downtown Virginia Beach Borough, the business center of Virginia Beach, it was a twenty- to twenty-five-minute drive to the city hall, located at former Princess Anne courthouse. Regardless of the exact point of departure, within a few minutes the city's landscape had become entirely rural. There were no stop lights or street signs and few intersections. Except for the rush hours created by employees at the nearby Oceana Naval Air Station, traffic was sparse. The terrain was flat, cultivated fields spread along both sides of the two-lane highway, and occasional farmhouses sat far back from the highway. After traveling approximately ten miles through this pastoral setting, the road forked at rural Nimmo Church, which dated from the eighteenth century. From the right fork at Nimmo Church, the road wound through woods for a few additional miles until it reached Princess Anne courthouse.

The city hall of consolidated Virginia Beach is the former county courthouse. The architectural style of the courthouse is colonial; there is a broad lawn with large shade trees and, of course, the inevitable statue of the Confederate soldier. In 1963 the settlement at Princess Anne courthouse included a firehouse, two gasoline stations, a post office, Kellam and Eaton Building Supplies, Audet's Courthouse Inn, and approximately thirty-five houses. The city manager's office was in the old courthouse building. The constitutional offices were located in an adjacent annex. A separate structure located behind the courthouse still bore a sign denoting the office of the sheriff of Princess Anne County in July 1963.

The courthouse is located at the approximate geographic center of the new city. By almost any other standard, however, Princess Anne courthouse is out of the way. In Virginia Beach, and in Chesapeake too, a citizen does not drop by city hall to pay a sewer service charge or question an assessment. Round-trip distances of well over fifty miles are involved if one resides in the urbanized Bayside or Lynnhaven boroughs of Virginia Beach. A similar situation exists in Chesapeake, where the city hall at Great Bridge is approximately twelve miles from the former City of South Norfolk and especially remote from the Western Branch Borough of Chesapeake. On a direct-access line, persons residing in the Western Branch Borough first must pass through the City of Portsmouth in order to reach their own city hall at Great Bridge.

But if the geographic size of the cities created difficulties for a citizen who wanted to reach the seat of his government, similar difficulties were also encountered when government tried to reach the citizen. In road maintenance, for example, a significant amount of time was spent just getting the proper equipment to the spot where it was needed. Inspectional services, such as the enforcement of building and plumbing codes, were rendered more difficult by the distances that had to be traveled. The preparation of city maps using aerial photographs for planning or assessment purposes was a task of major proportions. Police and fire protection, including highway patrol, was also difficult. In general, almost every municipal function or activity was affected in some way by geographic size.

Local leaders generally anticipated the problems emanating from geographic size in advance of the merger, and size was therefore a factor in the planning and provision of services for the merged cities. Size and population density dictated that some services be rendered on a city-wide basis while others had to be considered as special services and, accordingly, were limited to defined areas within the consolidated cities. So-called special services, such as sewer systems, trash collection, water supply, street lighting, and sidewalks had to be limited to urban enclaves. On the other hand, schools, the administration of justice, road construction and maintenance, and health and welfare programs were among those services that had to be rendered city-wide by all the merged governments.

Because of their smaller geographic areas and greater population densities, Newport News and Hampton initially furnished more city-wide services than did Virginia Beach and Chesapeake. The City of Newport News had traditionally supplied water from its own water system to all residents of the Lower Peninsula.[3] Sanitary sewers and trash collection were also provided on a city-wide basis in both Hampton and Newport News. Sidewalks, curbs and gutters, and streetlights were also made available city-wide with the city and the recipient of the service sharing the cost. The financial realities accompanying a large geographic area with a low population density worked to prevent Chesapeake and Virginia Beach, at least initially, from assuming full responsibility for these latter services.

Both Virginia Beach and Chesapeake inherited former county sanitary districts that had been created originally to provide some services to urbanized parts of the former counties, and both con-

[3] Before merger the water system was controlled by a special district of Newport News known as the Newport News Waterworks Commission. This commission supplied water to Warwick, Newport News, and Hampton. As a result of merger, the district was abolished, and the waterworks became a department of the City of Newport News. An extensive capital improvements project was completed in 1962 in the form of Diascund Creek Reservoir and Dam. Water is sold to residents of Hampton on an individual basis at a nondiscriminatory rate. No bulk sales are made to the City of Hampton. In the minds of certain officials who were interviewed, this enlightened policy is partly "merger bait" in the form of voter good will should the Newport News—Hampton merger proposal ever be resurrected.

tinued to use these special service districts for water supply, sanitary sewers, and selected other services. The Borough of Virginia Beach in the City of Virginia Beach and the Borough of South Norfolk in Chesapeake alone enjoyed what might be termed a full range of urban services in the two cities. Otherwise, these services were optional and were offered on a spot basis in the remaining city areas. Continuation of this policy was clearly necessitated by the size of the cities, for any attempt to undertake a city-wide sewer construction program, or some similar facility, was unquestionably not economically feasible.

As far as the problems relating to sewage disposal were concerned, however, all the consolidated cities benefited significantly from the existence of the Hampton Roads Sanitation District, a special district charged with preventing pollution in the Hampton Roads area of Chesapeake Bay. This special district functioned in both of the Standard Metropolitan Statistical Areas facing the harbor of Hampton Roads, and all the cities were connected with the district's sewer mains and treatment plants. Immediately before the Virginia Beach and Chesapeake mergers, approximately two-thirds of Princess Anne County and one-half of Norfolk County were served by the district. Following the merger referendum, both of the new cities immediately requested a feasibility study of including all former county areas within the district.

The policy of having to provide special urban services on a spot or demand basis because of geographic size was a source of irritation and, thus, a political issue, especially in Virginia Beach and Chesapeake. Although in the immediate postmerger period both cities adhered to the principle that only those who received the services should pay for them, there remained the question of the city's interest in the development of particular services. Should the residents of a small section of the city be permitted to construct a sewer system incapable of accommodating additional growth? If the pay-use theory was followed, it could be argued that the residents should not be compelled to pay extra to accommodate the future growth of the area. But if the system was to be overdesigned to accommodate growth, what portion of the cost should the city bear?

Had Virginia Beach and Chesapeake not been experiencing rapid population growth at the time of merger, many of the problems relating to the provision of services might have been resolved much more easily. But rapid and continued growth resulted in several legal snarls and also made the planning and engineering of services more difficult. As matters stood in 1963 in Virginia Beach and Chesapeake, one urban enclave might receive several city services while an adjacent enclave might be deprived of similar services because it was outside the boundaries of a special district. The latter area might not be of sufficient size to warrant the formation of a special service district, and citizen resistance to expansion of existing district boundaries was almost invariably a deterrent. From an engineering standpoint unforeseen growth could rapidly make inadequate any facility or system which was designed to accommodate the needs of an existing area.

Geographic size resulted in some rather curious responses by the merged cities to specific problems, such as the busing of school pupils in the Newport News–Warwick merger. Because of its geographic area and lack of public transportation facilities, Warwick required assurances prior to merger that its school children would continue to receive free bus service. This issue was resolved in the consolidation agreement by guaranteeing school buses to Warwick with the understanding that after four years school bus service would be extended to the former Newport News. Thus, expanded school bus service was a direct result of merger.

Organization

Legally speaking, all the consolidated cities are municipal corporations endowed with the powers, duties, responsibilities, and limitations that are common to all other municipal corporations in Virginia. They all routinely chose a council-manager form of government,[4] and there was little that was new or even different in regard to their powers or their governmental structure. Except for an occasional department such as farm and home demonstration, or an office such as that of high constable, the paper organization of the consolidated cities resembled that of other Virginia cities.

One of the first problems that confronted officials in the postmerger period was the need to gain insight and understanding into the operations of a city government. A municipal operation was a

---

[4] There is no evidence that the commission plan or mayor-council plan were even considered by the promergerites. This may be explained in part in terms of Virginia's affinity for council-manager government, although other reasons, to be explained later, were also present. The routine adoption of the council-manager plan may be explained, at least in part, by what one recent writer has referred to as Virginia's "love affair" with the plan. See John P. Wheeler, "Virginia and the Council-Manager Plan," 42 *University of Virginia News Letter* 33–36 (May 15, 1966).

completely new experience for the former officials of Princess Anne County, Elizabeth City County, and Norfolk County, while Warwick had been a city for only six years prior to its merger with Newport News. Although there were similarities in the structural arrangements and powers of each former county and consolidated city, there were also important differences. For example, there was a new relationship with the school board, which was now to be appointed by council; departmental organization was new and basically untried; new responsibilities had to be assumed, such as roads and highways and the addition of tort liability; the taxing power was changed; and the regulatory power of the consolidated entity represented a significant expansion of power. It was also discovered that certain functions formerly performed by the county or the state either (1) could not be undertaken by the city after consolidation or (2) had to be assumed by the new city.

The application of county sanitary district statutes within the consolidated cities provides a good example of the organizational problems that arose. County sanitary districts are special service and taxing districts empowered to provide a few or a wide range of urban services in urbanized county areas. Created by the circuit courts following a petition by residents in the proposed district, the oversight and administration of sanitary districts is vested in the county board of supervisors, often with the assistance of a district citizens advisory committee. Existing sanitary districts in Hampton, Virginia Beach, and Chesapeake were simply carried over into the consolidated governments.

In Hampton the former county sanitary districts apparently did not create any major problems for the new government. As Hampton began to undertake the provision of services on a city-wide basis, no need existed to expand the jurisdiction of localized districts, and they were continued mainly in order to repay long-term debt that had been incurred prior to merger. Perhaps as a result of the lack of difficulty in Hampton, neither Virginia Beach nor Chesapeake made any special plans during the transitional period to adjust their sanitary districts to the new city status. Apparently it was believed that the application of the statutes relating to sanitary districts and their operation would continue uninterrupted after consolidation.

Shortly after the legal date of merger, however, Chesapeake officials discovered that the state's county sanitary district law was not applicable to sanitary districts in the consolidated cities. Although the existing sanitary districts continued to operate, their future became a matter of concern as the state attorney general ruled in 1963 that the boundaries of a sanitary district within the corporate limits of Chesapeake could not be expanded.[5] In order to make such changes, the attorney general advised, it would be necessary to obtain a special act from the General Assembly.

This problem assumed concrete proportions at the Chesapeake council meeting on August 13, 1963, after the hunters had scotched the proposed rifle ordinance and departed. Involved was Broadmoor Section J of Deep Creek Sanitary District No. 2. A few residents were on hand to inquire about the progress on construction of their sewer system. Before consolidation the district residents had voted a $550,000 bond issue, equal to the permitted statutory maximum of 18 percent of the assessed valuation of district property, to provide the district with a sewer system. After the $550,000 had been committed, it was found that an additional $250,000 would be required to complete the project. Unless additional funds could be found, therefore, the residents of Section J were to be taxed at the rate of $1.00 per $100 of assessed valuation for thirty years to repay bonded debt for sewers they did not have and might not get. The sanitary district could not be expanded, there was no inclination within the district to raise the tax rate further to obtain the needed money, and the city could not advance money to the district as a county might do under similar circumstances.[6]

To make the matter even worse, all cities and towns in Virginia are subject to a maximum municipal debt limit equal to 18 percent of the assessed value of property in the city, a limit not applicable to Virginia counties. Councilman I. H. "Ike" Haywood, chairman of the Chesapeake council's finance committee, stated that even if the city could lend money to the sanitary district, it might not be economically judicious to do so because such a loan would push the city dangerously close to its maximum debt limitation.

Acting in part at the behest of Chesapeake officials, the General

[5] *O. A. G.*, 1962–63 (May 31, 1963), pp. 296–97.

[6] For an account of events at this council meeting, see Lloyd Lewis, "$250,000 Sewerage Problem Discussed, but Not Solved," *Ledger-Star*, Aug. 14, 1963. For subsequent developments see "Broadmoor Residents Slate Meeting on Sewer Dilemma," *ibid.*, Aug. 21, 1963; Lloyd Lewis, "Broadmoor Alphabet Dilemma Clouds Future Underground," *ibid.*, Aug. 22, 1963; "The Overspent Sewer Districts," *ibid.*, Jan. 17, 1964; and Lloyd Lewis, "Johnston Stumping New York Seeking Cash for Sewer Work," *ibid.*, Jan. 17, 1964. By this time the total amount needed for all sanitary districts had risen to $994,445, of which $875,268 represented overspending on 3 sewer system projects. Difficulties were compounded by the fact that the new city did not have a bond rating, although prior to merger Norfolk County had an Aa rating.

Assembly in 1964 made the county sanitary district law, in its entirety, applicable to all cities in Virginia.[7] This extension of the county sanitary district law to include counties and cities alike was a solution to Chesapeake's problem, as well as a similar one that might arise in Virginia Beach. Other cities have not taken advantage of the option for providing services made available by this act, a reluctance attributable to the fact that its constitutionality has never been tested in the Virginia Supreme Court, among other reasons.

The case of the Virginia Beach–Princess Anne Incinerator Commission illustrates another problem arising from a consolidated and corporate status. This particular commission was created by the 1942 General Assembly and was composed of the Princess Anne County supervisors from Kempsville and Lynnhaven magisterial districts, the mayor of the then Town of Virginia Beach, and certain other town and county officers serving ex officio. At the time of the merger negotiations, no official provision was made for the continuation of the commission; thus in 1963 it existed as a legal entity but was unable to act for want of a governing board because the legislation creating the commission specified that the board would include the members of the now nonexistent board of supervisors of Princess Anne County.[8] Again, the 1964 General Assembly provided a solution by repealing the 1942 act.[9]

The acquisition of city status also affected the application of certain other state laws within the new corporate limits. One such statute was the Seed Tree Law,[10] which after merger became unenforceable in Virginia Beach and Chesapeake. At the time of merger these two cities had large tracts of land in commercial forests. According to the Seed Tree Law commercial foresters were required to leave a specified number of trees per acre to provide for reseeding. This statute was enforced by the State Department of Conservation and Economic Development, but the law did not include trees that were located within a city. As the state attorney general ruled in 1963: "While no doubt this legislation is intended to apply to rural or farming properties, it does not appear that there is any way the Department of Conservation and Economic Development could enforce its provisions within the corporate limits of a city." [11]

[7] *Acts of Assembly*, 1964, p. 808.

[8] *O. A. G.*, 1962–63 (June 10, 1963), pp. 37–38.

[9] *Acts of Assembly*, 1964, p. 112.

[10] Code §§ 10-74.1–10-83.

[11] *O. A. G.*, 1962–63 (Feb. 1, 1963), pp. 200–201.

In this case, unlike the previous examples, the General Assembly has not enacted any legislation permitting the state forester to exercise authority in Virginia Beach or Chesapeake regarding the application of the Seed Tree Law.

Council-Manager Government

All the merging governments, with the exception of Norfolk County, had had some exposure to the concept of an appointed administrator. The cities without exception had the council-manager plan. Elizabeth City County and Princess Anne County each had an executive secretary who exercised many of the duties of the traditional city manager. The executive secretary in Virginia is a full-time employee of the county who is appointed by and responsible to the board of supervisors, serves at its pleasure, and is charged with such administrative duties and responsibilities as it may assign. In practice, therefore, the executive secretary is the county's chief administrative officer.

One significant difference between the governments of cities and counties, however, quickly came to the surface in the immediate postmerger period. While most Virginia cities elect their councilmen on an at-large basis, the counties at that time, with one exception, uniformly elected their supervisors by magisterial districts. Partly for this reason, all of the consolidated cities, with the exception of Newport News, chose initially to adopt the district system. In Chesapeake, Virginia Beach, and Hampton, former county magisterial districts were recast as boroughs, and each county supervisor was transformed into a city councilman. Each of the former cities also became a borough of the consolidated city, such as the Borough of South Norfolk in Chesapeake and the Borough of Virginia Beach in Virginia Beach. In these two cities, moreover, all members of the former city councils assumed posts on the consolidated city councils. In Hampton, as noted earlier, a slightly different scheme was used; the former City of Hampton did not become a borough, and only the mayors of the City of Hampton and the Town of Phoebus served on the first consolidated city council. Thus, the consolidated city council of Hampton had five members as opposed to eleven for Virginia Beach and ten for Chesapeake. Shortly after merger Hampton created four boroughs or election districts and elected one councilman at large. At a still later time Hampton abandoned the borough plan altogether and substituted election at large.

Selecting councilmen by districts has two important ramifications for council-manager government. First, because of his localized constituency, the district councilman is less likely to adopt a city-wide point of view in approaching the public business. Politics and policies are judged in terms of their probable impact upon the particular district or borough. Although this approach may have certain merits, it does operate to render agreement more difficult and sometimes casts public programs and policies at the level of the lowest common denominator. Because the "county councilmen" might not be especially interested in public housing or urban renewal, for example, they might accord any effort initiated along these lines only minimal interest and support.

Second, the district system tended to create a proprietary interest by the councilman in the implementation of services in his particular district. Again, this is not necessarily detrimental to the conduct of government, unless it reaches the stage of interference by individual councilmen in the day-to-day conduct of administration. Such interference may reach the point where the city manager is the chief administrative officer only in a limited sense.

It appears that the district system in operation worked to deter the establishment of typical council-manager government in the consolidated cities. At first there was the confusion of beginning an entirely new city government and simply getting acquainted. Within a short time after the actual mergers, the managers began to encounter certain of the compromises or arrangements that were necessary for the promotion of consolidation but restricted their operating flexibility. This was a particular problem in Chesapeake and Virginia Beach, where the city manager of Virginia Beach maintained his office at Princess Anne courthouse while his Department of Public Works and Department of Public Utilities were located in downtown Virginia Beach Borough.[12] Finally, the managers had to cope with the district system in operation and with councilmen who might or might not be inclined to cooperate. In its worst aspects, the managers operating in the borough system came to feel that they were overseeing the affairs of a number of separate cities. If the councilmen did not defer to the manager as the chief administrative officer, the result was a multiple number of amateur

[12] Physical decentralization was a problem not only for the manager but for department heads as well. One observed that he simply allotted one day per week for his trip to "city hall" to get the "proper signatures on the proper papers" and talk to the manager. As he put it, "A trip to city hall just about shoots the day."

managers with the full-time professional reduced to the role of chief clerk, record keeper, and errand boy.

Although the acuteness of the problems relating to the operation of council-manager government varied, the problem of developing and establishing satisfactory council-manager relationships was a significant phase of postmerger politics. Some officials recognized the need to begin to approach certain problems city-wide, yet who was to do this? In certain cases, the task of developing city-wide policies and programs was apparently left either to selected appointive officers whose political influence was limited or to the elected constitutional officers who operated from a city-wide electoral base. The involvement of the constitutional officers, however, added another dimension to the problem of developing orderly council-manager relationships. Merritt Sallinger of the *Ledger-Star* caught the nature of this undercurrent of the borough-city conflict in Chesapeake between the councilmen and other officials.

Developing now is a new system of government slightly strange to old Norfolk County political leaders who in January found themselves faced with heretofore unheard of organization control.

To survive, officials claim, the city's government must recognize the people as a whole and shake off the ghost of the old ward system in which a supervisor from one district might receive a blank check from fellow supervisors with the idea of "You run your district and I'll run mine." [13]

Since all the former cities had employed the council-manager plan with councilmen elected at large, one may wonder why the former city councilmen were not able to exercise influence to counter the ward attitude and to routinize council-manager relationships. There is no fully satisfactory answer to this question. The former "city boys" never constituted a majority on the Hampton, Virginia Beach, or Chesapeake councils. But even if they had been a majority, it is doubtful that they would have been able to counteract the influence of the district system. Minimally, unanimity among themselves would have been required, and achieving this condition was unlikely. Moreover, former city councilmen were under pressure from their constituents to look out for their own interests, which served to promote a district attitude among them. Finally, there is reason to believe that former city officials also experienced difficulty

[13] "Chesapeake Fight Brews over Apartment Project," *Ledger-Star*, Nov. 16, 1963.

in comprehending the operation of a vastly expanded consolidated city government. Their former cities had been relatively small in size with few employees and a comparatively simple government structure. For example, although former municipal officials had experience in such policy areas as street construction and maintenance before merger, this was hardly a sufficient preparation for assuming the responsibility for 175 to 600 miles of roadway.

These generalizations do not apply equally to all of the consolidated cities. Chesapeake seems to have encountered the greatest difficulty in the immediate postmerger period, due in part to the fact that Norfolk County had no prior experience with council-manager government. Hampton also seems to have experienced difficulty initially, and although many of the details are now lost or forgotten, responsibility for the sanitary district operation was apparently a source of some friction. Virginia Beach, of all the cities electing by districts, displayed the greatest outward stability with little overt evidence of the district attitude on its council. This was due to a variety of factors, not the least of which was the operation of the Kellam organization. The council of Virginia Beach displayed almost remarkable unanimity in approaching the problems of consolidated city government.

Newport News experienced little or no difficulty in adjusting to council-manager government in the postmerger period because the council-manager team that existed before merger was virtually the same for the consolidated city. Joseph Biggins had served as manager of the former City of Newport News for more than three decades; he was admired by many and respected by all. Because of his long tenure with the former city, his acknowledged managerial ability, his determination to preserve managerial prerogatives, and his apparent willingness to resign if necessary, Biggins was a force of no small consequence in the political world of Newport News. From the very outset of consolidated city government, he was able to grasp the administrative reins firmly by insisting upon his appointments, his budget preparation prerogative, and his power to direct the day-to-day affairs of the city's administration.[14] Consequently, the status of council-manager government in Newport News was quite different from that of the other three consolidated cities in the immediate post-merger period. It may be characterized

[14] Biggins's tenure in Newport News was apparently grounded on a firm political base of broad popular support. Even when control of council shifted to former Warwick, there was no concentrated effort to dislodge him. As one respondent put it, "If you campaign against him, you end up voting to raise his pay."

in part as a struggle between the old Warwick-based organization, which controlled the constitutional officers, and the former Newport News city council with its manager, Joe Biggins. At best, the results were probably a stand-off with an initial edge going to council. In any case, the conflict was sporadic, of short duration, and apparently left no permanent imprint on Newport News politics.

Thus, the experience of the four cities with council-manager government seems to have produced mixed results. Generally, the proprietary attitude of district councilmen toward affairs in their particular boroughs produced some administrative and political problems for the new governments. This was especially true in Chesapeake, where the first city manager resigned after six months of service, but it was not unique to that city. One respondent in Hampton concluded that real consolidation and effective council-manager government did not begin until an at-large election system for choosing councilmen was adopted by that city.

Operating Relationships

The problems of operating relationships result from the attempt to unite two formerly distinct political communities into a single operating government. Merger compelled the public business to be carried on by a single government, but this did not mean that each of the officers of the merged government necessarily abandoned previous attitudes, loyalties, or ideas as to how the public business should be performed. For each of the merging partners, there was frequently a tendency to look backwards with the goal of approximating conditions that existed in the former county or city. One result was the protection and defense of former local interests, a practice which hindered the evolution of coordinated city-wide policies and programs.

Much of the difficulty in defining operating relationships obviously stemmed simply from beginning a new government. Time alone appears to be the chief remedy for alleviating this problem. Gradually, the formal and informal processes that serve to routinize and expedite the business of government were established within each consolidated city. In the newly consolidated cities such relationships did not exist, however, and there were barriers to their evolution.

Certain problems of operating relationships emanated from requirements new to each of the merging partners. The branch offices of the treasurer and commissioner of the revenue in Virginia Beach

and Chesapeake were cases in point. Neither of the merger participants operated branch offices prior to consolidation, and questions
immediately arose as to the exact nature of the business that might
be conducted in the branches. What records, if any, should be kept
at the branch offices, and what had to be centrally maintained?
What business could the citizen conduct at a branch, and for what
purposes was it necessary for him to go to city hall? As a rule,
administrative experience with branch offices revealed serious shortcomings. There was some tendency for the branches to act independently, and there were problems stemming from duplicate record
keeping. Branch offices were not established uniformly in all functional areas, and there was some confusion as to where the citizen
should go to obtain a given service. Finally, management problems
resulted from what one observer termed "government by telephone." In some degree, and in certain functional areas, the administrative problems arising from the establishment of branch
offices were foreseen by those responsible for effecting the transition,
but considerations of distance, citizen convenience, and politics on
occasion outweighed administrative preference.

The general problem of developing new operating relationships
in the immediate postmerger period can be further illustrated by an
examination of one particular functional area, fire protection in
Chesapeake. The Chesapeake charter provided for the creation of a
department of public safety, of which the bureau of fire protection
was one of the component parts, with the director of public safety
being appointed by the city manager. The charter provided in
Chapter 10: "The bureau of fire protection shall consist of a fire
chief and such other officers and employees as may be provided by
the council or by the orders of the director of public safety consistent therewith. The bureau of fire protection shall be responsible
for the protection from fire of life and property within the city."
According to the charter, then, the fire department was to be an
integrated agency of the city's administrative structure with lines of
authority running from the fire chief to the council through the
director of the department of public safety and the city manager.

In addition, Chapter 18 of the Chesapeake charter provided: "The
department of personnel shall be responsible for the formulation
and administration of the personnel policy of the city, including a
civil service commission for policemen and firemen such as is
presently in effect for the City of South Norfolk." The City of South
Norfolk prior to merger maintained a small but full-time fire
department within the regular departmental structure. South Nor-

folk's chief, John Ben Gibson, was appointed fire chief of the consolidated city. Gibson was a professional fireman with some twenty-
five years of experience.

Fire protection in Norfolk County, on the other hand, was provided by the volunteer fire companies organized in each of the
county's magisterial districts. Each volunteer company was organized
independently of the others, and each had a fire station, a chief who
was appointed by the county supervisor from that magisterial district, and varying numbers of volunteer firemen. The several firehouses were manned with one or two full-time firemen per shift,
but the bulk of responsibility for fighting fires fell to the volunteers.

To appreciate the problem of establishing and operating a single
city-wide fire department, it should be recognized that the volunteer
fire company in the Virginia county is something more than a fire-
fighting unit. It is also a social and political club. The fire station
is frequently the focal point of political activity in the magisterial
district, and in former Norfolk County, each supervisor maintained
an office at the district fire station. Each supervisor "presided" over
his fire companies, obtained funds for equipment, and acted as chief
sponsor. Because a small sum was paid to those volunteers "answer-
ing the fire bell," the position was of some importance. At the time
of consolidation with South Norfolk, there were eight firehouses in
Norfolk County manned by an estimated 300 volunteers.

The creation of an integrated fire department by the city charter
did not, as one might suppose, abolish or significantly restructure
the former Norfolk County volunteer fire companies which continued to exist. One of the first outbreaks between the city and the
volunteers focused on who was to be accorded the title of chief.
Each fire company before merger had its own chief, and official
awarding of the title to Chief Gibson in line with the charter provisions settled nothing. Subsequently, each of the volunteer companies was allowed to retain its chief with that title. Thus, as
one observer put it, the fire department of Chesapeake consisted of
one "big chief" and eight "little chiefs." By early 1964 there were
nine deputy chiefs, or "little chiefs," twenty captains, and a staff
of sixty-five firemen in addition to the volunteers.[15] The "big chief"

---

[15] This information and much that follows is taken from Yarger and Associates, *Administrative Survey, City of Chesapeake* (Falls Church, Va.: The Author, 1964). The Yarger Report was highly critical of many phases of municipal
government in Chesapeake and caused something of a political furor because a
number of Chesapeake's officials felt they had been unfairly criticized.

maintained his office at Station No. 5 at Great Bridge with a secretary as an aide.

Besides fire fighting, a variety of local services were offered through the county firehouses, either as a result of tradition or at the behest of the individual borough councilmen. According to the report prepared by Yarger and Associates, a consulting firm employed by the city, oil and gasoline were dispensed at the firehouses. Most of the stations provided ambulance service, which drew two firemen from the duty shift. In another case, Yarger reported that the ambulance service appeared to be serving as a local taxi service. A branch office for the tax collector was located in one fire station, and a branch post office was attached to another. The deputy fire chief in one station supervised the collection and disposal of refuse from homes in that area. Three stations maintained a truck driver who served to pick up and deliver construction materials for citizens residing in that district. The citizen paid for the materials; delivery was free of charge. One station had a fireman who doubled as justice of the peace.

The mutiple role of the firehouse in Norfolk County clashed with that of former South Norfolk with its more traditional, professional, and centralized approach to fire fighting. From the standpoint of formal organization, the administration of fire protection was clearly centered in the hands of Chief Gibson, the director of public safety, and the city manager, but the charter provisions did not suddenly transform the firehouse or the volunteer fire company into a typical city fire station. Nor did the borough councilmen, who constituted one-half of the council, surrender their prerogatives of appointment of firemen or direction of the firehouse. Chief Gibson found that to operate his department he had to deal with the manager, the councilmen, the little chiefs, and the volunteers. Thus, even though there was an agreed-upon goal of providing the best possible fire protection for Chesapeake, the problem was essentially one of defining responsibilities and relationships.

Few would argue that the organization and operation of Chesapeake's fire department in 1963–64 conformed to any known standard for a city of more than 70,000 people. But, as has been stressed, the operation of government in the merged cities was really not comparable with that in other cities, at least in the immediate postmerger period. Doubtless, many officials in Chesapeake would have agreed that substantial doses of professionalism and centralization would have improved the state of its fire protection. But, at least in the immediate postmerger period, neither centralization nor professionalism could be implemented by fiat.

Certain criticisms of the Yarger survey provide some insight into the real difficulty of establishing meaningful operating relationships in a consolidated city. In commenting on the report, one Chesapeake official argued that "they just did not understand our situation." The Yarger report was criticized for (1) applying standards of measurement and performance applicable to a compact city of 70,000 persons, and (2) failing to understand and take into account the status quo approach to merger that was very much a part of consolidation in the former county government. Moreover, a portion of the county leadership simply did not accept what may be termed the usual city standards insofar as the provision of services and other governmental functions were concerned. In the absence of an agreed standard of performance, a conflict was unavoidable.

When compared with that of most Virginia counties at the time, fire protection in Chesapeake would probably have been rated as good to outstanding. Admittedly, the firehouse was politically oriented, but such was the case in almost every county. And if the firehouses were engaged in rendering extracurricular services, the former county supervisors could and did take justifiable pride in the fact that these services were available to their constituents. There was always the question of who would provide such services if the firehouse did not. The city was certainly not prepared to supply ambulance service, let alone free delivery service. But since the former city councilmen also did not understand these former county operations, the difficulties of evolving new operating relationships were compounded.

The Provision of Services

In the early months following the legal date of merger, a number of problems arising from consolidation were encountered in providing service. In that period, according to a department head in one of the consolidated cities, everything was in a state of confusion. Municipal services had to be provided with an untried organization, inadequate personnel, and generally insufficient funds. In the Hampton merger, for instance, there were three separate sewer systems at the time of consolidation, each different from the other; it was not until 1956 that a city-wide approach to sewer service was clearly fixed.

Of the several services, public schools involved the greatest single expense but presented the least difficulty. In Hampton and Virginia Beach the cooperative school arrangements that existed prior to merger made for a smooth changeover. In Newport News and Chesapeake some minor problems such as the adjustment of teacher pay scales and the provision of textbooks were encountered, but they were easily resolved.

In contrast with the easy meshing of the educational systems, other services did not fare so well. A case in point is trash collection in Chesapeake in the early days after merger. In 1963–64 trash collection was conducted both by city employees constituting a unit in the public utilities department and by private contractors. As a result, different collection schedules were in force throughout the city; residential pickup was either once or twice a week, and commercial collection occurred daily, once a week, or twice a week, depending upon the location. The details of these arrangements were complex, as the following summary shows:

1. City forces under the Sanitation Division Superintendent picked up and disposed of garbage and trash in Washington and South Norfolk boroughs. Residential collections were on a twice-a-week schedule, as was commercial collection in Washington Borough. In South Norfolk Borough, commercial collection was on a daily schedule.

2. Deep Creek Borough employed city forces under the direction of a deputy fire chief. Both commercial and residential collection was on a twice-a-week schedule.

3. Western Branch Borough was serviced by a private contractor who picked up trash and garbage in containers only. The borough had twice-a-week collection. Trash not in containers was collected by a truck operated from the Western Branch Firehouse. The "contract" was oral for the amount of $37,500.

4. Pleasant Grove Borough had a private contractor who collected on a once-a-week schedule except in the urbanized area around Great Bridge, which was on a twice-a-week schedule. The contractor also serviced the Civic Center. The contract was oral in the amount of $15,000.

5. The Butts Road Borough was serviced by a private contractor who collected on a once-a-week schedule, except for urbanized areas. This contractor alternated the "second collection" in these areas with the contractor in Pleasant Grove Borough. The contract was oral in the amount of $8,710.[16]

The city at the time of merger operated three dumps in Deep Creek, South Norfolk, and Washington boroughs. None of the disposal areas were owned by the city, but it used them on an informal

[16] See *ibid.*, pp. 105–13.

basis, with no payment to the owners. City-operated vehicles in South Norfolk and Washington boroughs used the Washington Borough dump. From downtown South Norfolk the distance to the Washington dump was about ten miles. The contractor in Pleasant Grove Borough maintained a small dump which received about 15 percent of his collection. Otherwise, both private contractors and city forces used the same dump.

The private contractors were essentially hired by the councilmen from the pertinent boroughs without the benefit of written contract. Although payments were on a lump sum basis, the method of paying the contractors varied, and council had occasionally appropriated specific sums for extra collections by the contractors. Yarger found no system of cost accounting for the entire utility operation. Needless to say, a variety of equipment was used in trash collection, and moreover, the city superintendent did not inspect the private collectors. The delivery-truck drivers who operated out of three firehouses made some pickups on special request. At the time the city had no comprehensive sanitation ordinance.

It should be clear that the adjustments necessary to provide uniform trash collection service in Chesapeake could not have been instituted at the time of merger. The city did not have the money, equipment, or personnel to undertake immediate centralization. According to Yarger, moreover, the utility department needed to improve practices and procedures within its immediate sphere of operation before more ambitious plans were made.

The construction and maintenance of roads and bridges were new and expensive services for all the consolidated cities except Newport News. Prior to merger, only former cities exercised any responsibility for streets, for county roads, both primary and secondary, were the responsibility of the State Department of Highways. Accordingly, at the time of merger, Hampton, Virginia Beach, and Chesapeake needed both highway personnel and equipment for road work. Fortunately, all three cities succeeded in recruiting many state highway employees in the area who otherwise would have been transferred elsewhere after merger. Each of the cities acquired a nucleus for its road crew, and most important, a skilled supervisor who was familiar with the roads and the highway system. Chesapeake and Virginia Beach arranged to share the services of a specialized bridge supervisor, while the state assisted the merged cities by making available the convict road force that had been previously used by the highway department in the former county areas.

The three cities had to obtain expensive road equipment with limited sums of money. Hampton waited until 1955, three years after merger, to buy construction equipment of any consequence. Purchases up to that time were limited largely to maintenance items. To begin their road operations, Virginia Beach and Chesapeake allocated about $350,000 each for road equipment. Certain equipment had to be duplicated by the neighboring cities, a duplication which did not exist when the roads were maintained by the state. Fortunately for both Chesapeake and Virginia Beach, the state declared some items of equipment to be surplus, and the cities were able to acquire a variety of tools and machinery at substantially reduced prices.[17]

All the consolidated cities counted on state financial aid for the maintenance of their primary and secondary road systems. Road aid funds were available to the cities from the state on the basis of a formula which, in 1963–64, allocated a minimum of $800 per mile for secondary maintenance and $10,000 per mile for primary maintenance. Before qualifying for such aid, however, the roads had to meet state highway specifications. This requirement presented some problems. When Hampton assumed full road responsibility in 1955, for example, about 40 miles of its 175 miles of highway were refused certification for failure to meet minimum state standards. This decision was upheld even though the State Department of Highways had maintained the very same roads before consolidation. In Chesapeake, in the Borough of South Norfolk alone, there were 47 miles of city streets that did not qualify for state assistance.

In 1963 official opinion within the consolidated cities held that the state allocation for roads was generally adequate for maintenance provided the system did not experience a major disaster. There were some special cost problems such as bridge maintenance for which there was no separate or special allocation. Bridge maintenance was expensive, and the state program of inspection and preventive maintenance for the bridges in the state system was relatively recent. The cities therefore inherited bridge problems; Chesapeake was especially hard hit as there were over 100 bridges of all types within the city limits. Ten of these bridges were classified as major structures. At the time of merger, virtually all the bridges in Chesapeake were in need of repairs and maintenance.

For the purposes of road construction and maintenance Chesapeake was divided into three geographic areas with an area superintendent located in each. The use of district divisions was intended

[17] See Lloyd H. Lewis, "Road Equipment Needed," *Ledger-Star*, May 31, 1963.

to counteract any tendency to play "road politics" in terms of borough lines. In fact, the Yarger report of 1964 generally commended the highway administration in Chesapeake as well as the efforts that were being made in road construction and maintenance. However, maintenance of the city streets was probably the most difficult of the services to inaugurate because Virginia Beach, Chesapeake, and Hampton had to build their street departments from scratch.[18]

Planning and Zoning

The creation of the consolidated cities offered exciting possibilities for coordinated planning. All the cities were basically in an infant stage of development, but all indicators projected significant growth in both population and the economy. The consolidated cities enjoyed the luxury of vast quantities of undeveloped land, much of which was in a rural or at most a semiurban state. Both Newport News and Chesapeake began consolidated government with sizable industrial bases, and many of the elements needed for the promotion of diversified or light industry were present in Hampton and Virginia Beach. Moreover, with the exception of some small enclaves in downtown Newport News as well as a few parts of former South Norfolk and Hampton, the problem of urban blight and slums common to older compact cities was almost nonexistent. Even so, redevelopment and housing programs had been undertaken in each of these cities to eliminate blight and slum conditions and to check their spread.

The charter of each of the consolidated cities called for the establishment of a planning commission to provide guidelines for future growth and development. The commission was to be appointed by council and was empowered to make recommendations to council on all phases of city planning, including the development of a master plan, zoning, and subdivision control. In addition, under the general laws of the state, city planning commissions had several other powers incidental to fulfilling their primary function. They

[18] Some measure of citizen forbearance was needed. The *Chesapeake Post* advised, "When a motorist hits a hole in one of Chesapeake's 600 miles of roadway—don't cuss and get upset—one should calmly count to ten and think of the tremendous responsibilities of Taylor's department. It just might take a few days to get that hole filled" ("Road Maintenance Big Task for City of Chesapeake," Aug. 22, 1963).

could retain planning consultants, hire a full-time planning director, and obtain state assistance for planning.

In its relationship with the city council and other city departments, the planning commission in Virginia is usually conceived to be a staff agency of the council. The powers of the planning commission are limited to making recommendations to council. The commission prepares a master plan and recommends it to council, but it is up to the council to adopt the plan and provide for its enforcement. The nature and kind of zoning and subdivision regulations to be utilized depend upon the ordinances that council is willing to enact, and council may make exceptions to its stated policies. Therefore, all the final decisions relating to planning and zoning rest with the elective city council.

The initiation of the planning function in the immediate postmerger period was characterized by important differences in the activities each city undertook. Newport News and Warwick began joint meetings of their respective planning bodies before the legal date of consolidation. Planning in Hampton was a gradual development. Virginia Beach and Princess Anne County had employed the same planner for five years before merger. South Norfolk had a small planning department which consisted of a planning aide and a secretary, but no provision had been made for planning in Norfolk County prior to merger.

Somewhat paradoxically, the large geographic area of the consolidated cities, on the surface one of the chief planning assets, seems to have been a major barrier to the initiation of planning in the immediate postmerger period. Shortly after the mergers were formally launched, planning and zoning activity was limited mainly to enforcing ordinances that existed before consolidation. Attempts to proceed with the evolution of new plans and ordinances were hindered by limited funds. Within a month after his appointment, for example, Durward Curling, the Chesapeake city planner, initiated a program of aerial photography for mapping purposes following council's appropriation of $160,000 for the mapping program and the hiring of two planning assistants. But the size of the city and additional duties combined to keep Curling from his task. Billboards began to appear throughout the consolidated city, subdividers had to be dealt with, inspections had to be made, unpiped drainage ditches were cross-stitching the new city, and unlicensed house trailers were being parked according to the whims of the owners. Eight months after the merger Curling stated his own dilemma: "I spent the past month doing nothing but administrative work for the planning commission—making field inspections on agenda items, arguing with subdividers, dealing with the public— and at work Saturdays and Sundays. We're not doing any planning, I have no time left for it." [19]

Nevertheless, Chesapeake made some progress in planning and zoning. On April 23, 1963, the council voted to end unrestricted zones in former Norfolk County and to zone such land for agricultural use.[20] Under this classification land could be used for farming or residential purposes but not for commercial or industrial uses. Although a stopgap measure, this move injected some control until a comprehensive zoning law could be adopted for the entire city. By June 25, 1963, Chesapeake was ready to consider a uniform subdivision ordinance.[21]

In Virginia Beach, significant progress in the planning process was made by undertaking initial land use and economic studies. But Virginia Beach was in the throes of a population boom; F. Mason Gamage, the city planner, calculated that the city had grown from 85,000 in 1960 to 110,000 by 1963. Frank Cox, the school superintendent, using school enrollment as a base, estimated a population of 125,000. The need for planning had reached critical proportions. Both Chesapeake and Virginia Beach had to plan and zone for residential areas, recreational facilities, schools, highways, and accessible shopping centers. Yet by late 1963 neither city had made an appreciable beginning on a master plan. In November 1963 City Mangaer Russell Hatchett of Virginia Beach called this matter to the attention of council. In what must have been a calculated understatement regarding a master plan, Hatchett stated: "I think we need one." [22]

To what extent did political considerations affect the course of planning and zoning in the postmerger period? Although no categorical answer is possible, it appears that both Hampton and Newport News managed to overcome whatever difficulties may have existed immediately following merger. When the control of council passed to former Warwick in 1962, there was some fear in former Newport News for the future of downtown redevelopment, while

[19] Lloyd H. Lewis, "Chesapeake's City Planner Flying SOS," *Ledger-Star*, Aug. 8, 1963.
[20] Lloyd H. Lewis, "Chesapeake Council Votes to End 'Unrestricted' Zones," *ibid.*, April 24, 1963.
[21] "Chesapeake Council to See New Subdivision Law Tonight," *ibid.*, June 25, 1963.
[22] "Master Plan Start Urged at Va. Beach," *ibid.*, Nov. 26, 1963.

some suggested a struggle might be brewing over the location of a proposed new city hall. In general, however, planning and zoning appeared otherwise to be relatively free of overt political meddling. Hampton and Newport News each established a planning department with adequate staffs and adopted a master plan, a comprehensive zoning ordinance, and subdivision regulations. In Chesapeake and Virginia Beach the full-scale commitment to planning and zoning was not so evident as in the older consolidated cities. A beginning had been made, but in each case the nature and extent of the commitment to planning and zoning could be questioned, especially in view of the operation of the borough system. The following episode during a Chesapeake council meeting is illustrative:

Councilman Howard P. McPherson of South Norfolk offered a resolution to rezone a small tract on the west side of Highway 168 in Councilman Eugene P. Wadsworth's Washington Borough. Wadsworth flinched, but held his peace.
Then South Norfolk Councilman Daniel W. Lindsey, Jr. began a meticulous inquiry into the location of the tract. Wadsworth was irked.
"It's in my borough," he snapped. "Mr. McPherson has moved on it. All right, I'll second it. Let's have the vote."
On the roll call, Lindsey voted "No."
"It's got so the recommendation of the councilman from the borough means nothing any more," Wadsworth growled.
"I'll vote as I want to and you vote as you want to," Lindsey retorted.[23]

At the same time, other evidence suggested that planning and zoning in Virginia Beach and Chesapeake were making significant headway. Effective efforts were being made to discourage strip development along Chesapeake's highways, which would have resulted in traffic problems as well as an undesirable mixture of residential and commercial properties. By December 1963 the mere existence of undeveloped Cedar Road near the Chesapeake Civic Center, a strip apparently ripe for commercial development, attested to the success of zoning. Planner Curling and the commission had managed to prohibit the creation of a jungle of retail service outlets and commercial establishments along this two-mile strip of highway.[24] Also, two months earlier the Chesapeake council had enacted a compre-

[23] "Break Appears in Honeymoon of Chesapeake Councilmen," *ibid.*, March 13, 1963.
[24] See Paul Rule, "City Planners Continue Battling Scattered Business Development," *The Chesapeake Post*, Dec. 17, 1964.

hensive trailer park ordinance to combat the haphazard scattering of trailers within the city limits.[25]

In Virginia Beach, Planner Gamage offered a number of challenging concepts for directing the future growth and development of the city, not the least of which was that of five or six self-sustaining satellite communities bound together under a common government.[26] He envisioned that the implementation of such a concept would cut down on highway travel by developing self-contained centers with parks, schools, churches, and shopping centers. Thus, although much remained in the formative or infant stage after a year of merger, there were signs of activity and interest in comprehensive planning and zoning.

Politics, Managers, Mayors, and Councilmen

If anyone had hoped that merger might cause an immediate breakup of the local organizations, that policies would be drastically reoriented or altered, or that new faces and personalities would suddenly emerge, they were to be disappointed. For the most part, there was little or no change in the immediate postmerger period. The implementation of consolidated government was firmly in the hands of the leadership of the former governments, and whatever dissent occurred was usually sporadic and ineffectual. In most of the elections during this period the voters duly returned the leadership to office. In several instances no opposing candidates even ran.

In the short run, the mergers appeared to achieve the goal of preservation of the political status quo. In the cities of Hampton, Virginia Beach, and Chesapeake merger did work to guarantee territorial integrity, even though Chesapeake eventually lost 10.6 square miles of territory and approximately 11,000 people to Portsmouth as a result of an annexation suit filed before the merger referendum. Moreover, the local organizations in Hampton, Virginia Beach, and Chesapeake were apparently strengthened by the successful mergers, at least initially. The Kellam organization in Virginia Beach, for example, emerged from the successful referendum and transition even more unified than it was before merger; its prestige had been increased, and the successful merger caused it

[25] See "Council Adopts Trailer Rules; Industry Asks Money Point Road," *ibid.*, Oct. 22, 1964.

[26] Ruby Jean Phillips, "Master Plan Would Bring City Together as Satellite Communities," *Virginia Beach Sun-News*, July 18, 1963.

to grow in public esteem. Sidney Kellam's reputation as one of the state's major political leaders was unquestionably enhanced by the adroit handling of merger. In Hampton, Court Clerk Stuart Gibson's leadership of promerger forces produced a similar effect, while in Chesapeake the political stature of the constitutional officers who promoted the consolidation, Cross, Waldo, Flora, and so on, also appears to have increased. Outwardly, then, there was little evidence that changes in consolidated city policies or politics would occur.

However, it now seems reasonably clear that certain forces which would bring about political change were at work in the immediate postmerger period. For the most part, the changes that occurred were gradual and evolutionary; yet, approximately four years after the effective legal date of each merger, it was indeed evident that political and administrative changes had taken place. The loosely defined status quo attitude that characterized merger politics during the first year of the cities' lives no longer prevailed.

Certain of the main features of this process of change have already been described. In the immediate postmerger period, an attempt was made, whether consciously or not, to carry on politics and administration in much the same manner as before merger. During this honeymoon period, overt or dramatic change was avoided. Officials and citizens alike tended to look backward to the practices and policies of their former governments. Potentially divisive issues arising from merger were either compromised or avoided. Although merger was a legal and political fact, politics and policy making were approached in terms of political realities that existed in each government prior to the merger.

At some point in the first year of each city's life, however, new issues and problems began to emerge with an accompanying impact upon political alignments and policy making. Cleavages manifested themselves not only according to former city-county divisions but also within former city or county organizations. Conflict generated new political alignments that, on occasion, crossed over former city-county boundaries. A new city-wide approach to politics, policy making, and issues was emerging, and by the end of four years, virtually all of the significant manifestations of former constituencies and governments had dwindled into relative unimportance.

Several forces had a major impact upon politics and policy making. Resolution of the conflicts over policy issues came to be focused in the consolidated city councils, with the net result that the political stature of the councils increased at the expense of that of the constitutional officers. Because of their broad decision-making powers, and because of expanded or new services and programs, the councils had to assume leadership and resolve conflicts. The increasing professionalization of the consolidated cities' administration also affected the formulation of policy and the conduct of politics. With the exception of Virginia Beach, where the Kellam organization subsequently experienced a dramatic internal split between Kellam and City Treasurer V. A. Etheridge, this process operated without any major overturn of elected public officials.

In assessing these changes, one must take into account an additional dimension provided by state political developments in the mid-1960's, particularly in Virginia Beach and Chesapeake. Paramount among these developments were a sharp increase in Republican Party strength, a split in the Democratic Party, and the subsequent decline of the Byrd Organization in power and prestige. The consequences were manifested at the local level although their impact on the local organizations was not uniform. The split in the Kellam organization, for example, seems to have been generated initially by opposing Democratic candidates for one of Virginia's seats in the United States Senate. In the 1966 Democratic primary Kellam supported incumbent Senator A. Willis Robertson, while Treasurer Etheridge served as the local campaign manager for challenger William Spong. Spong's subsequent victory in Virginia Beach and statewide probably served to split the Kellam organization, although the split may not have been complete until the 1968 election for the constitutional officers and council. Upon discovering that he had an opponent for the office of city treasurer who was endorsed by Kellam, Etheridge responded by helping to put together an antiorganization slate of candidates. The results were mixed. Etheridge was reelected by a resounding margin, and an anti-Kellam candidate won the post of Commonwealth's attorney. But Kellam men controlled the city council and won most of the other constitutional offices.

A different situation developed in Newport News and Hampton, perhaps because it occurred during a more tranquil period in Virginia politics. In Newport News the most significant evidence of change came in 1962 when control of council shifted to former Warwick with the defeat of four members of the 1958 council. Smith, Murchison, Bowen, and Christie, all of former Newport News, were defeated in the councilmanic election of that year, while Donald M.

Hyatt, a resident of Warwick and an employee of the Newport News Shipbuilding and Drydock Company, became the consolidated city's second mayor.

The results of the 1962 councilmanic election clearly indicated a shift in power from downtown Newport News to former Warwick. Because of developments in the interim between 1958 and 1962, however, the results of this election should not be cast solely in terms of a power struggle between former Newport News and Warwick. New political forces had been emerging in Warwick led by such persons as Councilman B. E. Rhodes and State Senator Fred Bateman, both of whom, it will be recalled, served as Warwick's representatives on the charter-drafting committee. In addition much of the opposition on both sides of the former boundary line had diminished during the four years of merger since 1958.

The shift of control to former Warwick was probably inevitable. Warwick contained a majority of the population, it was a growth area, and it was the "frontier" of the new city. While business and other interests in downtown Newport News continued to argue for preservation of the core, this was countered by a recitation of problems generated by growth in former Warwick. In part, the results of the 1962 election underscored the pressures generated by growth and development in Warwick rather than connoting an antidowntown sentiment. There was some opinion among Warwick leaders and residents, however, that the former council was perhaps too much oriented toward the downtown area.

The changes that occurred in Hampton's postmerger politics were gradual; yet change did take place. In 1963 there remained remnants of two factions known as the "Old Liners" and the "Jeffersonian Club," both of which existed before merger. With the death of Circuit Court Clerk Stuart Gibson in the mid-1950's, however, political leadership apparently was transferred to the council and other influential men not in the circle of the elected constitutional officers. About 1955 Hampton shook off the vestiges of the district system and the "ghosts" of government in former Elizabeth City County and began to approach politics and issues on a citywide basis.

The manner by which policy issues came to generate cleavages and political realignments in the immediate postmerger period can best be illustrated by the example of Chesapeake's council and its selection of a mayor for the consolidated city in June 1963. In the councilmanic elections held in Chesapeake on June 12, 1963, three incumbent councilmen were casualties, T. Ray Hassell of Butts

Road Borough in former Norfolk County, and Vice Mayor Charles L. Richardson and Councilman Daniel Y. Lindsey, Jr., of South Norfolk Borough. Nomination and election was by boroughs, and the defeat of incumbents Richardson and Lindsey in South Norfolk Borough was of particular significance to the merger. The winning candidates, James W. Overton, Jr., and Edward L. Trotman, had been opposed to merger and were sponsored by the antimerger South Norfolk Betterment League. The *Ledger-Star* interpreted the election as follows:

> In the South Norfolk councilmanic balloting, the election of political newcomers James W. Overton, Jr. and Edward L. Trotman, by a narrow margin, was by its very nature an expression of dissatisfaction with the "ins."
> Since the defeated councilmen, Vice Mayor Charles L. Richardson and Councilman Daniel W. Lindsey, backed the Chesapeake merger it is not unreasonable to assume that some of this was left-over dissatisfaction from previous anti-merger sentiment in South Norfolk.[27]

Nevertheless, both Trotman and Overton made it abundantly clear that they had no intention of scuttling the merger. Both pledged to work hard in the interests of Chesapeake as a whole and were quoted as observing that "the merger is now history."

In any case, Chesapeake had three new councilmen who would take office in September, at which time the charter provided for the selection of the mayor by the council. Although the post of mayor is primarily an honorary one under the council-manager form of government, the selection process became embroiled in other policy considerations. Two of the most visible centered on the proposed route of State Highway 168 and the overspent sanitary districts.

State Route 168 is Chesapeake's main arterial highway and connects the Borough of South Norfolk with the Civic Center at Great Bridge. In 1963 Route 168 was a narrow and twisting road completely unsuitable for heavy traffic; yet, with the location of the city offices at Great Bridge, it was Chesapeake's "main street." To accommodate traffic, a new or rebuilt Route 168 was proposed, the State Department of Highways was willing to schedule the project, and the city was asked to make recommendations regarding the route that the new road would follow.

---

[27] "The Election Tally in Two Cities," *Ledger-Star*, June 13, 1963. See also Lloyd H. Lewis, "Counting of South Norfolk Votes Done with Flourish, Parade," *ibid.*, June 12, 1963.

There were three alternatives. First, an entirely new road could be constructed following a straight line between South Norfolk Borough and Great Bridge. Second, the new road could follow the curves of existing Route 168. Third, the new road could follow a portion of existing Route 168 and then adopt a new straight-line course. Regardless of the route, however, the road was to have four lanes. On March 26, 1963, partly because it did not wish to isolate the business establishments that had grown up along existing Route 168, the council requested that the new road conform to the present route of Highway 168 "as far as current design standards will permit." [28]

On July 11 council decided to reconsider its vote, although the March 26 vote had been unanimous. It was plain that incumbent Mayor Hall wanted the straight-line route. On the other side, Councilman E. P. Wadsworth of Washington Borough, through which Route 168 ran its winding course, wanted to retain the old path. The curves could be straightened, he argued, and the estimated cost would be $180,000 less than the straight road. The straight-route proponents countered by arguing that the reconstructed Route 168 was something that the city was going to live with for a long time. At that point, by a 6–3 vote with Councilman G. A. Treakle of former Norfolk County abstaining, the council reversed its March stand and endorsed the straight-road route. Voting with Wadsworth in favor of the existing road were Councilman Lindsey and Vice Mayor Richardson of South Norfolk Borough.[29] At subsequent public hearings held by the highway department, the rift in council between Mayor Hall and Councilman Wadsworth became even wider.[30]

In August, Mayor Hall apparently incurred the enmity of Councilman Treakle on the matter of overspent Deep Creek Sanitary District No. 2. Hall took the position that sanitary districts were the individual councilman's responsibility and affirmed that he had no intention of voting to appropriate city funds to bail out the overspent sewer district. Rumors circulated that Mayor Hall would not stand for reelection as mayor when the council reorganized in September.[31]

[28] See "Great Bridge Road to Follow Present Curves of Route 168," *ibid.,* March 27, 1963.

[29] "Tongue-Lashing Doesn't Keep Council from 'Straight' OK," *ibid.,* July 12, 1963.

[30] See Joseph V. Phillips, "Va. 168 Routes Hotly Debated," *The Virginian-Pilot,* Aug. 21, 1963, and Lloyd H. Lewis, "Hightway Department Sifting Testimony on Chesapeake Road," *Ledger-Star,* Aug. 21, 1963.

[31] See, for example, Lloyd H. Lewis, "Mayor Hall Mum on Won't Run Talk," *Ledger-Star,* Aug. 9, 1963.

The balance of power in the mayoralty race lay in South Norfolk Borough, and three South Norfolk councilmen wanted the mayoralty removed from former Norfolk County, although none were announced candidates for the post. On the eve of the organization meeting of the new city council, political observers felt that the race for mayor was in doubt. Councilman Treakle of Deep Creek Borough, an announced candidate, apparently could count on four of the 10 council votes. Mayor Hall seemingly had three votes, but all hopes for a majority rested with the three South Norfolk councilmen.[32]

On September 10 Howard McPherson, one of the incumbent South Norfolk councilmen who had been reelected, was chosen to be mayor by a 6–4 vote. He received the support of former Mayor Hall and the two councilmen pledged to support Hall, Hudgins of Butts Road and I. H. Haywood of Western Branch Borough. McPherson's majority was gained by his own vote and that of incumbent councilmen H. S. Boyette and F. T. Allen of South Norfolk Borough. On the losing side were Treakle and Wadsworth, who had wanted to defeat Hall. They were joined by newly elected councilmen Overton and Trotman of South Norfolk. The post of vice mayor went to Haywood of Western Branch by the same 6–4 vote, in conformity with the charter requirement that prohibited electing both the mayor and vice mayor from one of the former governmental units. Mayor McPherson observed for the benefit of the press that: "The first thing we have to do is get a city manager. If we can get a strong one, he alone can deter a lot of problems that would occur. . . . One of the main things we need is harmony among the boroughs. We need to think city wide and not by boroughs."[33]

Actually, neither faction had emerged fully victorious. With the aid of two South Norfolk councilmen, Treakle and Wadsworth had prevailed in preventing Hall from continuing as mayor. Hall, at the same time, had seen his city-wide viewpoint sustained with the election of McPherson. The *Ledger-Star* was encouraged by the outcome:

While it is true that the post of mayor in Chesapeake's city manager system of government is officially only an honorary one, it is a substantial honor. And to the extent that Mr. McPherson's victory signifies a genuine intention to accord the South Norfolk Borough its rightful place in the consolidated sun, it is a healthy thing.

[32] See "Chesapeake Mayor Vote Showdown Set," *ibid.,* Sept. 10, 1963, and Lloyd H. Lewis, "Chesapeake Political Tiff Jells," *ibid.,* Sept. 11, 1963.

[33] "Contractor Catapulted into Chesapeake's Top Job," *ibid.,* Sept. 11, 1963.

At the same time, it is encouraging that the contest and vote for mayor did not finally fall into any hard and fast old-city vs. old-county alignment. (Councilman G. A. Treakle of Deep Creek, McPherson's opponent for mayor, received two of his four votes from South Norfolk Borough councilmen.) [34]

The search for a city manager in Chesapeake to replace Phillip Davis went on until November 1963. At that time, a divided council settled on Lewis Z. Johnston, city manager of Falls Church, Virginia.[35] Johnston's tenure in Chesapeake was to represent a major contribution to the establishment of a city-wide viewpoint, as well as fixing the role of city manager as the chief administrative officer in fact as well as in name.

By way of contrast, in adjacent Virginia Beach during the same period, the politics of outward tranquillity prevailed. Mayor Frank A. Dusch of Virginia Beach Borough was reelected on September 10 by a unanimous vote, while Paul Brown, former chairman of the Princess Anne County board of supervisors, was chosen to be vice mayor, also unanimously.[36] At that time, there was no doubt that Russell Hatchett would continue as city manager.

[34] "The New Mayor of Chesapeake," *ibid.*, Sept. 17, 1963.
[35] See Joseph V. Phillips, "Chesapeake Picks Manager in Discord," *ibid.*, Nov. 13, 1963.
[36] "Dusch Again Beach Mayor," *ibid.*, Sept. 10, 1963.

CHAPTER VII

THE MERGERS IN PERSPECTIVE

Each of the four consolidated cities, as the 1970's begin, has developed a style of politics and administration quite different from that which prevailed at the time of merger. Although an analysis of this political transformation must await a later inquiry, outward appearances in Tidewater suggest that the style of politics at present resembles that of other large Virginia cities much more closely than it did in the early days after merger. Some things, however, do not change. City supervision of 27,000 computerized cow management records in Virginia Beach [1] and the bears of the Dismal Swamp in Chesapeake remind us that the consolidated Tidewater cities will retain certain aspects of uniqueness for some time to come.

On the surface, the Tidewater mergers occurring between 1952 and 1963 constitute the realization of a metropolitan area reformer's dream. In the two Tidewater Standard Metropolitan Statistical Areas, four former counties disappeared completely as governmental units, along with four former cities and one town. By the time the mergers were completed, the number of governments in the two metropolitan areas had been reduced to six cities, one county, and one town, containing in 1970 more than 800,000 people and embracing more than 900 square miles.

As was suggested in the opening chapter, however, from the viewpoint of the traditional metropolitan area reformer the Tidewater mergers probably were undertaken for the wrong reasons and involved the wrong governments. The significant issues of the mergers did not include the overlap or duplication of functions or services, the establishment of uniform levels of service, or any other aspect of economy and efficiency. Little or no concern was given to promoting the unity of the metropolitan area. In fact, none of the

[1] See "A Balanced and Healthy Economy," in "Virginia Beach, 1969, Growth Challenge, A Professional Response, Annual Report of the City of Virginia Beach," supplement to *The Virginian-Pilot,* Jan. 30, 1969. This report is unpaginated and is issued in a newspaper format to the citizens of the city.

traditional reasons offered by reformers on behalf of local government consolidation since 1900 were factors in the Tidewater mergers
except on an incidental basis. And, because three of the four mergers
clearly aimed at confining the core cities to their existing boundaries, they could be said to have involved the wrong governments.

In spite of this, however, the mergers were accomplished. They
were approved by the voters with substantial majorities in each of
the consolidating local governmental units. And, in each case, there
were very good political and economic reasons for approval.

The Environment of Merger

Initially, two questions prompted this inquiry into the Tidewater
mergers. These were (1) why was consolidation an acceptable alternative in Tidewater Virginia when it has usually proved to be unacceptable elsewhere in the United States, and (2) to what extent
and in what ways were the Tidewater mergers sui generis, that is,
unique and therefore not likely to be repeated, the product of a
particular environment at a given point in time.

Several additional questions arose as the study progressed. One
such question was generated by interview responses to the why of
consolidation. Once a particular respondent noted an issue which
triggered the merger attempt, such as annexation or the threat of
annexation, he usually went on to list environmental and political
factors that helped to promote consolidation. The recurring mention of such factors suggested that the success of consolidation was
predicated upon their presence before the merger referendums.
Thus, the acceptability of merger seemed to depend in some way
upon the politics of merger itself.

Interest in the impact of political factors upon local government
reorganization proposals is not recent. In 1962, for example, the
Advisory Commission on Intergovernmental Relations noted four
factors that tended to promote local government reorganization
proposals:

1. a sympathetic and cooperative attitude by state legislators from
the area,

2. the use of locally knowledgeable individuals as staff to conduct
background research and to develop recommendations,

3. the conduct of extensive public hearings by the responsible
plan-preparing group, and

4. careful concern, in the design of the reorganization proposal,

for problems involving representation of various districts and population elements.[2]

At the same time the Advisory Commission observed that there were at least eight unfavorable factors that worked to deter the adoption of local government reorganization proposals, including:

1. absence of a critical situation to be remedied—or of widespread popular recognition of such a situation,

2. vagueness of specification as to some important aspects or implications of the reorganization proposal,

3. active or covert opposition by some leading political figures in the area,

4. discontinuity or lack of vigor in promotion of the reorganization proposal,

5. popular suspicion of the substantial unanimity expressed for the proposal by metropolitan mass media (newspapers, TV, and radio),

6. inability of the proponents to allay popular fear of the effects of the proposed reorganization upon local taxes,

7. failure by the plan proponents to communicate broadly, in a manner which reached relatively unsophisticated voters, and

8. failure by the proponents to anticipate and prepare for late-stage opposition efforts in the referendum campaign.[3]

Even the most cursory examination of the Tidewater mergers reveals the presence of the four favorable factors cited by the commission, even though the issue of representation in Virginia Beach and Chesapeake was more than likely decided on the basis of expediency rather than with "careful concern." However, those who drafted the consolidation agreements and charters were, in fact, concerned with voter acceptability of the proposals, and combining the two former governing bodies was both expedient and realistic.

Of equal importance in understanding the Tidewater mergers was the near absence of the unfavorable factors noted by the Advisory Commission. In fact, the exact opposite of each factor was more characteristic of the Tidewater mergers, with the exception of the fifth point, relating to mass media. The Tidewater merger proposals were not vague; there was near unanimity by political leaders in favor of merger; the proposals were promoted vigorously; assurances were supplied regarding local taxes; and promerger leaders reached

[2] U.S., Advisory Commission on Intergovernmental Relations, *Factors Affecting Voter Reactions to Governmental Reorganization in Metropolitan Areas* (Washington, D.C.: The Author, May 1962), pp. 16–18.

[3] *Ibid.*, pp. 19–23.

all levels of voters and were prepared to cope with late-stage opposition in the referendum campaigns.

Granting the influence of political factors in securing the acceptance of merger, a number of other factors can be identified as contributing to that cause. Which of these factors, and in what combination, were crucial to the end result? For example, it is clear that the threat of annexation by Norfolk was the crisis that initiated the Princess Anne–Virginia Beach merger and that the merger was accomplished through the efforts of the unified Kellam organization. The evidence suggests that both were crucial to the acceptability of merger. The Norfolk annexation threat alone probably would not have generated a merger proposal, nor would the Kellam organization have been able to win acceptance for a merger without the threat of annexation. However, the prospects for merger were also helped along by such events as the "water squabble" with Norfolk, Norfolk's "interference" during the campaign, the assurances given regarding taxes and services, the split in the Byrd Organization over massive resistance, and Sidney Kellam's control of the Tidewater Metropolitan Study Commission. On the surface, then, the why of the Virginia Beach merger was multidimensional. But it is arguable that only two of the variables were crucial to the merger, namely, the threat of annexation and the Kellam organization. Once the issue of annexation had been joined, what really mattered was the ability of the Kellam organization to exploit the water squabble, Norfolk's so-called interference, the Byrd Organization split, and any other factors that would contribute to promoting the promerger cause.

At the same time, there is no way to substantiate the proposition that the threat of annexation by the City of Norfolk plus the Kellam organizaion by themselves would have resulted in the Virginia Beach merger. What confounds the equation, at least as much as anything else, was the curious role that chance seemed to play in the Tidewater mergers. Certain situations and circumstances that eventually contributed to promoting merger were mere products of chance which the promerger leaders were sufficiently astute to exploit whenever they could. For example, all evidence seems to suggest that it was simply luck that transformed the state's merger statutes into general law in the 1960 General Assembly. The amended law was commonly assumed to apply only to the proposed Richmond–Henrico County merger; had the Norfolk and Portsmouth legislators perceived how the law was to be used, they would have opposed it vigorously. Neither the Kellam organization nor the political leaders of Norfolk County could claim credit for enacting this general law that was to make their respective mergers legally possible.

Chance also appeared at the local level. Had Norfolk County not moved the seat of its government from the City of Portsmouth to outlying Great Bridge in the late 1950's, the consolidation with South Norfolk would certainly have been much more difficult. Because South Norfolk's facilities were in no way adequate to house a government the size of Chesapeake's, the new city would have faced the ludicrous situation of having its city hall located inside the corporate limits of Portsmouth. Other examples of chance include the Warwick supermarket fire that dramatized the need for improved cooperative services and the blunder of the Norfolk city council in voting to cut off the water supply to Princess Anne County if merger was approved. Thus, although the mergers were carefully contrived and skillfully developed, there is no doubt that chance, and its timely exploitation, was one of the major contributors to the achievement of consolidation.

What was truly different about the Tidewater mergers, however, was their political nature. The employment of a practical political approach to consolidation by established political leaders was among the principal reasons, if not indeed the prime reason, that merger came to Tidewater. This political approach not only made the mergers, but in terms of the experience with consolidation elsewhere in the nation, it made the mergers unique.

Why Merger Came to Tidewater

To understand why merger came to Tidewater, it is necessary to cite a variety of contributing circumstances and events. Basically, merger resulted from (1) a state and local political environment which was favorable to local government consolidation, (2) the emergence of a crisis which suggested the merger response, (3) the presence of a skillful and unified political leadership which actively promoted and supported merger, and (4) the essentially conservative and pragmatic approach to consolidation adopted by promerger leaders.

Legal and Political Factors

The absence of any significant legal or constitutional barriers to local government consolidation and indeed the broad flexibility granted in the enabling legislation helped materially to promote the Tidewater mergers. Adjustments to take care of local desires were permitted in matters such as councilmanic representation, taxation, and the selection of officers, all of which were critical to achieving merger. Indeed, the enabling legislation was clearly intended to promote merger for the sake of merger; the ways and means of achieving consolidation were left largely to the participating governments to articulate and define.

Second, the idea of local government consolidation was not new to Tidewater. Consolidation had been explored at the local level as early as 1941; many of the advantages, disadvantages, and special problems had been identified; and there had been at least one major attempt prior to the Hampton consolidation in 1952. Although much of the thinking about merger emanated from the Newport News side of Hampton Roads, it was not confined solely to that area. Moreover, before the mergers, the Tidewater governments had successfully initiated limited regional approaches to common problems, which at least suggested the efficacy of large operating units. Of these, the bimetropolitan-area Hampton Roads Sanitation District was probably the most notable, although the Newport News Waterworks Commission also functioned in part on a metropolitan basis.

Third, the presence of the Byrd Organization contributed to merger, although, for the most part, that contribution was indirect. During the period in which the mergers were consummated, the organization controlled state politics, and this fact had several influential consequences. These included an electorate restricted by means of the poll tax and other devices as well as established lines of communication to that electorate, which historically had supported organization positions. Of equal importance was the fact that state and local leaders in the organization were not opposed to local government merger, which helped to make consolidation respectable and even desirable. It was the hallmark of Byrd Organization leaders that they enjoyed the image of being conservative, honest, and dedicated to economy and efficiency in government; at least a segment of this aura was transferred to the mergers. Although the prospective mergers encountered some local opposition, no one ever charged that they were the product of "fuzzy-thinking liberals" or that they were part of an alleged socialistic plot to undermine local government.

The organization also provided a framework for merger discussions and negotiations. The leaders of the several local governments were not isolated each from the other as they might have been in some other state. Although the presence of the organization certainly did not eliminate localism, its members shared common political interests and ideologies. Minimally, the presence of organizational ties worked to assure that bargaining would be in good faith, politically realistic, and undertaken in a serious manner.

Finally, the system of city-county separation operating in conjunction with the Virginia scheme of municipal annexation contributed significantly to the development of a favorable environment for merger. Had the Virginia cities been part of a county, as is the case with all but a handful of cities in other states, the consequences of municipal annexation for county government would have been less far-reaching. Under the Virginia plan of city-county separation, however, municipal annexation totally severs that part of the county which is annexed, including its resident population, from county jurisdiction. As a result, a county government must take into account a lesser population and a diminished tax base with the concomitant effect of these factors on the development of services. Moreover, if a county is to be threatened periodically with annexation by a neighboring city, meaningful long-range planning becomes difficult if not impossible. The economic consequences of annexation are paralleled by political considerations. Annexation alters the political base of elected county officials and, at the least, injects a measure of uncertainty into county politics. An expanding core city threatens county political leaders in such matters as legislative and congressional reapportionment. These combined economic and political stresses emanating from the Virginia system of annexation and city-county separation triggered three of the four merger attempts.

The Emergence of a Crisis

All the Tidewater mergers were, essentially, responses to a crisis situation. In each case, the government that initiated discussions and sought a merger did so in response to a threat to its existence or to the political status quo. This threat was immediate; it was neither remote nor incidental. In three of the four Tidewater consolidations the alternatives consisted of acquiescence to annexation or the promotion of consolidation. Virginia law provides no other alternative. Thus, even though consolidation had been considered in the abstract in Tidewater for more than a decade prior to the Hampton consolidation in 1952, three of the mergers were more closely akin to an emergency action. Had the counties not perceived annexation as a threat and responded to it, it is quite likely that the consolidations would never have been implemented.

Annexation was not a factor in the Newport News–Warwick merger because both governments were cities at the time of consolidation. Instead, depending upon one's perception of the situation in the mid-1950's, the crisis was either economic, racial, or a combination thereof. There was concern among business leaders in former Newport News for its economic future, as well as its gradual physical deterioration. But the most obvious issue appeared to be impending black control. Not only did this prospect generate apprehension among the business community, but it was also an issue that was readily comprehended by the white Newport News voters.

The emergence of a crisis had several implications for the government initiating the merger. Among these, perhaps the most important was a recognized need to make some concessions to its merging partner in the interest of promoting the consolidation. Even in the Virginia Beach merger where Kellam forces controlled most of the offices in both Virginia Beach and Princess Anne County, important concessions were made to the former city in terms of representation, jobs, and services. Both former Virginia Beach and South Norfolk, for example, were vastly overrepresented on the first consolidated city councils in terms of population.

No real counterpart to these crises faced the other former cities and the town that participated in the mergers. The former City of Hampton, for instance, did not have to join the Elizabeth City County–Phoebus merger; yet a realistic appraisal of circumstances clearly indicated that (1) the proposed Elizabeth City County–Phoebus merger would be consummated, (2) as a result, Hampton would be completely surrounded by the new city, and (3) this would have significant economic consequences for Hampton's future development. Business leaders in Hampton recognized that substantial growth and development was occurring in Elizabeth City County and that Hampton, with its small area and resident population, would be unable to compete effectively with the new city. Thus, the reasons for Hampton's decision to join the merger were largely economic, although there was a political community of interest with Elizabeth City County, and there was latent support for the merger anyway. When the city leaders found that Elizabeth City County was prepared to offer concessions, it was decided over some opposition to join the merger.

Somewhat similar circumstances prevailed in South Norfolk, although that city was also facing a budgetary crisis. It was plain that South Norfolk could hope neither to protect itself from the adjoining and aggressive cities of Portsmouth and Norfolk nor to compete with them. Moreover, when it became clear that the City of Norfolk could no longer expand into Princess Anne County because of the impending Princess Anne–Virginia Beach merger, it seemed to be only a matter of time before South Norfolk would be encircled by the cities of Norfolk and Portsmouth. With the prospect of encirclement and a restricted tax base, South Norfolk resolved to merge with larger and more affluent Norfolk County.

Unity of Leadership

Unity of leadership is the third key to understanding the successful promotion of the Tidewater mergers. With the exception of the Newport News–Warwick merger where special conditions existed, the principal incumbent local officers and most of the minor ones were unanimous in their endorsement and promotion of consolidation.[4] Since officials from all the participating governments actively promoted the merger, there was little or no skilled political talent available to the antimerger cause. Only in the Newport News merger, where the antis were led by the able George DeShazor, could a prominent local organization member be identified actively with antimerger sentiment.

Unity of leadership, while perhaps strange to localities in other states, is not especially difficult to understand if one considers the nature, traditions, practice, and experience of the Byrd Organization in Virginia. In achieving unity of leadership local political leaders promoting merger simply acted like most local organizations in the Old Dominion. Even though the salesmanship of consolidation was special in several respects, one of the most intriguing aspects of the Tidewater mergers was the fact that the leaders seemed to treat them much like any other political issue. They simply assumed full responsibility for the promotion of merger, and if novel tactics and strategy were used, they were not evident. The mergers were in the hands of ready-made organizations with established channels of political communication, the same channels that had put the leaders in power in the first place. There was no need to build new organizations for carrying on the referendum campaigns.

[4] For a discussion of leadership in the Nashville–Davidson County, Tennessee, consolidation, see Daniel R. Grant, "Metropolitics and Professional Political Leadership," 353 *Annals* 72–83 (May 1964) .

The organizations that existed could be used, with such special arrangements as the Merger Executive Committee of Virginia Beach and Princess Anne County. In sum, except for the Newport News merger, the consolidations were the work of professional politicians who displayed great inner cohesion, were well organized prior to merger negotiations, and were thoroughly familiar with local politics. Although the Newport News merger might be classified as an amateur undertaking by comparison, the special merger organization led by J. B. Woodward, Jr., was accorded the support of the professionals of former Newport News, while most of the Warwick leadership either chose the course of neutrality or openly endorsed the merger.

Even for Virginia, however, the extent to which unity of leadership was achieved represented a striking accomplishment. Certain pressures helped to encourage cohesion, and a potentially difficult problem was settled when jobs were eliminated as an issue. But the settlement of the job issue alone cannot explain the degree of cohesion. Time after time, local political leaders and public officials alike reiterated that merger was largely a battle for survival against eventual destruction through annexation. Although an outside observer might question whether annexation would indeed have resulted in destruction, this was not the point. The leadership believed that it would, and this contributed both a sense of urgency and a need for unity to meet the impending danger.

The existence of skillful and unified political leadership had several important consequences for the consolidators. First, promerger leaders by virtue of their positions commanded an attentive audience, whatever method was used to reach that audience. At a promerger rally, for example, at least two or more officials would likely be present to explain why merger was both necessary and desirable. Questions raised by citizens could be directed to the responsible public officer or officers, who were able to speak to the question with both knowledge and authority.

Second, because merger was recognized as being a political act, the campaigns were approached as political campaigns. Because they were skillful politicians, promerger leaders were rarely placed on the defensive. They were quick to exploit whatever opportunities arose during the course of the campaigns. All established channels of communication were used, as were a variety of propaganda and propaganda devices. The leaders anticipated questions, and they were aware that the burden of proof for supporting consolidation rested on them. Consequently, they took the initiative in presenting their case to the voters; they did not wait for the voters to come to them. If the promerger leaders ever assumed that the voter instinctively believed merger was a good thing, this assumption was not evident in their campaigning.

Finally, because the campaigns were in the hands of political leaders, consideration was given to such political intangibles as tactics, strategy, and timing. There was consultation on such matters, and in fact, there is evidence to show the mergers were programmed or timetabled in so far as possible. When a decision was made to try for merger, promerger leaders then considered what they wanted and how and when they intended to get there. Indeed, the only serious challenges the promerger leaders had to meet during the campaigns were those which would have upset the timing of the merger attempts. These included such diverse actions as a court suit challenging the constitutionality of consolidation and a general plea that more time was required for study.

A Conservative and Pragmatic Approach

As conceived and promoted, the Tidewater mergers were essentially conservative and pragmatic exercises in politics. The goals of merger were limited and were carefully defined as protection from annexation and/or preservation of the status quo. The leadership was studiously vague about regionalism; their statements simply implied that the prospects for greater metropolitan area-wide cooperation would be improved after merger.

In structuring the proposed consolidations, promerger leaders were guided by three general considerations: (1) merger should work as few outward changes as possible, especially avoiding changes that might alter or modify existing citizen-government relationships; (2) no important community interest or service should be adversely affected by merger; and (3) except in Newport News, no public employee or elected official should suffer loss of employment, a reduction of salary, or loss of retirement or other benefits as a consequence of consolidation.

These three general considerations suggest a broad hypothesis regarding the promotion of city-county consolidation in Tidewater. Merger leaders apparently felt that the chances for promoting merger varied inversely with the number of changes, either real or imagined, that merger might bring. If the changes were few or seemed to be relatively unimportant, the chances for merger improved. Thus, the strategy and tactics of the promergerites aimed at casting the proposed consolidated entity in the same general image as the existing local governments. Similarities would be stressed while changes would be played in low key. In any consolidation some change is inevitable, and the burden ultimately rested on the promergerites to demonstrate that vital community interests would not be affected. The determination of such interests in each locality was a matter for political judgment as exercised by persons who were actively involved in and familiar with the local political scene.

In all the new cities except Newport News, a third aspect of the conservative and pragmatic approach to consolidation involved the allocation of jobs. The merger leaders recognized that jobs might well be crucial to realizing consolidation and agreed early that consolidation would not include the removal of elected or appointed public officials. Those officials who promoted merger did so with every reasonable assurance that consolidation would work no personal political hardship on them.

The practice of arranging to retain incumbent officeholders had a number of advantages for merger. Their retention underscored the point that consolidation was not a revolutionary undertaking. Second, it served to ensure that experienced persons would hold the major policy posts in the consolidated cities. Third, by retaining all officeholders, usually in the principle-deputy arrangement, it was possible to continue a geographic division of labor which followed former city and county lines, a further indication that merger was not revolutionary. Fourth, the practice of bargaining for office helped to ensure that the consolidated governments would be in friendly hands. Because they had formulated the merger, there was no reason for officeholders to make political capital from uncertainties or mistakes that might occur in the process of merger. The merger leaders needed some time to begin the consolidated governments without internal dissension, and the presence of former officeholders in the major policy posts permitted adjustments without unduly disrupting the new governments or magnifying minor shortcomings before the public. Fifth, the precept that no employee should be deprived of his job as a result of consolidation promoted unity of leadership in the referendum campaigns. Had such a working agreement not been evolved before the beginning of the campaigns, a possible schism might have resulted over the distribution of jobs, and excluded officeholders would likely have been a source of serious opposition.

The foregoing represent the principal characteristics of the Tidewater mergers that led to the acceptance of consolidation. That there were particular local circumstances and conditions which also promoted the cause of each merger is easily demonstrable. Nevertheless, the one recurring theme in all the mergers was the primacy of political considerations in all phases of the premerger period. If any lesson emerges, it is that consolidation must be approached in terms of existing political circumstances and realities if there is to be a real chance of winning the support necessary to bring it into being. Or, in the words of the late Stuart M. Gibson, the chief architect of the Hampton consolidation: "The plan of consolidation admittedly gave priority to political expediency and economy where there was conflict with preferred governmental procedure. Its primary purpose was not for the removal of elected, or appointed office-holders, but to effect a merger of governments." [5]

The Consequences for Consolidation

If the Tidewater mergers were largely an exercise in political realism conceived and promoted by political leaders whose orientation was fundamentally conservative and pragmatic, what then were the consequences of this approach to merger? Or, if politics was a vital consideration in winning acceptance for merger, how did this fact influence the subsequent operation of consolidated city government?

Problems confronting all the consolidated cities in the immediate postmerger period stemmed from their physical size, which included both large land areas and low densities of population; from the duties, functions, and responsibilities of corporate existence; from adapting council-manager government to the consolidated entity; and from blending two formerly distinct governmental units. These difficulties had several consequences for consolidated city government.

First, planning and transitional arrangements by public officials helped to alleviate many potential difficulties, although certain problems could not be solved and other difficulties were unforeseen. Second, all the difficulties were interrelated to some extent. Problems of corporate existence, for example, were related to the sprawling semiurban nature of the consolidated cities. There is no

[5] Gibson, "The Tale of Two Cities," 6 *Virginia and the Virginia County* 7 ff. (Oct. 1952).

real solution to size per se; rather it is a factor that must be taken into account in the operation of a merged government.

Consolidated city government has two basic objectives. The first, common to local government in Virginia, entails the responsibility to provide services and to fulfill statutory and constitutional assignments. The second objective involves the responsibility of the merged city to provide the framework for an orderly and reasonable development of the area under its jurisdiction. Regardless of the circumstances leading to merger, these additional responsibilities were incumbent upon the new cities. These were not, however, the primary objectives of the proconsolidation forces. With the exception of the Newport News–Warwick merger, the consolidations were clearly intended to preserve what existed rather than undergo piecemeal annexation by the core cities of the metropolitan areas.

Paradoxically, the reasons, processes, and arrangements that worked to promote merger also deterred the implementation of consolidated city government. In one way or another, political realism, including a conservative and pragmatic approach to merger, returned to haunt the promergerites under consolidated city government. In drawing up their agreements and charters and in working out the details of government, the consolidationists were motivated as much by status quo considerations as by problems of future adjustments necessitated by growth and development. Since they had no intention of upsetting existing political arrangements, they tended to view the consolidation agreements and charters as perpetual contracts. Adjustments to change, under such circumstances, were simply made more difficult by the status quo orientation of merger.

Except perhaps for Newport News, none of the cities were adequately prepared for the responsibilities of consolidated government in the immediate postmerger period. Merger and incorporation did little more than place an additional burden upon already strained resources, and most of the efforts of the merged cities had to be directed toward meeting immediate service needs. With limited resources, large areas, and low population densities, the new cities were unable to provide city-wide services even if they had wanted to.

When the status quo attitude was confronted with area growth and development, a political schism resulted, at least temporarily, in each of the merged cities. Although it cannot be claimed that city-wide progressives won a decided victory, the hard-line status quo position was in fact subsequently abandoned by most political leaders. The political cost in terms of unity of leadership was significant, however, and a certain disunity prevailed until a new working consensus was formed on a consolidated city political base. But the long-range impact of consolidation upon the politics and government of a particular city is, more properly, the subject of another study. The evidence at present suggests only that political change was necessitated by merger, that the process was complex, and that it was incremental in nature. In the immediate postmerger period, political adjustments represented a balance between a recognized need for change and a need to maintain some semblance of unity.

The Tidewater mergers, then, underscore the importance of the political side of merger. A hard assessment of what was politically possible in the premerger period, an ordering of priorities in which practical political considerations were at least coequal with good government objectives, the skillful exploitation of a crisis, and authoritative reassurances to the voter that merger would make few changes in his relationship to government constituted the realpolitik of the Tidewater mergers. But the realpolitik of consolidation had consequences for the transition and for the conduct of government once merger had to be implemented.

In balance, however, the developments of the immediate postmerger period should in no way detract from the achievement of promerger leaders. Quite clearly, certain of the problems encountered by the consolidated governments would have had to be faced by the former governments had no merger taken place. And although some might argue that the normal annexation procedure by the core cities would have been a preferable solution, there is no conclusive evidence that the metropolitan areas would somehow be better governed or administered than is now the case.

Appendixes

Bibliography

Index

CONSOLIDATION AGREEMENT FOR THE CITY OF VIRGINIA BEACH AND PRINCESS ANNE COUNTY, VIRGINIA

I. Names of City and County Proposing to Consolidate

The names of the city and county proposing to consolidate are City of Virginia Beach and Princess Anne County.

II. Name of Consolidated City

The name of the city into which it is proposed to consolidate is City of Virginia Beach.

III. Property and Value

The property, real and personal, belonging to the City of Virginia Beach and Princess Anne County and the fair value thereof in current money of the United States is as follows:

	City of Virginia Beach	County Princess Anne
Real Estate	$2,719,590	$20,522,046
Personal Property	3,168,550	1,740,450
Total	$5,888,140	$22,262,496

IV. Indebtedness of Units

The indebtedness, bonded and otherwise, of the City of Virginia Beach and Princess Anne County is as follows:

	City of Virginia Beach	Princess Anne County
General Bonded Debt	$3,053,000.00	$7,413,924.80
North Virginia Beach Sanitary District	——————	34,000.00
Kempsville and Bayside Magisterial Districts	——————	443,562.00

From the legal advertisement in *The Virginian-Pilot*, Nov. 16, 1961.

	City of Virginia Beach	Princess Anne County
Pungo Magisterial District	—————	48,000.00
Total	$3,053,000.00	$7,939,486.80

(Figures do not include interest in future years.)

V. Source of Valuations and Debts

The above valuations were established by the City of Virginia Beach for property and indebtedness of the city and by Princess Anne County for property and indebtedness of the county, and such valuations are accepted by the city and county solely for the purposes of this agreement.

VI. Effective Date

Subject to the outcome of the referendum provided for in paragraph VII hereof and subject to approval by the General Assembly of Virginia of an amended charter for the City of Virginia Beach as hereinafter provided, the consolidation shall become effective on January 1, 1963.

VII. Referendum

1. As soon as practicable following the execution hereof, the governing bodies of the City of Virginia Beach and Princess Anne County shall file with one of the judges of the Circuit Court of Princess Anne County the original of this consolidation agreement, together with a petition on behalf of such governing bodies, signed by the chairman and clerk of each such bodies, asking that a referendum on the question of the consolidation herein provided for be ordered to be held at a special election within the city and the county pursuant to Article 4, Chapter 9, of Title 15 of the Code of Virginia of 1950, as amended, on January 4, 1962, or on such other date as may be fixed by the Court. Thereafter, the governing bodies of the city and county shall cause a copy of this consolidation agreement to be printed at least once a week for four successive weeks in some newspaper having a general circulation in the city and county.

2. If this consolidation receives an affirmative vote by a majority of the qualified voters in the referendum in the City of Virginia Beach and a majority of the qualified voters voting in the referen-

dum in Princess Anne County, then governing bodies of the City of Virginia Beach and Princess Anne County shall submit an amended charter for the City of Virginia Beach in substantially the form annexed hereto to the 1962 session of the General Assembly of Virginia and shall urge its adoption. Such governing bodies shall have authority to agree to such revisions in the charter that may be proposed by the General Assembly.

VIII. Disposition of Property and Assumption of Debts

1. Upon the effective date of consolidation all property, real and personal, of Princess Anne County, including any sanitary districts therein, shall become the property of the City of Virginia Beach, and any and all indebtedness and other obligations of the county, including all magisterial and sanitary districts therein, shall be assumed by the City of Virginia Beach.

2. The areas comprising the City of Virginia Beach, Princess Anne County, North Virginia Beach Sanitary District, and Bayside, Kempsville and Pungo Magisterial Districts on the effective date of consolidation shall be continued in effect as special taxing districts for a period of not more than 20 years for the purpose of repaying any indebtedness chargeable to such areas. The council of the consolidated City of Virginia Beach shall levy a special tax on real property within such districts in such amount as may be necessary to repay such indebtedness, to the end that all indebtedness existing on the effective date of consolidation shall be repaid by the area creating the indebtedness.

3. From the date of this agreement until the effective date of consolidation neither the present City of Virginia Beach nor Princess Anne County, or any magisterial or sanitary district therein, shall issue any bonds which shall not mature on or before 20 years after the effective date of consolidation, unless the issuance of such bonds shall have been approved by the Council of the present City of Virginia Beach and by the Board of Supervisors of Princess Anne County.

IX. Boroughs and Elections

1. The present City of Virginia Beach and the six present magisterial districts of Princess Anne County shall become boroughs of the consolidated City of Virginia Beach which shall be known by the following names, i.e., Virginia Beach, Bayside, Blackwater,

Kempsville, Lynnhaven, Princess Anne (formerly known as Seaboard) and Pungo, respectively.

2. The council shall consist of eleven members, five to be elected from the borough of Virginia Beach and one from each of the other six boroughs. At such time as may be determined by the affirmative vote of seven councilmen, which shall not be earlier than five years after the effective date of consolidation but not later than September 1, 1971, the council shall submit to the qualified voters of the city a new plan for election of councilmen.

3. The initial council shall consist of five members of the council of the City of Virginia Beach and the six members of the Board of Supervisors of Princess Anne County in office on the effective date of consolidation who shall hold office until beginning of the terms of their successors. Councilmen in each borough shall be elected in the same manner and for the same terms as councilmen or supervisors were elected in such borough immediately preceding the effective date of consolidation; provided, however, that the three councilmen of the present City of Virginia Beach elected in June 1962 shall serve until September 1, 1967. Two councilmen from the Borough of Virginia Beach shall be elected in June 1964 and shall serve until September 1, 1967. All other councilmen shall be elected in June 1963 and shall serve until September 1, 1967. Beginning in 1967 all councilmen shall be elected on the second Tuesday in June for terms of four years and shall take office on the first day of September following their election.

X. Constitutional Officers

1. Upon the effective date of consolidation the constitutional officers of the city and the county shall continue in office for the full terms to which they were elected.

2. The sheriff of Princess Anne County and the present City of Virginia Beach shall continue to perform the same duties during the remainder of the term to which he was elected. From and after January 1, 1964, the consolidated City of Virginia Beach shall have a sergeant who shall be elected in lieu of a sheriff. No election shall be held in the present City of Virginia Beach to elect a sergeant for the term beginning January 1, 1963, but the sergeant of the present city of Virginia Beach shall become the high constable of the consolidated City of Virginia Beach and shall serve at the pleasure of the council. He shall perform such of the duties now performed by the sergeant of the present City of Virginia Beach and such other duties as the council may prescribe.

3. The treasurer and the commissioner of revenue for the consolidated city shall be determined by agreement between those persons holding such respective offices. In the event that no agreement is reached before the effective date of consolidation, the Circuit Court of Princess Anne County shall designate one officer as principal and the other as deputy.

4. The salaries of the constitutional officers shall not be diminished during the remainder of the terms to which they were elected.

XI. Municipal Seat of Government

The municipal seat of government shall be located at the present county seat of Princess Anne. Offices for municipal services shall be maintained at the city hall in the present City of Virginia Beach for the convenience of citizens.

XII. Higher Taxes for Additional Services

The council of the City of Virginia Beach shall have power to levy a higher tax in such areas of the city as desire additional or more complete services of government than are desired in the city as a whole, provided that such higher tax shall not be levied for school, police or general government services but only for those services which prior to consolidation were not offered in the whole of the city and the county. The proceeds of such tax shall be segregated and expended in the areas in which collected.

XIII. Preparation of 1962–63 Budgets

1. The city and the county shall prepare and adopt separate budgets for the fiscal year July 1, 1962–June 30, 1963, in accordance with present practices on the assumption that each would operate independently for the entire fiscal year. Before January 1, 1963, the city and county budgets shall be consolidated into a single budget under which the consolidated City of Virginia Beach shall operate from January 1 through June 30, 1963.

2. All funds from the issue of bonds by the city or the county, the use of which is restricted by the terms thereof, shall be set aside in a special fund for disposition in accordance with such requirements.

XIV. Personnel Pay and Retirement Benefits

1. In order to carry on an efficient administration, the City of Virginia Beach will need the experience and skills of the employees

of both the city and the county. Therefore, it is agreed that the city will adhere to the principle that all employees of the two governmental units will be retained and will be compensated at no lower rate of pay than they received at the effective date of consolidation and that they will occupy positions as comparable as practicable to those occupied at the time of consolidation.

2. The obligation of the present City of Virginia Beach under its existing pension plan for the police and fire departments on the effective date of consolidation shall become the indebtedness and obligation of the consolidated City of Virginia Beach. The consolidation agreement shall be deemed an agreement between the consolidated City of Virginia Beach and the employees and retired employees having vested rights covered by such pension plan on the date of consolidation to the end that the rights and equities of employees and retired employees under such pension plan shall not be diminished, curtailed or impaired in any way. From and after the effective date of consolidation such pension plan shall be continued in effect for the exclusive benefit of such employees and retired employees having vested rights thereunder and for no others.

3. All other employees and retired employees of the present City of Virginia Beach and all employees and retired employees of Princess Anne County having vested rights under any retirement plan of the city or county on the effective date of consolidation shall continue to be covered by such plan. The consolidation agreement shall be deemed an agreement between the consolidated City of Virginia Beach and such employees and retired employees that in the event that the consolidated City of Virginia Beach shall combine, consolidate or amend any such retirement plan, such action shall not in any way diminish, curtail or impair the vested rights of any such employee or retired employee.

XV. Schools

For the safety and welfare of the school children the school board of the City of Virginia Beach shall continue substantially the school bus service formerly maintained in Princess Anne County, unless in the opinion of the school board, considering various factors including increased density of population, availability of school facilities, changes in traffic patterns and availability of public transportation, such services or part thereof should be altered or discontinued.

In witness whereof, the Council of the City of Virginia Beach and the Board of Supervisors of Princess Anne County have entered into this consolidation agreement and the city and county have caused this consolidation agreement to be executed in their respective names and their respective seals to be hereunto affixed and attested by their respective officers thereunto duly authorized.

CITY OF VIRGINIA BEACH
By: /S/ FRANK A. DUSCH, *Mayor*
Attest: /S/ LEWIS E. SMITH, *Clerk*
(Seal)

PRINCESS ANNE COUNTY
By: /S/ S. PAUL BROWN, *Chairman,*
Board of Supervisors
Attest: /S/ JOHN V. FENTRESS, *Clerk*
(Seal)

CHARTER OF THE CONSOLIDATED CITY OF VIRGINIA BEACH

Chapter 147 of the Acts of the 1962 General Assembly

An Act to effectuate the consolidation of Princess Anne County and the city of Virginia Beach, a city of the second class, into the city of Virginia Beach, a city of the first class; and to this end to validate, ratify and confirm the consolidation agreement between Princess Anne County and the city of Virginia Beach; to provide a charter for the new city of Virginia Beach, and to repeal Chapter 33 of the Acts of Assembly of 1952, approved February 14, 1952, which incorporated the city of Virginia Beach, and all amendments thereto.

Approved February 28, 1962

Be it enacted by the General Assembly of Virginia:

1. The consolidation of the city of Virginia Beach and Princess Anne County into the consolidated city of Virginia Beach, a city of the first class, as provided in the consolidation agreement to which reference is hereby made and which is made part hereof, is hereby validated, ratified and confirmed in all respects and such consolidation shall be effective on and after January one, nineteen hundred sixty-three.

2. Chapter 33 of the Acts of Assembly of 1952 and all amendments thereto, which is entitled "An act to incorporate the city of Virginia Beach; and to repeal Chapter 76 of the Acts of Assembly 1906, approved March 6, 1906, which incorporated the town of Virginia Beach, and all amendments thereto," approved February 14, 1952, is repealed as of the first moment of January one, nineteen hundred sixty-three.

3. *Be it further enacted by* the General Assembly of Virginia:

Chapter 1

Incorporation and Boundaries

§ 1.01. Incorporation. The inhabitants of the territory comprised within the limits of the City of Virginia Beach, as they are or hereafter may be established by law, shall continue to be a body politic and corporate under the name of the City of Virginia Beach and as such shall have perpetual succession, may sue and be sued, contract and be contracted with and may have a corporate seal which it may alter at its pleasure. The inhabitants of the territory comprised within the limits of Princess Anne County as it exists at the effective date of this charter shall also be a part of such body politic and corporate.

§ 1.02. Boundaries. The boundaries of the City of Virginia Beach shall coincide with the outside boundaries of Princess Anne County so as to include all of the territory comprising Princess Anne County and the City of Virginia Beach as existing immediately preceding the effective date of this charter.

Chapter 2

Powers

§ 2.01 General Grant of Powers. The powers set forth in §§ 15–77.1 through 15–77.70 of the Code of Virginia as in force on January 1, 1962, are hereby conferred on and vested in the City of Virginia Beach.

§ 2.02 Additional Powers. Without limiting the generality of the foregoing, but in addition thereto, the City of Virginia Beach shall have the following additional powers:

(a) To spend not exceeding five per cent of its annual revenue from all sources in advertisement of and giving publicity to its resources and advantages.

(b) To levy a higher tax in such areas of the City of Virginia Beach as desire additional or more complete services of government than are desired in the city as a whole, provided that such higher tax rate shall not be levied for school, police or general government services but only for those services which prior to the effective date of this charter were not offered in all the territory within the boundaries of the city and provided further that the proceeds from such higher tax rate shall be so segregated as to enable the same to be expended in the areas in which raised.

(c) To levy a special tax on real property in any borough, sanitary district or other special taxing district or combination thereof, for a period of not exceeding 20 years, which may be different from and in addition to the general tax rate throughout the city, for the purpose of repaying indebtedness existing on the effective date of this charter and chargeable to such borough, sanitary district or other special taxing district or combination thereof.

(d) To exercise all powers possessed by the City of Virginia Beach and Princess Anne County immediately preceding the effective date of this charter, consistent with general law and not inconsistent with this charter; provided, however, that except as otherwise specifically provided in this charter, all laws heretofore applicable to Virginia Beach or Princess Anne County, respectively, shall continue to apply to the areas theretofore comprising such political subdivisions, now incorporated under this charter as a single such subdivision, until otherwise provided by law.

Chapter 3

City Council

§ 3.01. Composition. The city shall be divided into seven boroughs. One of such boroughs shall comprise the City of Virginia Beach as existing immediately preceding the effective date of this charter and shall be known as the borough of Virginia Beach, and the remaining six boroughs shall comprise the six magisterial districts of Princess Anne County as existing immediately preceding the effective date of this charter and shall be known as the boroughs of Bayside, Blackwater, Kempsville, Lynnhaven, Princess Anne (formerly known as Seaboard) and Pungo. The council shall consist of eleven members, five of whom shall be elected by and from the borough of Virginia Beach and one by and from each of the other six boroughs. The five members of the council of the City of Virginia Beach and the six members of the Board of Supervisors of Princess Anne County holding office immediately preceding the effective date of this charter shall constitute the council of the city and shall hold office until the beginning of the terms of their successors. At such time as may be determined by the affirmative vote of seven councilmen, which shall not be earlier than five years after the effective date of this charter but not later than September 1,

1971, the council shall submit to the qualified voters of the city a new plan for election of councilmen.

§ 3.02. Election of Councilmen. Councilmen in each borough shall be elected in the same manner and for the same terms as councilmen or supervisors were elected in such borough immediately preceding the effective date of this charter; provided, however, that the three councilmen of the present City of Virginia Beach elected in June 1962 shall serve until September 1, 1967. Two councilmen from the borough of Virginia Beach shall be elected in June 1964 and shall serve until September 1, 1967. All other councilmen shall be elected in June 1963, and shall serve until September 1, 1967. Beginning in 1967 all councilmen shall be elected on the second Tuesday in June for terms of four years and shall take office on the first day of September following their election.

§ 3.03. Filling Vacancies. Vacancies in the office of councilmen, from whatever cause arising, shall be filled within 60 days for the unexpired portion of the term by a majority vote of the remaining members of the council, provided that so long as any councilmen are elected by and from wards or boroughs the vacancy shall be filled by a qualified voter residing in the same ward or borough.

§ 3.04. Compensation. Councilmen shall receive as compensation for their services such amounts as the council may determine, not to exceed $200 per month for councilmen and $250 per month for the mayor. No member of the council shall be appointed to any office of profit under the city government during the term for which elected and for one year thereafter.

§ 3.05. Powers. All powers vested in the city shall be exercised by the council except as otherwise provided in this charter. In addition to the foregoing, the council shall have the following powers:

(a) To provide for the organization, conduct and operation of all departments, bureaus, divisions, boards, commissions, offices and agencies of the city.

(b) To create, alter or abolish departments, bureaus, divisions, boards, commissions, offices and agencies other than those specifically established by this charter.

(c) To create, alter or abolish and to assign and reassign to departments, all bureaus, divisions, offices and agencies except where such bureaus, divisions, offices or agencies are specifically assigned by this charter.

(d) To provide for the number, titles, qualifications, powers, duties and compensation of all officers and employees of the city.

(c) To provide for the form of oaths and the amount and condition of surety bonds to be required of certain officers and employees of the City.

(f) To provide for the submission of any proposed ordinance to the qualified voters of the city at an advisory referendum to be initiated by a resolution to the circuit court of the city and held not less than 30 nor more than 60 days thereafter in the manner provided by law for general elections.

§ 3.06. Procedural Powers. The council shall have power, subject to the provisions of this charter, to adopt its own rules of procedure. Such rules shall provide for the time and place of holding regular meetings of the council which shall be not less frequent than once each month. They shall also provide for the calling of special meetings by the mayor or any three members of the council and shall prescribe the methods of giving notice thereof. A majority of the council shall constitute a quorum for the transaction of business. No ordinance, resolution, motion or vote, other than motions to adjourn, to fix the time and place of adjournment and other motions of a purely procedural nature, shall be adopted by the council except at a meeting open to the public.

§ 3.07. Mayor. At its first regular meeting of the term the council shall choose by majority vote of all the members thereof one of its members to be mayor and one to be vice-mayor. Until such time as the representation on the council is changed as provided in § 3.01, one of such officers shall be a councilman elected by and from the borough of Virginia Beach and the other shall be a councilman elected by and from one of the other boroughs. The mayor shall preside over the meetings of the council, shall act as head of the city government for ceremonial purposes and shall have such other rights and duties as the council may prescribe, in addition to all the rights and privileges of councilmen of the city. The vice-mayor shall perform the duties of mayor in the absence or disability of the mayor.

§ 3.08. City Clerk. The council shall appoint a city clerk who shall serve at the pleasure of the council. He shall be clerk of the council and custodian of the corporate seal of the city and he shall have such further duties as the council may prescribe.

Chapter 4

City Manager

§ 4.01. Appointment and Qualifications. The council shall appoint a city manager who shall be the executive and administrative head of the city government. He shall be chosen solely on the basis of his executive and administrative qualifications and shall serve at the pleasure of the council.

§ 4.02. Powers and Duties. The city manager shall have the power and it shall be his duty:

(a) To appoint all officers and employees of the city and to remove such officers and employees, except as he may delegate such power to appoint and remove to his subordinates and except as otherwise provided in this charter.

(b) To perform such other duties and to exercise such other powers as may be imposed or conferred upon him by the council.

§ 4.03. Council Not to Interfere in Appointments or Removals. Neither the council nor any of its members shall direct the appointment of any person to or his removal from any office or employment by the city manager or by his subordinates.

Chapter 5

Budget

§ 5.01. Fiscal Year. The fiscal year of the city shall be established by ordinance and shall also constitute the tax year and the budget and accounting year.

§ 5.02. Submission of Budget. The city manager shall submit to the council a budget and a budget message at least 90 days prior to the beginning of each budget year.

§ 5.03. Preparation of Budget. It shall be the duty of the head of each department, the judges of the courts not of record, each board or commission, including the school board, and each other office or agency supported in whole or in part by the city, to file at such time as the city manager may prescribe estimates of revenue and expenditure for that department, court, board, commission, office or agency for the ensuing fiscal year: The city manager shall hold such hearings as he may deem advisable and shall review the estimates and other data pertinent to the preparation of the budget and make such revisions in such estimates as he may deem proper, subject to the laws of the Commonwealth relating to obligatory expenditures for any purpose, except that in the case of the school board he may recommend a revision only in its total estimated expenditure. The budget shall be prepared in accordance with accepted principles of municipal accounting and budgetary procedures and techniques.

§ 5.04. Balanced Budget. In no event shall the expenditures

recommended by the city manager in the budget exceed the receipts estimated, taking into account the estimated cash surplus or deficit at the end of the current fiscal year, unless the city manager shall recommend an increase in the rate of ad valorem taxes on real estate and tangible personal property or other new or increased taxes or licenses within the power of the city to levy and collect in the ensuing fiscal year the receipts from which estimated on the basis of the average experience with the same or similar taxes during the three tax years last past, will make up the difference. If estimated receipts exceed estimated expenditures the city manager may recommend revisions in the tax and license ordinances of the city in order to bring the budget into balance.

§ 5.05. Budget Message. The budget message shall contain the recommendations of the city manager concerning the fiscal policy of the city, a description of the important features of the budget and an explanation of all significant changes in the budget as to estimated receipts and recommended expenditures as compared with the current and last preceding fiscal years.

§ 5.06. Appropriation and Additional Tax Ordinances. At the same time that he submits the budget the city manager shall introduce and recommend to the council an appropriation ordinance which shall be based on the budget. He shall also introduce at the same time any ordinances levying a new tax or altering the rate on any existing tax necessary to balance the budget as provided in § 5.04.

§ 5.07. Public Hearing. The council shall hold a public hearing on the budget as submitted, at which all interested persons shall be given an opportunity to be heard. The council shall cause to be published a notice of the time and place of the hearing not less than seven days prior to the date of the hearing.

§ 5.08. Adoption of Budget. After the public hearing the council may make such changes in the budget as it may determine, except that no item of expenditure for debt service shall be reduced or omitted. The budget shall be adopted by the vote of at least a majority of all members of the council not later than 30 days prior to the end of the current fiscal year. Should the council take no action prior to such day, the budget shall be deemed to have been finally adopted as submitted. In no event shall the council adopt a budget in which the estimated total of expenditures exceeds receipts, unless at the same time it adopts measures to provide additional revenue estimated to be sufficient to make up the difference.

§ 5.09. Additional Appropriations. Appropriations in addition to those contained in the general appropriation ordinance may be made by the council only if there is available in the general fund an unencumbered and unappropriated sum sufficient to meet such appropriations.

Chapter 6

Borrowing

§ 6.01. Borrowing Power. The council may, in the name of and for the use of the city, incur indebtedness by issuing its negotiable bonds or notes for the purposes, in the manner and to the extent provided in this chapter.

§6.02. Purposes for Which Bonds or Notes May Be Issued. Bonds or notes of the city may be issued for the following purposes:

(a) To finance capital projects.—Bonds, and notes in anticipation of bonds when the issue of bonds has been authorized as hereinafter provided, may be issued for the purpose of financing the whole or any part of the cost of any capital improvement project.

(b) To anticipate the collection of revenue.—Notes may be issued, when authorized by the council, at any time during the fiscal year in anticipation of the collection of revenue of such year.

(c) To refund outstanding bonds.—Bonds may be issued for the purpose of refunding existing bonds, provided that the director of finance shall certify in writing that such refunding is necessary to prevent default on the interest or principal of the city's outstanding bonds or in the case of callable bonds to secure a lower rate of interest.

§ 6.03. Limitations on Indebtedness. In the issuance of bonds and notes the city shall be subject to the limitations as to amount contained in Section 127 of the Constitution.

§ 6.04. Form of Bonds. Bonds and notes of the city shall be issued in the manner provided by general law.

§ 6.05. Authority for Issuance of Bonds. No bonds of the city shall be issued until their issuance shall have been authorized by a majority of the qualified voters of the city voting at an election held for the purpose and in the manner provided by general law; provided, however, that the council may issue bonds in an amount not exceeding $500,000 in any calendar year or notes in anticipation of the collection of revenue without submitting the question of their issuance to the qualified voters.

§ 6.06. Payment of Bonds and Notes. The power and obligation of the city to pay any and all bonds and notes issued pursuant to this charter, except revenue bonds made payable solely from revenue producing properties, shall be unlimited and the city shall levy ad valorem taxes upon all taxable property within the city for the payment of such bonds or notes and the interest thereon, without limitation as to rate or amount. The full faith and credit of the city are hereby pledged for the payment of the principal of and interest on all bonds and notes of the City of Virginia Beach and of Princess Anne County and any sanitary districts therein issued and outstanding on the effective date of this charter, and of the city hereafter issued pursuant to this chapter, except revenue bonds made payable solely from revenue producing properties, whether or not such pledge be stated in the bonds or notes or in the bond ordinance authorizing their issuance.

Chapter 7

Administrative Departments

§ 7.01. Creation of Departments. The following administrative departments are hereby created:
    (a) Department of Finance
    (b) Department of Law
    (c) Department of Public Safety
    (d) Department of Public Works
    (e) Department of Public Utilities
    (f) Department of Public Health
    (g) Department of Public Welfare
    (h) Department of Farm and Home Demonstration
    (i) Department of Education
    (j) Department of Parks and Recreation
    (k) Department of Personnel
The council may create new departments or subdivisions thereof, combine or abolish existing departments and distribute the functions thereof or establish temporary departments for special work; provided, however, that the council shall not have the power to abolish, transfer or combine the functions of the departments of finance, law and education.

§ 7.02. Department Heads. There shall be a director at the head of each department, and the same person may be the director of several departments. The director of each department, except the departments of law and education, shall be appointed by the city manager and may be removed by him at any time; provided, however, that the council may provide that the city manager shall be director of one or more departments. The director of each department shall be chosen on the basis of his general executive and administrative ability and experience and of his education, training and experience in the class of work which he is to administer.

§ 7.03. Responsible to City Manager. The directors of each department, except the departments of law and education, shall be immediately responsible to the city manager for the administration of their respective departments, and their advice may be required by him on all matters affecting their departments. They shall make reports and recommendations concerning their departments to the city manager under such rules and regulations as he may prescribe.

Chapter 8

Financial Administration

§ 8.01. Department of Finance. The department of finance shall consist of a director of finance, a comptroller or accounting officer, the city treasurer and the commissioner of revenue and their respective offices, insofar as inclusion of these offices is not inconsistent with the Constitution and general laws of the Commonwealth of Virginia, and such other officers and employees organized into such bureaus, divisions and other units as may be provided by the council or by the orders of the director consistent therewith.

§ 8.02. Director of Finance. The head of the department of finance shall be the director of finance who may also be the city manager. He shall be a person skilled in municipal accounting and financial control. He shall have charge of the financial affairs of the city, including such powers and duties as may be assigned by the council not inconsistent with the Constitution and general laws of the Commonwealth of Virginia.

§ 8.03. City Treasurer. The city treasurer shall be the custodian of all public monies of the city and shall have such powers and duties as are provided by general law. He shall perform such other duties as may be assigned by the director of finance or the council not inconsistent with the laws of the Commonwealth.

§8.04. Commissioner of Revenue. The commissioner of revenue

shall perform such duties not inconsistent with the laws of the Commonwealth in relation to the assessment of property and licenses as may be assigned by the director of finance or the council.

§ 8.05. Division of Purchasing. There shall be a division of purchasing which shall be in charge of purchasing all supplies of the city. The head of the division of purchasing shall be the purchasing agent who shall have such duties as may be assigned by the council.

§ 8.06. Annual Audit. The council shall cause to be made an independent audit of the city's finances at the end of each fiscal year by the auditor of public accounts of the Commonwealth or by a firm of independent certified public accountants to be selected by the council. One copy of the report of such audit shall be always available for public inspection in the office of the city clerk during regular business hours.

Chapter 9

Department of Law

§ 9.01. Department of Law. The department of law shall consist of the city attorney and such assistant city attorneys and other employees as may be provided by the council.

§ 9.02. City Attorney. The head of the department of law shall be the city attorney. He shall be an attorney at law licensed to practice law in the Commonwealth of Virginia. He shall be appointed by the council and shall serve at its pleasure.

§ 9.03. Powers and Duties. The city attorney shall be the chief legal advisor of the council, the city manager and of all departments, boards, commissions and agencies of the city in all matters affecting the interests of the city. He shall have such powers and duties as may be assigned by the council.

§ 9.04. Restrictions on Actions for Damages Against City. No action shall be maintained against the city for injury or damage to any person or property or for wrongful death alleged to have been sustained by reason of the negligence of the city or of any officer, employee or agent thereof, unless a written statement by the claimant, his agent, attorney or representative, of the nature of the claim and of the time and place at which the injury is alleged to have occurred or been received shall have been filed with the city attorney within sixty days after such cause of action shall have accrued, except that when the claimant is an infant or non compos mentis, or the injured person dies within such 60 days, such statement may be filed within 120 days. Neither the city attorney nor any other officer, employee or agent of the city shall have authority to waive the foregoing conditions precedent or any of them.

Chapter 10

Department of Public Safety

§ 10.01. Department of Public Safety. The department of public safety shall include the bureaus of police and fire protection and may include such other bureaus, divisions and units and have such powers and duties as may be provided or assigned by the council or by the director consistent therewith. The council may continue the Police and Trial Board as authorized for Princess Anne County by Acts of 1954, Chapter 101, as amended by Acts 1960, Chapter 44.

§ 10.02. Director of Public Safety. The head of the department of public safety shall be the director of public safety. He shall have general management and control of the several bureaus, divisions and other units of the department.

§ 10.03. Bureau of Police. The bureau of police shall consist of a chief of police, who may be the director of public safety, and such other officers and employees as may be provided by the council or by the orders of the director of public safety. The bureau of police shall be responsible for preservation of the public peace, protection of the rights of persons and property and enforcement of laws of the Commonwealth and ordinances of the city. The chief of police and the other members of the police force shall have all the powers and duties of police officers as provided by general law.

§ 10.04. Bureau of Fire Protection. The bureau of fire protection shall consist of the fire chief and such other officers and employees as may be provided by the council or by the orders of the director consistent therewith. The bureau of fire protection shall be responsible for the protection from fire of life and property within the city.

Chapter 11

Department of Public Works

§ 11.01. Department of Public Works. The department of public works shall consist of the director of public works and such other officers and employees organized into such bureaus, divisions and other units as may be provided by the council or by the orders of the director consistent therewith.

§ 11.02. Functions. The department of public works shall be responsible for the construction and maintenance of all public buildings, streets, roads, bridges and drains, for garbage and refuse collection and disposal and for all other public works, and for the care of all public buildings. It shall also have such other powers and duties as may be assigned by the council.

§ 11.03. Director of Public Works. The head of the department of public works shall be the director of public works. He shall have general management and control of the several bureaus, divisions and other units of the department.

Chapter 12

Department of Public Utilities

§ 12.01. Department of Public Utilities. The department of public utilities shall consist of a director of public utilities and such other officers and employees organized into such bureaus, divisions and other units as may be provided by the council or by the orders of the director consistent therewith.

§ 12.02. Functions. The department of public utilities shall be responsible for the construction, operation and maintenance of the waterworks system and the sewers and sewage disposal and such other powers and duties as may be assigned by the council.

§ 12.03. Director of Public Utilities. The head of the department of public utilities shall be the director of public utilities. He shall have general management and control of the several bureaus, divisions and other units of the department.

Chapter 13

Department of Public Health

§ 13.01. Department of Public Health. The department of public health shall consist of the director of public health and such other officers and employees organized into such bureaus, divisions and other units as may be provided by the council or by the orders of the director consistent therewith.

§ 13.02. Functions. The department of public health shall be responsible for the exercise of all health functions imposed on municipalities by general law and such other powers and duties as may be assigned by the council.

§ 13.03. Director of Public Health. The head of the department of public health shall be the director of public health. He shall be a physician licensed to practice medicine in the Commonwealth of Virginia. He shall have general management and control of the several bureaus, divisions and other units of the department. He shall have all the powers and duties with respect to the preservation of the public health which are conferred or imposed on municipal boards of health and health officers by the laws of the Commonwealth of Virginia.

Chapter 14

Department of Public Welfare

§ 14.01. Department of Public Welfare. The department of public welfare shall consist of the director of public welfare, a welfare board constituted as provided by general law and such officers and employees organized in such bureaus, divisions and other units as may be provided by the council or by the orders of the director consistent therewith.

§ 14.02. Functions. The department of public welfare shall be responsible for the duties imposed by the laws of the Commonwealth of Virginia relating to public assistance and relief of the poor and such other powers and duties as may be assigned by the council.

§ 14.03. Director of Public Welfare. The head of the department of public welfare shall be the director of public welfare. He shall have general management and control of the several bureaus, divisions and other units of the department.

Chapter 15

Department of Farm and Home Demonstration

§ 15.01. Department of Farm and Home Demonstration. The department of farm and home demonstration shall consist of an agricultural agent, a home demonstration agent and such other officers and employees organized in such bureaus, divisions and other units as may be prescribed by the council or by the orders of the director consisting therewith.

§ 15.02. Functions. The department of farm and home demonstration shall exercise all powers which are conferred upon counties relating to county farm and home demonstration work and shall have such other powers and duties as may be assigned by the council.

§ 15.03. Director of Farm and Home Demonstration. The director of the department of farm and home demonstration shall be the agricultural agent. He shall be selected from a list of eligibles submitted by the Virginia Polytechnic Institute. He shall have general management and control of the several bureaus, divisions and other units of the department.

Chapter 16

Department of Education

§ 16.01. Department of Education. The department of education shall consist of the city school board, the division superintendent of schools and the officers and employees thereof. Except as otherwise provided in this charter, the city school board and the division superintendent of schools shall exercise all the powers conferred and perform all the duties imposed upon them by general law.

§ 16.02. School Board. For a period of three years after the effective date of consolidation the school board shall consist of all members of the school boards of the City of Virginia Beach and Princess Anne County holding office immediately preceding the effective date of this charter. Thereafter the school board shall be composed of seven members who shall be appointed by the council for terms of three years; provided, however, that in the appointment of the initial school board, two members shall be appointed for terms of one year, two for two years and three for three years. Vacancies shall be filled by the council for any unexpired term.

§ 16.03. Division Superintendent. The person holding office as division superintendent in both the City of Virginia Beach and Princess Anne County shall continue for the unexpired portion of his term.

Chapter 17

Department of Parks and Recreation

§ 17.01. Department of Parks and Recreation. The department of parks and recreation shall consist of the director of parks and recreation and such other officers and employees organized into such bureaus, divisions and other units as may be prescribed by the council or by the orders of the director consistent therewith.

§ 17.02. Functions. The department of parks and recreation shall be responsible for operating and maintaining public parks, playgrounds and recreation facilities and organizing and conducting recreation programs and shall have such other powers and duties as may be assigned by the council.

§ 17.03. Director of Parks and Recreation. The head of the department of parks and recreation shall be the director of parks and recreation. He shall have general management and control of the several bureaus, divisions and other units of the department.

Chapter 18

Department of Personnel

§ 18.01. Department of Personnel. The department of personnel shall consist of a director of presonnel and such other officers and employees organized into such bureaus, divisions and other units, including a personnel board, as may be prescribed by the council or by orders of the director consistent therewith.

§ 18.02. Functions. The personnel department shall be responsible for the formulation and administration of the personnel policy of the city.

§ 18.03. Director of Personnel. The head of the department of personnel shall be the director of personnel. He shall have general management and control of the several bureaus, divisions and other units of the department, except as the council may assign such duties to a personnel board.

Chapter 19

City Planning

§ 19.01. Planning Commission. There shall be a city planning commission which shall consist of not less than five nor more than fifteen members, and shall be organized as provided by general law. All members of the commission shall be qualified voters of the city and shall be appointed by the council for terms of four years.

§ 19.02. Functions of Planning Commission. The planning commission shall be responsible for making recommendations to the council on all phases of city planning, including a master plan, zoning, and subdivision control. It shall have the powers and duties provided by general law and such other powers and duties as may be assigned by the council.

§ 19.03. Board of Zoning Appeals. There shall be a board of zoning appeals which shall consist of five members appointed for three-year terms by the circuit court of the city or the judges thereof in vacation.

§ 19.04. Powers of the Board of Zoning Appeals. The board of zoning appeals shall have all powers granted to boards of zoning appeals by general law.

§ 19.05. Appeals from Actions of the Board of Zoning Appeals. Appeals from any action of the board of zoning appeals may be taken to the circuit court of the city in the manner prescribed by general law.

Chapter 20

Administration of Justice

§ 20.01. Circuit Court. The city shall continue to be in and a part of the Twenty-Eighth Judicial Circuit. The Circuit Court of Princess Anne County shall be known as the Circuit Court of the City of Virginia Beach and shall have the same jurisdiction in the City of Virginia Beach as is conferred by general law upon circuit courts of cities of the first class.

§ 20.02. Transition of Circuit Court. All actions of every kind, criminal as well as civil, pending in the circuit court of the county on the effective date of this charter shall automatically be transferred to, and shall proceed to final judgment in the circuit court of the city. The circuit court of the city shall have full authority to issue writs, enforce judgments and decrees and exercise every manner of judicial function in relation to former actions in the circuit court of the county as though no change had been made in the status of the latter.

§ 20.03. Municipal Court. There shall be a municipal court for the City of Virginia Beach. Such court shall have both civil and criminal jurisdiction, shall have such other judicial powers as are conferred by general law on municipal courts of cities of the first class, and shall hold court at such times in the boroughs of Princess Anne and Virginia Beach and at such other places as may be determined by the circuit court of the city.

§ 20.04. Judges of the Municipal Court. There shall be a judge of the municipal court and such associate and substitute judges as may be deemed necessary by the council. The judges of such court shall be appointed for terms of four years by the circuit court of the city or the judges thereof in vacation. Appointments to vacancies shall be made by the circuit court or the judges thereof in vacation and shall be for the unexpired term.

§ 20.05. Juvenile and Domestic Relations Court. There shall be a juvenile and domestic relations court for the city. Such court shall possess the same jurisdiction and powers as are conferred by law upon juvenile and domestic relations courts of cities of the first class.

§ 20.06. Judges of the Juvenile and Domestic Relations Court. There shall be a judge of the juvenile and domestic relations court and such associate and substitute judges as may be deemed necessary by the council. The judges of such court shall be appointed for terms of four years by the circuit court of the city or the judges thereof in vacation. Appointments to vacancies shall be made by the circuit court or the judges thereof in vacation and shall be for the unexpired term.

§ 20.07. Judges of Courts Not of Record. Any judge, associate judge or substitute judge of the municipal court may also be the judge, or associate judge or substitute judge of the juvenile and domestic relations court.

§ 20.08. Transition of Courts Not of Record. All actions of every kind, criminal as well as civil, pending in the county court of Princess Anne County or the police court of the City of Virginia Beach on the effective date of this charter shall automatically be transferred to, and shall proceed to final judgment in the municipal court or the juvenile and domestic relations court of the city, as the judges thereof may determine.

§ 20.09. Clerk of Courts Not of Record. The council may, at its discretion, provide for a single clerk for all courts not of record or a separate clerk for each court not of record. Each clerk shall be appointed by the court he serves.

§ 20.10. Transfer of Records. Upon the effective date of this

charter all records and papers of the county court of Princess Anne
County and the Police court of the City of Virginia Beach shall be
transferred to the appropriate courts of the city.

§ 20.11. High Constable. The council shall appoint a high constable who shall serve at the pleasure of the council. He shall be the
ministerial officer of the courts of the city and shall have such duties
as the council may prescribe.

§ 20.12. Justices of the Peace. The circuit court of the city shall
appoint such number of justices of the peace as it deems necessary,
not to exceed eleven, to serve at its pleasure. The justices of the
peace holding office in the City of Virginia Beach and Princess Anne
County immediately preceding the effective date of this charter shall
continue in office until the expiration of the terms for which they
were elected.

§ 20.13. Notaries Public. Notaries public for Princess Anne
County shall have full power and authority in the city until their
commissions expire.

Chapter 21

Miscellaneous and Transition Provisions

§ 21.01. Assets and Liabilities. Upon the effective date of this
charter, all property, real and personal, of the City of Virginia
Beach and Princess Anne County, including sanitary districts
therein, shall be vested in and owned by the city, and any and all
debts due the city and the county, including any sanitary districts
therein, shall become due to the city. The city shall assume the payment of all the then outstanding indebtedness, bonded or otherwise,
including interest thereon, and all of the then existing contracts
and any other obligations of the city and the county, including any
sanitary districts therein, in the same manner and to the same extent
as if they were originally issued, made, entered into or arose directly
by or with the city.

§ 21.02. Election of Constitutional Officers. The offices of clerk
of the circuit court, attorney for the Commonwealth, commissioner
of revenue, city treasurer and city sergeant shall be elective and
filled in accordance with the provisions of the Constitution of the
Commonwealth and in accordance with the provisions of general
law.

§ 21.03. Powers and Duties of Constitutional Officers. The clerk of the circuit court of the city, attorney for the Commonwealth, commissioner of revenue, city treasurer, and city sergeant shall have such powers and perform such duties as are provided by the Constitution of the Commonwealth and, except as otherwise provided in this charter, as are provided by the provisions of general law for cities of the first class.

§ 21.04. Present Ordinances and Rules and Regulations Continued in Effect. All ordinances, rules, regulations and orders legally made by the City of Virginia Beach and Princess Anne County in force at the effective date of this charter, insofar as they or any portion thereof are not inconsistent herewith, or with the consolidation agreement between the City of Virginia Beach and Princess Anne County, shall remain in force and effect within the same area to which they were applicable at the effective date of this charter, until amended or repealed in accordance with the provisions of this charter or general law.

§ 21.05. Preliminary Meetings of Council. At any time after the General Assembly shall have enacted this charter the councilmen for the consolidated city are authorized and directed to meet at such times and places as they may determine for the purpose of considering the appointment of a city manager, the preparation of ordinances, appointments which are required of them and such other matters as may be necessary to effectuate the transition resulting from the consolidation of the city and the county.

§ 21.06. Representation in the General Assembly. The granting of this charter shall in no way operate to affect or change the representation in the General Assembly of Virginia to which the people of the city were entitled at the time the charter was granted.

§ 21.07. Saving Clause. In the event that any portion, section or provision of this charter shall be declared illegal, invalid or unconstitutional by final judgment of any court of competent jurisdiction, such judgment shall not invalidate any other portion, section or provision hereof, but all parts of this charter not expressly held to be invalid shall remain in full force and effect.

BIBLIOGRAPHY

Interviews

Most of the material for this study was gathered during the summer of 1963 in the course of field interviews with merger leaders in the four consolidated cities. A few additional and informal follow-up interviews were conducted during the summer of 1968.

Merger leaders were identified initially from newspaper and other accounts of each consolidation. A reputational type question was asked of respondents in each city to help insure that major influentials were identified. For the most part, however, with the exception of two or three general questions regarding merger, interviews were entirely open-ended.

In conducting field interviews, the author benefited immensely from a former association with the Institute of Government of the University of Virginia. At that time, while serving as the Institute's representative in the conduct of certain conferences and training sessions for local officials, the author came to know personally a number of those officials who were later to be interviewed.

A list of persons interviewed follows. For personal and other reasons, three other respondents did not wish to be identified in any way.

W. C. Andrews, Jr., Commissioner of the Revenue, Newport News, July 30, 1963.

F. B. Barham, Clerk of the Corporation Court and Circuit Court, Newport News, July 31, 1963.

Fred W. Bateman, State Senator, 31st District, Newport News, July 31, 1963.

Harold I. Baumes, Executive Secretary, Virginia Municipal League, May 17, 1963.

Joseph C. Biggins, City Manager, Newport News, July 29, 1963.

Frank Blackford, reporter, *The Virginian-Pilot* (Virginia Beach Branch), July 22, 1963.

William L. Carelton, attorney, Aug. 22, 1963.

E. W. Chittum, Superintendent of Schools, Chesapeake, Aug. 8, 1963.

Charles B. Covington, Treasurer, Newport News, July 30, 1963.

F. W. Cox, Superintendent of Schools, Virginia Beach, Aug. 5, 1963.

Charles B. Cross, Jr., Clerk of the Circuit Court, Chesapeake, Aug. 8, 1963.

E. A. Culverhouse, Director of Personnel, Virginia Beach, Aug. 7, 1963.

Philip P. Davis, City Manager, Chesapeake, July 26, 1963.

George DeShazor, Clerk of the Corporation Court, Part II, Newport News, July 31, 1963.

Giles Dodd, Comptroller, Virginia Beach, July 24, 1963.

V. A. Etheridge, Treasurer, Virginia Beach, July 25, 1963.

John V. Fentress, Clerk of the Circuit Court, Virginia Beach, July 24, 1963.

Jack Frost, Deputy Clerk, Hampton, Aug. 14, 1963.

Matt Fulgham, Managing Editor, *Daily Press,* Newport News, Aug. 1, 1963.

F. Mason Gammage, Director of Planning, Virginia Beach, Aug. 6, 1963.

John Ben Gibson, Fire Chief, Chesapeake, July 26, 1963.

W. Russell Hatchett, City Manager, Virginia Beach, July 23, 1963.

Clifton W. Holdzskom, Director of Public Utilities, Chesapeake, Aug. 21, 1963.

Samuel P. Hoyle, Director of Finance, Newport News, July 29, 1963.

W. H. Huneycutt, Director of Public Works, Hampton, Aug. 15, 1963.

L. D. James, former City Manager, City of Hampton, July 18, 1967.

Clarence Johnson, City Manager, Hampton, Aug. 1, 1963.

Sidney S. Kellam, Virginia Beach, Aug. 6, 1963.

George Kelley, political writer, *The Virginian-Pilot,* July 22, 1963.

Lloyd Lewis, Jr., reporter, *Ledger-Star,* July 26, 1963.

C. Alton Lindsay, Superintendent of Schools, Hampton, Aug. 14, 1963.

George R. Long, Field Secretary, Virginia Association of Counties [then the League of Virginia Counties], July 19, 1963.

Ivan Mapp, Commissioner of the Revenue, Virginia Beach, July 24, 1963.

E. Sclater Montague, Hampton, Aug. 16, 1963.

R. O. Nelson, Superintendent of Schools, Newport News, Aug. 13, 1963.

..:..

A. W. Petty, Assistant Director of Public Utilities, Virginia Beach, Aug. 7, 1963.

B. F. Dyck Rhodes, Member of Council, Newport News, Aug. 13, 1963.

E. H. Smith, Deputy Commissioner of the Revenue, Chesapeake, Aug. 9, 1963.

Robert B. Smith, former Mayor, Newport News, Aug. 22, 1963.

William B. Speck, Field Secretary, League of Virginia Counties, July 17, 1963.

C. W. Taylor, Director of Highways and Engineering, Chesapeake, Aug. 21, 1963.

Robert H. Waldo, Commissioner of the Revenue, Chesapeake, Aug. 20, 1963.

Richard Webbon, Director of Public Works, Virginia Beach, July 23, 1963.

Victor P. Wilson, former State Senator, Hampton, Aug. 2, 1963.

J. B. Woodward, Jr., Newport News, Aug. 23, 1963.

Merger Records

Besides data gathered in interviews, certain of the records and working papers connected with three mergers were used. Of these, the most complete were those related to the Virginia Beach merger. At the time the interviews were conducted, these records had been stored in cardboard boxes in the vault at Princess Anne courthouse. Among other items, they contained the Minutes of Merger Executive Committee meetings and a vast quantity of miscellaneous papers related to merger. The author was allowed to make Xerox copies of certain of these papers. For ease of reference, they have been designated collectively as the Princess Anne Papers.

Although not as detailed or complete, certain of the records of the Chesapeake merger were also made available for reproduction. For the most part, these focused on the transition to a consolidated city. Again, for ease of reference, the source has been designated as the Chesapeake Papers. The reproduced copies of both the Virginia Beach and the Chesapeake papers have been preserved in the files of the Institute of Government.

State Senator Fred Bateman, who served as one of Warwick's representatives in drafting the consolidated charter for Newport News, preserved certain of his notes and working papers related to this phase of merger. Senator Bateman very kindly allowed me to examine these notes and provided working space in his law office in Newport News.

Additional primary source materials were obtained from selected respondents. Where possible, an attempt was made to reinforce data gathered from interviews, working papers, and other documents by newspaper accounts. Finally, an attempt was made in interviews to verify the accuracy of certain newspaper accounts in reconstructing the merger process in each city. Some discrepancies were uncovered, and where a discrepancy was unresolved, or a particular account could not be verified by a responsible source, it has either been qualified in the text or omitted altogether.

Selected Publications

Bain, Chester W. *Annexation in Virginia: The Use of the Judicial Process for Readjusting City-County Boundaries.* Charlottesville: Published for the Institute of Government, University of Virginia, by the University Press of Virginia, 1966.

——. *"A Body Incorporate": The Evolution of City-County Separation in Virginia.* Charlottesville: Published for the Institute of Government, University of Virginia, by the University Press of Virginia, 1967.

Bain, Chester W., and Weldon Cooper. "Two Virginia Cities Consolidate," 46 *National Municipal Review* 409–10 (Sept. 1957).

Blackford, Frank R. "A Democrat's Democrat: Sidney Severn Kellam," 87 *Virginia Record* 6 ff. (March 1965).

Bollens, John C., and Henry J. Schmandt. *The Metropolis: Its People, Politics, and Economic Life.* New York: Harper and Row, 1965.

Booth, David A. *Metropolitics:* The Nashville Consolidation. East Lansing: Institute for Community Development and Services, Michigan State University, 1963.

Bowen, John. "The Newport News–Warwick Merger," 25 *The Commonwealth* 27–29 (Aug. 1958).

Cooper, Weldon. "The Charter and Virginia Local Government," 45 *University of Virginia News Letter* 29–32 (April 15, 1969).

——. *Metropolitan County: A Survey of Government in the Birmingham Area.* University, Alabama: Bureau of Public Administration, University of Alabama, 1949.

Deming, George H. "An Approach to the Solution of Metropolitan Government Problems," 36 *Virginia Municipal Review* 292–94 (Nov. 1958).

Dye, Thomas. "Metropolitan Integration by Bargaining Among Sub-Areas," 5 *American Behavioral Scientists* 11 ff. (May 1962).

Elazar, Daniel J. *A Case Study of Failure in Attempted Metropolitan In-tegration: Nashville and Davidson County, Tennessee.* Chicago: Na-tional Opinion Research Center and Social Science Division, University of Chicago, Aug. 1961.

Gibson, Stuart M. "The Tale of Two Cities," 6 *Virginia and the Virginia County* 7 ff. (Oct. 1952).

Grant, Daniel R. "Metropolitics and Professional Political Leadership: The Case of Nashville." 353 *Annals* 72–83 (May 1964).

Greer, Scott. *Metropolitics.* New York: John Wiley and Sons, 1963.

Gunther, John. *Inside U.S.A.* New York: Harper and Brothers, 1947.

Harvard, William C., and Floyd C. Corty. *Rural-Urban Consolidation: The Merger of Governments in the Baton Rouge Area.* Baton Rouge: Louisi-ana State University Press, 1964.

Hawkins, Brett W. *Nashville Metro: The Politics of City-Council Consoli-dation.* Nashville: Vanderbilt University Press, 1966.

Hoyle, Samuel P. "Fiscal Problems Arising When Two Cities Consolidate," 31 *Municipal Finance* 144–48 (May 1959).

Institute of Government [then the Bureau of Public Administration]. Uni-versity of Virginia. *City Consolidation in the Lower Peninsula.* Charlot-tesville: The Author. 1956.

——. "Report on the Problems and Procedures of Incorporating the Pro-posed City of Warwick," Feb. 11, 1952. Typescript.

Key, V. O., Jr. *Southern Politics in State and Nation.* New York: Alfred Knopf, 1949.

Makielski, S. J., Jr. *City-County Consolidation: A Guide for Virginians.* Charlottesville: Institute of Government, University of Virginia, 1971.

——. "City-County Consolidation in the United States," 46 *University of Virginia News Letter* 5–8 (Oct. 15, 1969).

Makielski, S. J., Jr., and David G. Temple. *Special District Government in Virginia.* Charlottesville: Institute of Government, University of Vir-ginia, 1967.

Muse, Benjamin. *Virginia's Massive Resistance.* Bloomington: Indiana University Press, 1961.

Pate, James. "Virginia Counties Turn Cities," 41 *National Municipal Review* 216–23 (Sept. 1952).

Rush, John A. *The City-County Consolidated.* Los Angeles: The Author, 1941.

Sullivan, Frank. "Fledgling Atlantic Seaboard Cities, Chesapeake and Virginia Beach, Rank Among Nation's Top Ten in Area," 51 *Municipal South* 15–18 (Oct. 1964).

U.S., Advisory Commission on Intergovernmental Relations. *Factors Af-fecting Voter Reactions to Governmental Reorganization in Metro-politan Areas.* Washington, D.C.: The Author, May 1962.

Virginia Association of Counties [then the League of Virginia Counties]. *Statement Pertaining to Annexation, Consolidation and the Structure of Local Government in Virginia.* Charlottesville: The Author, 1963.

Wheeler, John P. "Virginia and the Council-Manager Plan," 42 *University of Virginia News Letter* 33–36 (May 15, 1966).

Wilkinson, J. Harvie, III. *Harry Byrd and the Changing Face of Virginia Politics, 1945–1966.* Charlottesville: University Press of Virginia, 1968.

Wood, Robert C. *Suburbia.* Boston: Houghton Mifflin Co., 1958.

INDEX